Medicine for the Body, Mind, and Soul,
The Mozart Effect®

- Stimulates learning and memory

- Plays a beneficial role in the treatment of stroke, dementia, head injuries, and chronic pain

- Reduces the number of seizures in people with epilepsy—hailed as a sound prescription for epilepsy by the *Journal of the Royal Society of Medicine*

- Helps lower blood pressure

- Provides successful results in therapeutic treatment, including listening problems, autism, attention deficit disorder, learning disabilities, and other sensory processing disorders

- Successfully assists treatment in substance abuse, migraines, anxiety, dyslexia, and many other common conditions

- Strengthens concentration abilities

- Boosts creativity among people of all ages

BOOKS AND TAPES BY DON CAMPBELL

Books

Music and Miracles

100 Ways to Improve Teaching Using Your Voice & Music

Music: Physician for Times to Come

Rhythms of Learning (with Chris Brewer)

The Roar of Silence

Master Teacher: Nadia Boulanger

Introduction to the Musical Brain

The Mozart Effect®

The Mozart Effect® for Children

Spoken Tapes

The Power of Music (five-tape set)

Mozart as Healer

Healing Yourself with Your Own Voice

Healing with Great Music

Healing with Tone and Chant

Sound Pathways: Accelerated Learning and Music

Music Tapes and Compact Discs

Essence

Music for the Mozart Effect®

Vol. I—Strengthen the Mind: Music for Intelligence and Learning

Vol. II—Heal the Body: Music for Rest and Relaxation

Vol. III—Unlock the Creative Spirit: Music for Creativity and Imagination

Vol. IV—Music for Stress Reduction

Vol. V—Music for Study

The Mozart Effect®—Music for Children

Vol. I—Tune Up Your Mind

Vol. II—Relax, Daydream, and Draw

Vol. III—Mozart in Motion

Vol. IV—Mozart to Go!

The Mozart Effect®—Music for Babies

Vol. I—From Playtime to Sleepytime

Vol. II—Music for Newborns

Vol. III—Nighty-Night Mozart

The Mozart Effect®—Music for Moms and Moms-to-Be

Audio Books

The Roar of Silence

The Mozart Effect®

The Mozart

Effect®

Tapping the Power of Music to Heal the Body,
Strengthen the Mind, and Unlock the Creative Spirit

DON CAMPBELL

HARPER

NEW YORK · LONDON · TORONTO · SYDNEY

Note to the Reader

Please bear in mind that it is advisable to seek the guidance of a physician or appropriate health-care professional in conjunction with the healing methods described in this book. If you have any reason to suspect a serious illness, it is essential that you contact a physician promptly.

A hardcover edition of this book was published in 1997 by Avon Books, Inc.

THE MOZART EFFECT. Copyright © 2001, 1997 by Don Campbell. All rights reserved. Printed in the United States of America. No part of this book may be used or reproduced in any manner whatsoever without written permission except in the case of brief quotations embodied in critical articles and reviews. For information address HarperCollins Publishers Inc., 10 East 53rd Street, New York, NY 10022.

HarperCollins books may be purchased for educational, business, or sales promotional use. For information please write: Special Markets Department, HarperCollins Publishers Inc., 10 East 53rd Street, New York, NY 10022.

First Quill edition published 2001.

Designed by Kellan Peck

The Library of Congress has catalogued the hardcover edition as follows:

Campbell, Don G.
   The Mozart effect : tapping the power of music to heal the body, strengthen the mind, and unlock the creative spirit / Don Campbell.
—1st ed.
      p.   cm.
Includes bibliographical references (p. 293) and index.
   1. Music therapy.   I. Title.
ML3920.C17   1997   97-27570
615.8'5154—dc21   CIP

ISBN 0-06-093720-3 (pbk.)

11 12 JTC/RRD 20 19 18 17 16 15 14 13

To Donna Lee Strieb,
who has inspired me throughout my life

Acknowledgments

I am deeply grateful to the hundreds, perhaps thousands, of musicians, therapists, and creative artists who have given me a wider view of music than I ever dreamed of as a student. Special regard to Nadia Boulanger who allowed me, at age thirteen, to enter into the grand "Boulangerie" of great students in Paris. To Bess Hieronymus who filled my childhood years with quality choral and organ music; to Dale Peters, Merrill Ellis, and Finn Viderø, all of whom gently mentored me through my university studies. Thanks to Norman Goldberg, who has brilliantly supported the publication of innovative music education and music therapy materials to bring music to many generations.

I am especially grateful to Dr. Alfred Tomatis, who has researched the use of Mozart's music for nearly thirty years and who introduced me to the Mozart Effect a dozen years ago. Rather than list the hundreds of other people who are mentioned in this book individually, I must thank them collectively for the hours of interviews, discussions, and preparation of studies and stories that made their own lives significant in music and health. I am grateful to Vidya Shankar in Madras, Pat Cook in Seattle, and Jean Houston, who showed me the power of indigenous musics that heal cultures throughout the world. I am also grateful to the intuitive musicians who have shown me, through their improvisations, that music must not always be impeccably structured to create rest and calm in our chaotic world.

This work was inspired by Eileen Cope, my visionary literary agent. Special thanks go to Alex Jack and to my editor, Rachel Klayman, who together brilliantly translated sound, idea, and my voice into the clarity of words. Special appreciation goes to Lyne

Besner-Lauzon, Wendy Young, Brenda Rosen, Mary Mayotte, Janet Benton, and Barbara Lowenstein, all of whose seasoned editorial skills greatly enhanced this book. And I am thankful to Mozart, Hildegard of Bingen, Vivaldi, Bach, and Paul Winter, whose serene music played quietly in the background while most of this book was written.

The greatest contribution to my work was made by my students and professional colleagues over the past decade, who arrived with their own visions, hopes, and desires to find greater meaning through music. The trust, questions, and immense challenges they brought with them as health professionals, artists, and lovers of sound have provided me with an opportunity to sail in this vast ocean of music and sound with quickened attentiveness.

Contents

Preface

Looking Back . . . and Gazing Forward:
A Few Words from Don Campbell

The Mozart Effect® was first published in 1997. The book was the result of years of research, study, and hands-on experience—a true labor of love, passion, and belief in the awesome power of music. Nonetheless, even I was not prepared for the amazing response engendered by the book's appearance—a response that has been enormously gratifying and exciting. Since the book's initial publication I have traveled from big cities to small towns; I have visited schools, community centers, and major corporations; I have spoken with people of all ages and backgrounds—from toddlers to golden-agers—sharing in the wonder of the Mozart Effect. The Mozart Effect® has been published around the world, in more than fifteen countries, and it has contributed to a global movement as the ears of the world have begun to explore sound's potential in newly integrated and creative ways.

Another happy by-product of this book's worldwide popularity is that much creative and heretofore unknown research supporting the Mozart Effect theory has come to the public's attention. The naïve assumption that music—any music—somehow makes us smarter has been replaced by the more sophisticated understanding and acceptance of music's powerful effect on multiple levels of neurological and physical responses. Classrooms, hospitals, and homes are being utilized as environments in which music can make dynamic changes in emotional, physical, and mental atmospheres. Teachers and health professionals alike are adapting the suggestions in this book for use in their own environments; researchers have been motivated to look at new ways in which the ear can be stimulated and educated.

Recently, the *Journal of the Royal Society of Medicine* in Great Britain published an important paper on the Mozart Effect, which reported that it appears Mozart's music affects the electrical impulses in the brain. Twenty-three out of twenty-nine patients with severe epilepsy showed reduced epileptic activity while listening to Mozart's music. And many other studies in health and education are currently looking at the importance of auditory stimulation and how it affects multiple systems in the body.

For three years, *The Mozart Effect*® music albums have continuously been among the top-ranked classical selections on the *Billboard* bestseller charts. Around the country, schools are integrating more music into their curricula, and major corporations are inaugurating programs to keep and/or expand music education in our schools. Even symphony orchestras have gotten into the act—many actively educate their audiences about how to listen to great music in order to reap multiple benefits (beyond the obvious one of listening pleasure!).

In my most recent book, *The Mozart Effect*® *for Children*, I explored the overwhelming new evidence of music's essential role in language development, physical movement, and higher brain functioning. Our children are our most precious resource, and music must be acknowledged as a fundamental, primary component of learning and processing multiple patterns of visual, auditory, kinesthetic, and emotional information.

Wolfgang Amadeus Mozart was a prodigy, a child star who saw, spoke, and listened to the world in creative patterns. His music creates a unique effect on the listener; it has a sense of order and clarity without being overly sentimental or emotional. Whether it is before study, after surgery, or in the midst of a meal, auditory stimulation can "re-orchestrate" the moment. As we learn more about this phenomenon, the techniques for listening to sound are changing, and the Mozart Effect is finally understood to be far more than a simple way to temporarily improve one's concentration.

From time immemorial, music has always been an important element of the human experience. But it is enormously gratifying to know that music is finally, rightfully, finding its central place in society—not merely as a form of entertainment or fine performance art but as a fundamental nutrient for physical well-being, mental development, stress release, and emotional expression.

—Don Campbell
March 2001

The Speech of Angels and Atoms

"How powerful is your magic sound."
—MOZART, THE MAGIC FLUTE

What is this magical medium that moves, enchants, energizes, and heals us?

In an instant, music can uplift our soul. It awakens within us the spirit of prayer, compassion, and love. It clears our minds and has been known to make us smarter.

Music can dance and sing our blues away. It conjures up memories of lost lovers or deceased friends. It lets the child in us play, the monk in us pray, the cowgirl in us line dance, the hero in us surmount all obstacles. It helps the stroke patient find language and expression.

Music is a holy place, a cathedral so majestic that we can sense the magnificence of the universe, and also a hovel so simple and private that none of us can plumb its deepest secrets.

Music helps plants grow, drives our neighbors to distraction, lulls children to sleep, and marches men to war.

Music can drum out evil spirits, sing the praises of the Virgin Mary, invoke the Buddha of Universal Salvation, enchant leaders and nations, captivate and soothe, resurrect and transform.

Yet it is more than all these things. It is the sounds of earth and sky, of tides and storms. It is the echo of a train in the distance, the pounding reverberations of a carpenter at work. From the first cry of life to the last sigh of death, from the beating of our hearts to the soaring of our imaginations, we are enveloped by sound and vibration every moment of our lives. It is the primal breath of creation itself, the speech of angels and atoms, the stuff of which life and dreams, souls and stars, are ultimately fashioned.

A Healing Breeze of Sound

"There are two ways to live your life.
One is as though nothing is a miracle.
The other is as though everything is a miracle."
—ALBERT EINSTEIN

Something was terribly out of kilter. The comfortably brisk mountain air did nothing to soothe the pounding in my skull, and from my front porch overlooking the sharp, iron-shaped mountains in Boulder, I could hardly distinguish the white light of the pale March sky from the flashes of light in the right side of my head.

A bump on the head had brought on these symptoms, but instead of abating over time, they had grown worse. I could barely see with my right eye, and the lid began to droop. My headaches became so severe that I had to take naps in the afternoon, yet at night I could barely sleep. Relaxation was impossible; every fiber of my being was awake with pain. During classes I taught, I found that because of the sensations in my head I could no longer reach the top register in my voice. Since my life's work was as a composer, a musician, and an authority on the healing aspects of sound, tone, and music, I was especially sensitive to all this—and fearful.

After three alarming weeks of flashing lights, headaches, and visual impairment, I consulted a neuro-ophthalmologist, who diagnosed my condition as Horner's Syndrome, an inflammation in part of the fifth cranial nerve that affects the sympathetic nerves in the eye and eyelid. The next step was determining the cause. So on April 1—both Good Friday and April Fool's day—I was wheeled into the tomblike capsule of the magnetic resonance imager (MRI) at the Kaiser Permanente Center in Denver.

I imagined myself as a character in a *Star Trek* episode. I had always wanted to see my own brain, to see the amygdala and differ-ent parts of the limbic system. What did they look like? Was my brain normal? I was soon bathed in a pulsating field about thirty thousand times the intensity of the Earth's magnetism, charging the protons in my head so that they could be measured and imaged.

The two hours in the MRI tube—a cross between a gigantic tin can and a space capsule—were intense. I began to hear sounds, loud hammers that turned into loud drums. The powerful rhythmic pattern would per-sist for seven or eight minutes and then stop, to be followed by a minute or two of silence and then another steady, concentrated rhythm. It would have been natural to feel claustrophobic, but the drumbeats that shot through me were among the most compelling manifestations of sound, vibration, and magnetism I had ever experienced.

With increasing excitement, I moved through tunnel after tunnel of light and sound. I had visions of men dancing. Eventually, the pulses evolved into songs, chanting, women singing, followed by the strangest tones—like Balinese rhythms in a gamelan orchestra and a Lutheran hymn, all in beautiful concordance. But it wasn't my ears that were hearing all this. It seemed as if my entire body were being tuned into one spiritual FM station after another and now played back some vital truth that was already encoded inside me.

Back in the radiologist's office, I was told it was essential I be moved to another hospital immediately so that a vascular surgeon could perform more tests. The radiologist had found a blood clot more than an inch-and-a-half long in the right carotid artery, just beneath the right hemisphere of the brain.

Given my three weeks of torture, the diagnosis did not come as a complete surprise. But the shock was nonetheless tremendous. I was forty-seven, relatively young and healthy, and I had been told that I had a potentially fatal condition.

Thirty minutes later, I was in the emergency room of Saint Joseph's Hospital in Denver, where the vascular surgeon told me that the blood clot had formed because there had been a hemorrhage in my skull. Because of the surrounding bone, the hemorrhage had reentered the bloodstream and coagulated, creating a large spiral, shaped like a crescent moon, around the inside of the right artery. Even a small aneurysm or clot can get into the bloodstream, travel to the brain, and cause a massive stroke. I was lucky to be alive.

After several hours and many tests, I was faced with three options. One was to undergo an operation as soon as possible, with no guarantees. Because the clot was positioned behind so much bone, surgery would involve removing a third of my skull on the right side. The second option was to be admitted to a hospital and remain there for six or eight weeks to be monitored hourly. The third was simply to wait for a few days and see what would transpire.

I knew that I wasn't ready for surgery that night—and possibly ever. Since I had lived for three weeks, I felt there was a good chance that my body, in its own natural, magnificent way, knew the secret of how to heal itself.

⟩ An Awakening

*"A solemn air [melody], and the best comforter
To an unsettled fancy, cure thy brains . . ."*
—SHAKESPEARE, *THE TEMPEST*

The awareness that my life had been in jeopardy for the past three weeks led me to remember my dreams and reflect deeply. For years I had pondered the nature of the soul, asking what is eternal and what is ephemeral, what is essence and what is superfluous. As a musician, I searched for the fundamental tone that uplifts and sustains the universe. I knew that from time immemorial, sound and music have been associated with the creation—or primary vibration—of the universe itself. In the East, the *Mahabharata* epic of India explains that out of the ineffable One came the symmetrical and numerical variations that underlie physical structures. In China, the *I Ching*, or Book of Changes, reflects a similar harmonic understanding. In the West, the Gospel tells us that in the beginning was the Word. In Greek, *logos* means not only "word" but also "sound." Once people listened to the sacred lyre of David, Orpheus, and Apollo, intoned the mystic Sufi poems of Rumi, or sought the legendary music of the spheres in the expectation of being healed. Music in the ancient world was a mysterious and powerful tool for the attunement of mind and body.

Over the years, in Haiti, Japan, Indonesia, India, Tibet, and other traditional societies, I had met and studied with shamans and healers who had incorporated sound and music into their treatments. Late that night, upon returning from the hospital, I realized that all the musical healing knowledge and wisdom I had absorbed was now being put to the ultimate test. I did not pray for health as much as the ability to be truly present, not dissociated from my body or my feelings. I knew I was at a crossroads, not only physically, but spiritually.

Somehow, I slept well. My last words before drifting off were that childhood prayer: "Now I lay me down to sleep, I pray the Lord my soul to keep. If I should die before I wake, I pray the Lord my soul to take . . ." The next morning, I reflected on the meaning of those words, especially the phrase, "If I should die before I wake." I wondered if I had been fully awake at any time in my life. What did it mean to be awake, to stay awake? The Buddha was once asked, "Why are you enlightened?" and he said, "It's only because I'm awake." In Sanskrit, "Buddha" means the Awakened One. Could it be that if we are truly awake, conscious, and responsible we do not die but live in a continuity of sound, presence, and knowing?

I called my friends Larry and Barbie Dossey, a medical doctor and nurse who have been pioneers in introducing principles of holistic health and prayer into the medical profession. Larry wrote *Space, Time, and Medicine, Healing Words,* and *Prayer Is Good Medicine,* all major contributions to the new paradigm shift in medicine and healing. They had helped me to develop my career and had inspired me through their friendship. Within hours, my name was pulsating through prayer circuits throughout the country, and I felt myself to be part of a global network. As I sensed my deep autonomic systems struggling to survive, I felt a quiet vibratory energy fostering inner awareness and well-being.

Now it was time to use that enhanced self-awareness, along with my ten years spent investigating the effects of tone and the voice upon the body, to heal myself. The answer seemed simple.

I began to hum.

Quietly, almost inaudibly, I hummed while concentrating on the right side of my skull.

Intuitively I knew I had to be very careful and not generate too powerful a sound, lest the blood clot disengage from the walls of the artery and bring about a stroke. You may remember the scene in *Seven Brides for Seven Brothers* in which high-spirited singing is used to cause an avalanche, thus separating the irate townspeople from their abducted daughters. Or you may have seen a soprano shatter a crystal glass merely by holding a high note. I needed to use tone to gently massage away the blood clot from within; otherwise, I might cause it to be abruptly—and fatally—released into the bloodstream.

In humming a tone, I sensed the power of a sound that had warmth, brightness, and clarity. I envisioned the sound as a vibrating hand coming into my skull on the right side, simply holding the energy within. I held my right hand above my head, closed my eyes, and exhaled. Then I imagined a vowel sound coming into my left hand, traveling through my heart and body, up to my right hand, and then back into my head, heart, and down through my feet. Each tone made a circuit through my body lasting two to three minutes.

This exercise grounded me and slowed down my breathing, pulse, and metabolism. I was able to control my basic physiological state and allow my breath, blood, and energy flow to integrate my mind and body. I felt an immense stillness and extraordinary presence—a state that scientists associate with the release of endorphins and with other positive hormonal and neurological changes.

⦃ An Inaudible Sound

> *"The Great Instrument is uncompleted.*
> *The Great Tone has an inaudible sound."*
> —LAO TZU, *TAO TE CHING*

The next day, I spoke on the phone with Jeanne Achterberg, the mind/body researcher whose books on imagery and heal-

ing have empowered my own experimentation with imagery and
sound. For nearly two hours, Jeanne explored with me ways to
access my own healing knowledge. She asked me what images I
could sense in that part of my head. My first response was "water
flowing through." Immediately, she said, "That is not a correct
image. It might create a stroke. See if you can exhale and go deeper."

I concentrated harder. Finally, I sensed a new and unusual
sound—only soundless. It was a vibration in my ears, and then a
warm hand that passed through my body. An image appeared: I was
sitting in a wonderful wooden chair, in a wooden room, with my
right side next to an open window with a hand-crocheted lace curtain. The curtain moved gently in a cool breeze from a peaceful
ocean shoreline. The breeze and the curtain very gently brushed
my head at the right temple.

Immediately, I knew this image was appropriate, and I knew
that what had ushered it in was not an actual, physical sound but
something more peculiar: an inaudible sound. It is difficult to describe. Close your eyes and imagine the sensation of a trumpet
blowing in your right ear without being able to hear it, or the
energy of a refrigerator humming into your right side.

I felt chills on my right side, and had that goose-pimpled effect I
know from hearing great music or being lifted to a place of spiritual
awareness. Unlike those experiences, this one continued for nearly
two hours, as I felt this breeze, this breath, this spirit, these wings
of angels simply entering the right side of my body. When I opened
my eyes and the phone was still in my hand, I asked if we were
finished. Jeanne simply said, "Keep this image as you sit, five or six
times a day for five minutes each, and we will see what happens."

Several days later, already feeling some improvement, I traveled
to the East Coast to lecture at the New York Open Center. The large
size of the group made it necessary to rent a room in a nearby
building. Halfway through the first morning, I was overcome by a
dynamic influx of energy from my right side, and I sat down to
steady myself. Suddenly, I realized I was actually sitting in a
wooden chair, next to an open window, in a wooden-floored room
where a lace curtain was ever so gradually moving near the right
side of my face. Although there was no quiet ocean directly outside
this window, the overpowering sense of that image and the inner
sound came over me.

The next day, I visited my friend Jean Houston, whose groundbreaking work in psychology had radically changed my consciousness in the 1980s. As director of the Foundation for Mind Research, Jean and her husband, Robert Masters, have explored for thirty years the most essential connections between mind, myth, and body. She and her friend Peggy Rubin listened to my story of the past few weeks and simply placed their hands on the right side of my body, which caused me to feel that inner amplification of the sound once again. There was a warmth and tingling, and again I felt the angelic wings that surrounded me during my childhood prayers.

Three weeks later, my second series of medical tests was exhaustive. Again in the MRI tube, I heard the songs, the chants, the drumming. I felt somewhat better, without severe headaches, and yet I was concerned that the clot might have worsened, in which case I would need to have surgery immediately.

The results of the tests came back: the clot had decreased from more than an inch and a half to less than an eighth of an inch. The doctor was astounded—it usually took four to five months, he said, for that kind of shrinkage. On the most recent MRI scans, he showed me how the crescent moon had almost disappeared from the artery beneath my brain. The greatest danger, he said, had passed.

And I knew I had been healed by the music of the spheres—or should I say hemispheres?

⟩ A Universal Language

Nothing in my life as a classical musician, a professional music critic in Japan, or the educational director of the largest guild of children's choirs in the United States had prepared me for this experience. The doctor was intrigued by my spontaneous remission but responded to my account of using sound to heal with the comment, "We know so little of this kind of medical miracle."

Although you may not have as dramatic a healing experience as mine, you too can benefit from the life-giving powers of sound and music. In this book, you will meet the leading therapists, practitioners, and educators in the field, as well as many ordinary individuals and families whose lives have been enhanced as a result of these explorations. You will learn how music heals and how to integrate this powerful transformational medium into your daily life.

You are already more musically inclined than you think. Everyone is. The world is inherently musical. Cutting across all ages, sexes, races, religions, and nationalities, music is a language with universal components. Its adherents outnumber the speakers of Mandarin, English, Hindi, Spanish, Russian, and all other tongues combined. Music rises above all income levels, social classes, educational achievements. Music speaks to everyone—and to every species. Birds make it, snakes are charmed by it, and whales and dolphins serenade one another with it. With the dawn of the space age, the music of the spheres became a reality. The Voyager spacecraft carried on board ninety minutes of music, including Bach, Beethoven, rock, and jazz, together with folk music from several countries, for the enjoyment and edification of any extraterrestrial civilization listening in.

Music is rapidly becoming the common tongue of the modern world. People today spend more money, time, and energy on music than on books, movies, and sports. The most popular cultural icons of our era are not statesmen or saints, but singers and vocalists. Beyond our addiction to rock concerts and CDs, stereos, and MTV, our daily communication and commerce is largely based on a musical model.

Interestingly, the word *health* comes from Old English *hal,* a root word signifying whole, healing, hale, and inhaling. *Heal,* in Northern Middle English, means "to make sound," to become healthy again. We use the word *sound*—a synonym for health and wholeness—to signify basic vitality and the unshakable foundation for whatever we do. Thus we speak of sound judgment, sound advice, sound investments, and sound business procedures. When things are going smoothly, we are *in tune* and *in harmony* with others and the world around us. When things are stuck, we are *out of tune* and *out of sync.* In romance or relationships of any kind, we hope to *set the right tone, strike a sympathetic chord,* or *communicate on the same wavelength.* When the unexpected happens, we decide to *play it by ear.* We admire the executive who can *orchestrate a deal* and cheer the team that can administer the opposition a *sound beating.* We commonly crave or shun an *audience*—from the root *audio,* to hear. Bombarded from morning until evening with modern advertising, we put up with the *pitches* of salespeople and commercials that are aimed (all too successfully) at drumming images and rhythmic jingles into our psyches. When we need a lawyer to navigate through the complexities of modern life, we want one who doesn't *miss a beat*. On the psychiatrist's couch, the board of the local PTA, or at a job interview, we strive to assert our identity as strong, independent *persons*, train ourselves to develop our *personalities*, and carefully construct our *persona* or public mask—all from the Greek roots *per son*, or "the sound passes through." Although we may not see ourselves as particularly musical, music metaphors and sonic imagery permeate our lives.

Millions of people today—one out of three Americans, according to the medical profession's own surveys—are seeking alternative healing methods. They are searching for techniques and comprehensive programs that can be used to maintain their basic health, stabilize their emotions, and relieve common ailments. They are tired of invasive, costly, potentially harmful treatments in which the remedy is often worse than the disease. On the other hand, they are dubious of alternative therapies that involve surrendering themselves to specialists of another kind, to strange belief systems that accompany the programs, and to training fees and supplementary paraphernalia that sometimes make doctors' visits look cheap. They want something easy to follow, safe, effective, inexpensive, and preferably self-administered.

If you are one of these people seeking healthful alternatives, you don't have very far to look. Your own inner sound system—your ears, voice, and choice of music or self-generated sounds—is the most powerful healing medium available. It costs nothing, is not controlled by some expert or guru, and you can't leave home without it. *The Mozart Effect* is your manual to this superb natural audio works.

CHAPTER 1

Sound Beginnings

THE MOZART EFFECT

*"The vocal nourishment that the mother
provides to her child is just as important
to the child's development as her milk."*
—ALFRED TOMATIS, M.D.

Weighing just over one-and-a-half pounds, Krissy was born prematurely in a Chicago hospital with a life-threatening condition. Doctors put her on total life support. Other than an occasional pat on the head, the only positive stimulation she received was from constant infusions of Mozart that her mother begged nurses to pipe into the neonatal unit. Doctors did not think Krissy would live; her mother believes that music saved her daughter's life.

Krissy could not sit up at age one and did not walk until she was two. Her motor skills were poor, and she was anxious, introverted, and uncommunicative. Despite all this, at age three she tested far ahead of her years in abstract reasoning. One evening, her parents took Krissy to a short chamber music concert. For days afterward, Krissy played with an empty tube from a paper towel roll, which she placed under her neck and "bowed" with a chopstick. Enchanted, her mother enrolled Krissy in Suzuki violin lessons with Vicki Vorreiter in Chicago, and the four-year-old girl could immediately reproduce from memory pieces several levels beyond her physical ability. Over the next two years, her strength and coordination on the instrument began to catch up with her mental capacity. With the support and encouragement of her parents, teachers, and fellow students, who were trained to perform in a group spirit, Krissy stopped wringing her hands in fear and began to socialize. Through a combination of pluck and grace, the little girl who was born weighing less than her violin could now express herself—and be whole.

In the last several years, many stories like Krissy's have emerged. The enhanced effects of music—especially Mozart and his contemporaries—on creativity, learning, health, and healing have become more widely appreciated. Let's look at a few examples:

- In monasteries in Brittany, monks play music to the animals in their care and have found that cows serenaded with Mozart give more milk.
- In Washington State, Immigration Department officials play Mozart and Baroque music during English classes for new arrivals from Cambodia, Laos, and other Asian countries and report that it speeds up their learning.
- "Beethoven Bread"—set to rise to Symphony No. 6 for 72 hours—is offered as a specialty item by a bakery in Nagoya.
- At Saint Agnes Hospital in Baltimore, patients in critical care units listen to classical music. "Half an hour of music produced the same effect as ten milligrams of Valium," Dr. Raymond Bahr, director of the coronary care unit, reports.
- The city of Edmonton, Canada, pipes in Mozart string quartets in the city squares to calm pedestrian traffic, and, as a result, drug dealings have lessened.
- In Tokyo, noodle makers sell "Musical Udon" made with tapes of Vivaldi's *The Four Seasons* and the chirping of birds playing in the background.
- In northern Japan, Ohara Brewery finds that Mozart makes the best sake. The density of yeast used for brewing the traditional Japanese rice wine—a measure of quality—increases by a factor of ten.

♩ Another Rosetta Stone

The power of Mozart's music has come to public attention largely through innovative research at the University of California in the early 1990s. At the Center for the Neurobiology of Learning and Memory in Irvine, a research team began to look at some of the effects of Mozart on college students and children. Frances H. Rauscher, Ph.D., and her colleagues conducted a study in which thirty-six undergraduates from the psychology department scored eight to nine points higher on the spatial IQ test (part of the Stanford-Binet intelligence scale) after listening to ten minutes of Mozart's "Sonata for Two Pianos in D Major" (K. 448). Although the effect lasted only ten to fifteen minutes, Rauscher's team concluded that the relationship between music and spatial reasoning was so strong that simply listening to music can make a difference.

Mozart's music "may 'warm up' the brain," suggested Gordon Shaw, a theoretical physicist and one of the researchers, after the results were announced. "We suspect that complex music facilitates certain complex neuronal patterns involved in high brain activities like math and chess. By contrast, simple and repetitive music could have the opposite effect."

The day after the Irvine findings were reported, music stores in one major city sold out of Mozart recordings. The researchers, intrigued, likened the Mozart Effect to a "Rosetta stone for the 'code' or internal language of higher brain function."

In a follow-up study, the scientists explored the neurophysiological bases of this enhancement. Spatial intelligence was further tested by projecting sixteen abstract figures similar to folded pieces of paper on an overhead screen for one minute each. The exercise tested whether seventy-nine students could tell how the items would look when they were unfolded. Over a five-day period, one group listened to the original Mozart sonata, another to silence, and a third to mixed sounds, including music by Philip Glass, an audiotaped story, and a dance piece.

INTERLUDE

Lost in Space—Not!

Designers, decorators, landscapers, pilots, golfers, and others attuned to visual cues in their work rely on what Howard Gardner, a professor of education at Harvard's Graduate School of Education, has christened "spatial intelligence." Researchers at the University of California at Irvine discovered that listening to Mozart's "Sonata for Two Pianos" (K.448) could boost these abilities. My own preference is for Mozart's violin concertos, especially numbers 3 and 4, as well as other string music. In my experience, they produce even stronger effects.

The researchers reported that all three groups improved their scores from day one to day two, but the Mozart group's pattern recognition soared 62 percent compared to 14 percent for the silence group and 11 percent for the mixed group. The Mozart group continued to achieve the highest scores on subsequent days, but the other groups did not differ significantly, probably as a result of a learning curve. Proposing a mechanism for this effect, the scientists suggested that listening to Mozart helps "organize" the firing patterns of neurons in the cerebral cortex, especially strengthening creative right-brain processes associated with spatial-temporal reasoning. Listening to music, they concluded, acts as "an exercise" for facilitating symmetry operations associated with higher brain function. In plain English, it can improve your concentration, enhance your ability to make intuitive leaps, and, not incidentally, shave a few strokes off your golf game!

In their most recent study, Rauscher and Shaw's team observed thirty-four preschool children given piano keyboard training during which they learned pitch intervals, fine motor coordination, fingering techniques, sight reading, music notation, and playing from memory. After six months, all the children could play basic melodies by Mozart and Beethoven. They also exhibited dramatic enhancement in spatial and temporal tasks (up to 36 percent improvement) compared to twenty children receiving computer lessons and twenty-four children provided other stimulation. In contrast to the college students, whose improvement lasted for only ten to fifteen minutes, the preschoolers' increased intelligence lasted at least one full day, representing "an increase in time by a factor of over one hundred."

Following the Irvine studies, a number of public schools introduced Mozart pieces as background music and reported improvements in their pupils' attention and performance.

⟩ Sonic Rebirth

"Our little girl was born to a Mozart string quartet and placed on my chest for me to hold. This was the most wonderful moment of my life."
—A mother quoted in ADRIENNE LIEBERMAN, *EASING LABOR PAIN*

The powers of music may be even more dramatic than this research indicates. Although the Irvine team brought the Mozart Effect to the attention of the public, it is undoubtedly the research of Alfred Tomatis, M.D., that has established the healing and creative powers of sound and music in general, and the Mozart Effect in particular.

Over the last half century, the French physician has devoted his life to understanding the ear and the many dimensions of listening. To his associates, he is the Einstein of sound, the Sherlock Holmes of sonic detection. To many of his patients, he is simply Dr. Mozart. In the course of this time, Tomatis has tested more than 100,000 clients in his Listening Centers throughout the world for listening disabilities and vocal and auditory handicaps, as well as learning disorders. From his headquarters in Paris, he works with a wide range of people, including professional musicians, children with psychological and learning disabilities, and those with severe head injuries. His comprehensive view of the ear establishes new paradigms for education, healing, and rehabilitation.

Tomatis's accomplishments are legion. He was the first to under-

stand the physiology of listening as distinct from hearing. He clari-
fied understanding of the dominance of the right ear in controlling
speech and musicality and developed techniques to improve its
function. He is credited with the discovery that "the voice can only
reproduce what the ear can hear," a theory with profound practical
applications for language development—one first ridiculed, but later
widely accepted and dubbed the Tomatis Effect by the French Academy of Medicine. He created a new model of the ear's growth and
development by looking at how the vestibular system, or the ability
to balance and regulate internal muscle movement, works.

But possibly his most important contribution was to recognize
that the fetus hears sounds in the womb.

In his early thirties, Tomatis's scientific curiosity led him into
the world of embryology, where he discovered that the mother's
voice serves as the sonic umbilical cord for her developing baby
and a primal source of nurturing. This led to the development of a
technique that he calls Sonic Rebirth, in which simulated uterine
sounds are filtered to treat listening disabilities and emotional
disorders.

The story begins in the early 1950s when Tomatis heard about
the pioneering work of V. E. Negus, an English scholar. Negus observed that in many cases baby birds that are hatched by foster
parents will not sing, or will imitate the sounds of the birds who
hatched them. This led Tomatis to investigate the role of sound in
utero and to ask whether postnatal development problems, especially autism and speech and language disorders, might be related
to a breakdown in communication or trauma in the womb.

Contrary to then prevailing medical opinion, Tomatis declared
that the fetus is capable of hearing. Despite the ridicule of his peers,
who treated him as something of a renegade, he persevered and
found that the ear begins to develop as early as the tenth week of
pregnancy and is functional by the age of four and a half months.
To measure acoustic impressions in the womb, he devised an underwater system using microphones, loudspeakers, and large sheets of
India rubber, which eliminated the effects of air pockets on his
experiments.

"The fetus hears an entire range of predominantly low-frequency sounds," Tomatis explains in *The Conscious Ear*, his autobiography. "The universe of sound in which the embryo is submerged

is remarkably rich in sound qualities of every kind . . . internal rumblings, the movement of chyle at the time of digestion, and cardiac rhythms at a sort of gallop. It perceives rhythmic breathing like a distant ebb and flow. And then its mother's voice asserts itself in this context." Tomatis likens it to an African bush at twilight with its "distant calls, echoes, stealthy rustlings, and the lapping of waves." When the audiovocal circuit is properly established, he concluded, "the embryo draws a feeling of security from this permanent dialogue which guarantees it will have a harmonious blossoming."

Tomatis further observed that after birth, the newborn often relaxes very little—until its mother speaks. "At this moment, the infant's body leans over and falls in her direction. . . . The newborn reacts to the sound of a particular voice, *the only voice of which he or she was aware while still in the fetal stage.*" As though instinctively sensing this, the mother is likely to sing to the infant, lulling it to sleep with lullabies, pressing it to her breast with sweet melodies, and using nursery rhymes to foster its development.

Suspecting that a breakdown in this usual chain of sonic contact may be responsible for many childhood disorders, Tomatis began devising ways to recreate the auditory environment within the womb. The unborn baby hears sounds in a liquid medium. About ten days after birth, when the amniotic fluid in the ear drains, the infant begins to hear in an aerial environment. The outer and middle ear adapt to the air, while only the inner ear retains the watery environment of the amniotic liquid in which it was immersed for nine months. With his primitive electronic device, Tomatis set about simulating the auditory environment the developing fetus experiences. Tape recording the mother, he used filters to eliminate all the low frequency sounds, thus recreating what her voice sounded like in the womb. The results were uncanny: instead of the woman's voice, he heard sounds similar to the gentle calls, echoes, and rustling of the African savanna that he had detected earlier.

The first substantiation of the theory came with the family of an engineer whom he had been treating for voice problems. One day the man came to visit his laboratory accompanied by his nine-year-old daughter. Tomatis demonstrated his new apparatus, and for a while they all listened to a rendering of "marvelously fluid noises, like the sounds of a fairyland," corresponding to the intrauterine environment. Suddenly, the little girl, whose presence they had forgotten, spoke up excitedly, "I am in a tunnel. I see two angels at the end of it, two angels in white clothes!" As the girl continued to narrate a "fantastic waking dream," Tomatis and her father watched in amazement. The conclusion was inescapable: she was visualizing the process of her own birth. The two angels were clearly the doctor and midwife in white smocks.

After a few minutes, the girl exclaimed that she saw her mother. Her astonished father asked how she saw her. The girl demonstrated by falling back and curling up in the fetal birth position. Remaining in this posture until the tape ended, she jumped up and resumed her normal activity level as if nothing unusual had transpired. "I had just recreated for the child the conditions of her birth," Tomatis realized in astonishment.

The next major breakthrough came when a medical colleague brought one of his patients, a chubby boy about twelve years old who had been diagnosed as mentally ill. "He screamed so piercingly that he emptied my waiting room," Tomatis recalls in his autobiography. "Every five or six seconds he jumped so high in the air that he could kick himself in the back with both feet, a performance I have never seen from anyone else. He did not speak, but his face was always alive with an extremely vivid mimicry. He looked as if he were sucking something without stopping. His mother accompanied him, but he repelled her as if they were two electromagnets of the same polarity!"

The boy's psychiatrist also arrived and explained that the boy was autistic. She did not know the cause of the disorder, but observed that children like that are psychologically "not yet born."

"Not yet born?" Dr. Tomatis said. "You intrigue me. At this very moment I am carrying out an investigation into intrauterine life and birth."

"Yes, I know," the psychiatrist replied. "That's why I am here with this child. I think you may be able to help him. May we try?"

Tomatis arranged to tape-record the mother's voice in his laboratory for about 20 minutes. On the day of the first session, the boy lay flat on the floor and scribbled with some chalk he had found in the office. The two analysts sat nearby, with his mother, and Tomatis remained next to the door operating his equipment.

First, he played the filtered high frequency sounds of the mother's voice, aiming them with a directional loudspeaker at the boy's head. Immediately, the boy stopped drawing, jumped up, and turned out the light. "In the twinkling of an eye we were plunged into darkness. This gesture took my breath away—not that it was difficult for me to understand," Dr. Tomatis recounts. "On the contrary, it was perfectly clear that the child was only trying to recreate the lighting conditions of his fetal life."

As the tape continued, the boy got up and went to his mother. Sitting on her knees, he took her arms and put them around him and began to suck his thumb. He stayed in this posture until the tape ran out. "It was almost as if he were back inside his mother," Tomatis marveled. When the recording ended, the boy got up and turned the light back on. Everyone was speechless. It was the first time in ten years the boy had showed any signs of recognition for his mother, much less affection.

A week later, another session was held to try to bring about a sonic birth. The boy went through the same reactions as in the first experiment and on one occasion even caressed his mother's face. Recognizing that the beginnings of a reconciliation had taken place, Dr. Tomatis switched from acoustical sounds representing the watery environment in the womb to those in the outside world of air. This elicited a new reaction—babbling or chatter—which the medical team recognized as the genuine birth of language. "We had awakened in him the desire to communicate with his mother, a desire which had remained dormant until that moment," Tomatis said. At the close of the session, the boy again stood up and turned on the light, but this time he returned to the mother and buttoned her coat, which she had draped over her shoulders. "That's it!" the psychiatrist exclaimed. "He's finally been born!"

Over the years, Tomatis has refined Sonic Birth, but the essential method remains the same. The young listener is exposed to filtered sounds of his or her mother's voice, generating a sense of emotional nourishment—the theory being that he or she experiences a kind of unconscious primal return to earliest awareness. Tomatis has been particularly successful treating children with delayed speech development—individuals who are physically capable of hearing but who neither listen nor respond.

Today the Sonic Birth process takes place more gradually than in some of Tomatis's early experiments. The preparatory phase, the

Sonic Return, is accompanied by a musical theme, usually the music of Mozart. As a substitute for an absent parent, Mozart's music produces the best effects. "Mozart is a very good mother," Dr. Tomatis declares. "Throughout fifty years of clinical and experimental process, I have voluntarily chosen one composer and one only. I continue to test new forms of music and willingly use forms of chanting, folk music, classical, but the powers of Mozart, especially the violin concertos, create the greatest healing effect on the human body."

Under the steady influence of this music, which the subject perceives in the guise of filtered sounds (reproducing intrauterine hearing), the listener is massaged by a succession of sound waves. As these sounds are integrated into neural pathways, the subject develops the ability to speak and communicate with others. "Listening to Mozart is like a kiss from my mom," a six-year-old taking the Tomatis training exclaimed. "It makes you want to listen carefully so you don't miss anything," an architect said exuberantly, noting the tonal pattern of call and response in Mozart's music. "Now I know where learning to take turns comes from."

Premature infants have also been treated successfully with this method. At a children's hospital in Munich, Tomatis arranged an experiment with triplets born prematurely. The infants weighed 1.5 pounds each and were incubated after delivery. The first lay in the incubator without any auditory stimulation; he remained motionless and struggled to survive. The one exposed to filtered Mozart music showed signs of normal activity. Its breathing quickened and its pulse rate stabilized between 140 and 160. The third baby, exposed to filtered tapes of his mother's voice, moved vigorously, showed signs of pleasure, and smiled. Deep breathing ensued, and his pulse rose to 160. Interestingly, neither the mother's voice nor Mozart had any effect on the infants without the filtering out of low frequency sounds.

Even when a child is perfectly healthy, Tomatis emphasizes how important it is after birth for parents to speak with him or her often. "Each child must truly know the deep and wise voice of both of their parents . . . Without time for the family to eat together, to discuss, and to share, it will not mature in the most natural ways."

Like that of many trailblazers, Tomatis's childhood was filled with portents of what would come to be his life's passion. The son of an Italian mother and French father, Alfred nearly died during his own premature birth in Nice in 1920—it was only when his grandmother picked up the tiny infant by the ear (prescient!) that his parents and doctor realized the baby was alive. Since his father was an opera singer, Tomatis grew up in a musical environment. Although he never became a musician himself, he has done as much as anyone in the last quarter century to bring the healing power of music to people who might otherwise have been deaf to its wonders. His use of the mother's voice, Mozart's music, and Gregorian chants has allowed the damaged and defensive self to be reborn as curious and trusting, eager to explore and engage the outer world. In this way, he points out, the child's nervous system will be prepared to "encode and stabilize the structures and rhythms on which the future social language will be built."

≀ The Science of Lullabies

In 1962, Dr. Lee Salk demonstrated that the fetus is aware of the mother's heartbeat. Today embryologists agree that the ear is the first organ to develop in embryo, that it becomes functional after only eighteen weeks, and that it listens actively from twenty-four weeks on. In *The Secret Life of the Unborn Child*, Dr. Thomas Verny tells the story of Boris Brott, conductor of the Hamilton Philharmonic Orchestra in Ontario. Over the years, Brott was puzzled at how he could play some music by ear, while he had to labor to master most pieces. He later learned from his mother that she had played the selections that came to him effortlessly while pregnant. In his book, Verny also cites recent scientific experiments showing that fetuses preferred Mozart and Vivaldi to other composers in early as well as later stages of pregnancy. Fetal heart rates invariably steadied and kicking declined, while other music, especially rock, "drove most fetuses to distraction," and they "kicked violently" when it was played to their pregnant mothers.

The evidence is mounting that babies—before and after they are born—are as responsive to music as the most avid concertgoers. In a study in the mid-1980s, psychologists at the Pacific Medical Center in San Francisco found that playing "Twinkle, Twinkle Little Star"—a tune that inspired Mozart to create a set of variations—and "Hickory, Dickory, Dock" on a Sony Walkman helped hospitalized babies keep from kicking and yowling. And Philips Records recently released an album, *Mozart for Mothers-to-Be,* citing pre- and postnatal studies showing that mothers, as well as babies, respond positively to this music. (According to legend, Mozart held the hand of his wife, Constanza, during the delivery of one of their children while humming and composing with the other.)

In a study of fifty-two premature babies and newborns with low birth weight at the Tallahassee Memorial Regional Medical Center in Tallahassee, Florida, a researcher reported that playing sixty-minute tapes of vocal music, including lullabies and children's songs, reduced hospital stay an average of five days. Mean weight loss of babies was also about 50 percent lower for the group of babies listening to music, formula intake was less, and stress levels were reduced.

INTERLUDE

Rockabye Unborn Baby

Speaking, reading, and singing to a baby before birth enhances its ability to distinguish among sounds after birth. This is known as "auditory tracking." Although that may sound like science fiction, the fetus really does begin to hear sounds from the outside world between the third and fourth months of development. Years later, children have been known to recognize songs, lullabies, and even classical music that had been played to them while they were still *in utero.* Here are several suggestions.

Read to your baby in the womb, and have your partner do the same. Classics like *The Little Prince* and *Winnie the Pooh* are recommended. It's better not to read stories with scary images; your child will have plenty of experience with them after he or she has been born.

Make up songs with lyrics like, "Hello, baby, this is dad. We'll be welcoming you soon," or, "Hello, baby, this is mom, loving you with song." Don't be self-conscious; it will be quite a few more years before your child has the capacity to be judgmental.

Play music, including children's songs, lullabies, hymns, and excerpts from "The Nutcracker Suite."

After birth, repeat these same songs and stories from time to time to calm the child and reinforce his or her listening ability and neural development.

Several years ago, Terry Woodford, a music producer for such groups as the Temptations and the Supremes, produced a tape of lullabies echoing the sound of a human heartbeat that could be used to calm infants and small children and help them sleep better. Initially, he gave away tapes to 150 day care centers, but several hospitals also obtained copies and put them to the test. At Helen Keller Hospital in Alabama, an experiment with fifty-nine newborns found that 94 percent of crying babies immediately fell asleep without a bottle or pacifier when exposed to the music. At the University of Alabama at Birmingham, nurses used the *Baby-Go-to-Sleep* tape for infants recovering from open heart surgery. One baby, struggling on a respirator, was near death when desperate nurses turned to Terry's tape. To their astonishment, the baby calmed down, fell asleep, and lived.

"I could hardly breathe," Terry admitted when he heard this story. "Babies were recovering from open heart surgery, and to see their immediate response to a lullaby tape, instead of having to be injected with sedatives, changed my whole value system. In the music business, you measure success by your last record, how high it went on the charts. But the minute you see that music can calm a baby, give it the rest it needs to survive and live . . . well, that's real success." Over the next few years, Terry gave away thousands of free tapes, and the lullaby melodies have been used in more than 7,000 hospitals and special care centers, including 400 of the 460 neonatal intensive care units in the United States. They have even been adopted by the U.S. Army and Air Force, who give them to military parents. The tapes have also proved helpful with tiny burn victims, babies born addicted to crack cocaine, and children undergoing chemotherapy.

Just as Tomatis's work first suggested, current research indicates that the unborn baby is sensitive not only to music but also to the emotional tenor of the mother's voice, and perhaps even the meaning of her words. In 1993 *Science* reported new research describing electrical activity in infants' brains that could be linked to their ability to recognize simple syllables. Meanwhile, at the University of North Carolina in Greensboro, Dr. Tony DeCasper and Dr. Melanie Spence asked pregnant women to read Dr. Seuss's *The Cat in the Hat* out loud during the last trimester of pregnancy. After the babies were born, sucking tests showed that they were able to recognize verses from the book, and distinguish them from other reading material.

I believe that a mother's strong emotions—from anger and resentment to deep calm, gratitude, and acceptance—can create hormonal changes and neurological impulses that affect the fetus. In many traditional societies, it has long been recognized that all the influences to which the growing baby is exposed contribute to its health and well-being. In Japan, *Tai-kyo*, or embryonic education, was, until the early part of the twentieth century, a part of how families prepared for newborns. The voices, thoughts, and feelings of the mother and father, grandparents, and other family members were believed to influence the fetus, and disharmonious vibrations of all kinds were avoided. Today that would include blaring television sets, violent films, loud music, and other sounds that might upset a growing baby.

"Birth recapitulates 2.8 billion years of biological evolution in water," explains educator Michio Kushi. "The womb simulates the primordial ocean in which life began. Pregnancy extends for 9 months or approximately 280 days. Each day in the womb represents about 10 million years' of evolution. Improper diet, loud sounds, disharmonious thoughts, and wild erratic behavior or lifestyle can have a tremendous impact on the person's entire future mental, physical, and spiritual constitution and development."

♪ Why Mozart?

Why not call the transformative powers of music the Bach Effect, the Beethoven Effect, or the Beatles Effect? Is it merely that Mozart is held in greater esteem than even geniuses like Beethoven, Gershwin, and Louis Armstrong? Or does his music have unique properties, eliciting universal responses that only now are yielding to measurement?

Tomatis has posed the same questions. And he has found, again and again, that regardless of a listener's tastes or previous exposure to the composer, the music of Mozart invariably calmed listeners, improved spatial perception, and allowed them to express themselves more clearly—communicating with both heart and mind. He found that Mozart indisputably achieved the best results and long-term reactions, whether in Tokyo, Cape Town, or Amazonia.

Clearly, the rhythms, melodies, and high frequencies of Mozart's music stimulate and charge the creative and motivational regions of the brain. But perhaps the key to his greatness is that it all sounds so pure and simple. Mozart doesn't weave a dazzling tapestry like that great mathematical genius Bach. He doesn't raise tidal waves of emotions like the epically tortured Beethoven. His work doesn't have the stark plainness of a Gregorian chant, a Tibetan prayer, or a Shaker hymn. He doesn't soothe the body like a good folk musician or slam it into motion like a rock star. He is at once deeply mysterious and accessible, and above all without guile. His wit, charm, and simplicity allow us to locate a deeper wisdom in ourselves. To me, Mozart's music is like the great architecture of Moghul India—the Amber Palace in Jaipur, or the Taj Mahal. It is the transparency, the arches, the rhythms within the open space that so profoundly stir the human spirit.

Although Mozart shares affinities with Haydn and the other composers of his period, Tomatis asserts in *Pourquoi Mozart? (Why Mozart?)*, "he has an effect, an impact, which the others do not have. Exception among exceptions, he has a liberating, curative, I would even say, *healing* power. His efficacy exceeds by far what we observe among his predecessors . . . , his contemporaries, or his successors."

The unique and unusual power of Mozart's music likely springs from his life, especially the circumstances surrounding his birth.

Mozart was conceived in a rare space. His prenatal existence was daily suffused in music, especially the sounds of his father's violin playing, which almost certainly enhanced his neurological development and awakened the cosmic rhythms in utero. His father was a *kapellmeister*, or music director, in Salzburg, and his mother, the daughter of a musician, played a lifelong role in his musical education, beginning with songs and serenades during pregnancy. Because of this superior musical environment, Mozart was born already saturated in—and shaped by—music.

A gifted performer from the age of four, Mozart was one of the most famous child prodigies in history. Like young Jesus, who amazed the elders in the temple, young Wolfgang astonished the royal heads of Europe; and musicians, composers, and audiences everywhere applauded his youthful brilliance and virtuosity. He first composed a minuet and trio for the keyboard when he was six years old, and his last piece came 626 major compositions later. By the time he was twelve, he was writing constantly, creating in the course of his career seventeen operas, forty-one symphonies, twenty-seven piano concertos, dozens of piano sonatas, and music for organ, clarinet, and other instruments. He could imagine one piece as he wrote down another; he seemed to see a whole composition before he committed it to paper. In a letter to his father, he explained, "Everything has been composed but not yet written down."

Perhaps because his talent manifested itself at such a tender age, he never lost his aura of the Eternal Child. He also had a famously antic disposition. "Soon notions of Mozart's irresponsibility and childishness coalesced with other reports and fictions about the supposedly automatic, almost somnambulistic nature of his creative process," Maynard Solomon observes in his magisterial new biography *Mozart*. "All this seemed to imply a channel between childhood and creativity that early Romantic aestheticians found irresistible, for it echoes their rediscovery in childhood of the mourned Golden Age."

The Irvine researchers intuitively grasped the connection between Mozart's early upbringing and the creative power of his music. Drs. Rauscher and Shaw explained that they selected Mozart's music for their experiments since he was composing at an early age and was "exploiting the inherent repertoire of spatial-temporal firing patterns in the cortex."

Like many young virtuosos, Mozart's compositional and performing genius was accompanied by chaos in his personal life. As an adult he was greatly concerned with his appearance and spent money freely on wigs and clothes, perhaps compensating for the fact that he was only five feet four inches tall, his face scarred in childhood by pox. He was unlucky in love, marrying the plain sister of the strong-willed beauty who jilted him. Even after his marriage, he continued to fall hopelessly in love with his young female students, leading to tension in his family. He enjoyed playing practical jokes and remained a tease to the end of his life.

Yet, paradoxically, the chaotic aspects of his personality fed his art and today help feed the legend that surrounds him: they accentuate the elegance of his music and silhouette his mature achievements. Vain and innocent, worldly and naïve, Mozart never tried to understand who he was, but his ingenious naïveté was a perfect vessel for his seemingly heaven-sent compositions. No matter how absurd and tragic his life (and his death, at thirty-five), the channel to celestial harmony was never interrupted. He could write the most transparent, sweet, and loving melodies in the midst of the most gruesome personal circumstances. In the last year of his life, amid marital discord and court intrigues, he wrote his joyful, life-affirming, profoundly esoteric opera, *The Magic Flute,* and the somber yet inspiring *Requiem,* a potent confrontation with death.

Mozart both embodied and transcended his era. Musically, he stands between the high flourishes of the Baroque and the florid highs of Romanticism. But he also lived in the radical age of John Wesley, Voltaire, Thomas Jefferson, Mary Wollstonecraft, and Goethe, when all ranks of Western society were being reorchestrated in politics and religion. And so his work celebrates the freedom of human thought that was beginning to show its colors beneath the pale makeup and powdered wigs of a feudal caste society in Europe and a colonial empire in America. More important, there is an elegance and deeply felt sympathy in Mozart's music. His art remains serene, never becoming strident. Like modern western civilization itself, which emerged from the classical, medieval, and Renaissance worlds, Mozart embodies the innocence, inventiveness, and promise of the birth of a new order of the ages.

Musicians, scholars, and the listening public recently hailed the discovery that Mozart contributed about twenty minutes of music to *The Philosopher's Stone,* a Viennese opera written in the last year of his life. Little did Mozart know that his own compositional body of work would become the philosopher's stone—the universal key—to the healing powers of music and sound.

The word *music* derives from the Greek root *muse.* Mythology tells us that the nine muses, celestial sisters presiding over song, poetry, and the arts and sciences, were born of Zeus, the King of the Gods, and Mnemosyne, the Goddess of Memory. Thus, music is a child of divine love whose grace, beauty, and mysterious healing powers are intimately connected to heavenly order and the memory of our origin and destiny. In their own ways, Krissy, Tomatis, and Mozart himself are luminous examples of how the muses begin to weave their magic in us from the very inception of life and—as we shall see in the pages that follow—into this world, and beyond.

CHAPTER 2
Sound Listening

THE ANATOMY OF SOUND, HEARING, AND LISTENING

*"What comes with a carriage and goes with a carriage,
is of no use to the carriage, and yet the carriage
cannot move without it?"*
—OLD RIDDLE

In the mid-eighties, I began to receive dozens of phone calls each week from people throughout the country interested in how music heals: professional musicians who reported physiological changes in themselves and their clients; people who were controlling high blood pressure and reducing tension through their voices and through improved listening; teachers who wanted to know why playing certain music in their classroom improved attention spans and memory.

In response to this groundswell, I founded the Institute for Music, Health, and Education in 1988 in Boulder, Colorado. Beginning with the basics, I explained to my students that sound is energy that can be organized into shapes, patterns, figures, and mathematical proportions, as well as into music, speech, and utterances of agony and bliss. Sound is what our ancestors called "the beginning." It is the *Om* of the East and the *Word* of the West. It is the background noise of galaxies forming; the symphony of wind and water; the companion of carriages and all moving objects; and the dialogue we have with each other (and ourselves) at home, work, and play.

Sound travels in waves through the air and is measured in frequencies and in intensities. *Frequency* refers to pitch, the high or low quality of sounds, and is measured in *hertz,* the number of cycles per second at which the wave vibrates. The higher the pitch, the faster the vibration, the lower the pitch, the slower. Sound waves that are extremely low are much longer in length and take up an enormous amount of space. Perhaps you've seen organs with pipes that measure 32 or 64 feet in length. (Some of the pipes in the Mormon Tabernacle in Salt Lake City create waves of sound more than sixty feet long.) Think of the flutelike sound you produce when you blow across the top of a soda bottle—the pitch of these pipes is produced in a similar way.

A normal ear can detect sounds ranging from 16 to 20,000 hertz. On a piano, for instance, the lowest key registers at 27.5 hertz and the highest at 4,186 hertz. Thresholds of hearing vary from culture to culture and environment to environment. In Africa, the Maabans live in such tranquillity that they can hear a whisper from more than 90 feet away. No doubt they would regard the ability of New Yorkers, Parisians, and other modern tribal people to follow a conversation in a roaring subway or busy shopping mall equally astonishing. Tomatis believes that high-frequency sounds (3,000 to 8,000 hertz or more) generally resonate in the brain and affect cognitive functions, such as thinking, spatial perception, and memory. Middle frequency sounds (750 to 3,000 hertz), he says, tend to stimulate the heart and lungs and the emotions. Low sounds (125 to 750 hertz) affect physical movement A low drone tends to make us groggy; a low, fast rhythm, on the other hand, makes it difficult to concentrate or be still.

Intensity, or loudness, is measured in *decibels* (named after Alexander Graham Bell, the inventor of the telephone). The rustle of leaves registers at 10 decibels, a whisper at 30 decibels. A quiet home or office usually measures 40 to 50 decibels, and a normal conversation is about 60 decibels. Rush-hour traffic averages about 70 decibels. Shouted conversations, jackhammers, and motorcycles take us up to about 100 decibels, power saws 110 decibels, loud rock music and blaring car horns to about 115 decibels. A rocket at launch can reach 180 decibels. Pain begins at 125 decibels. The decibel scale—like the Richter scale in earthquake measurement—is logarithmic, so that each 10 decibels increment is ten times the intensity of the previous number. For example, loud music at 110 decibels is ten times as loud as a jackhammer at 100 decibels and 10,000 times as loud as an ordinary conversation at 60 decibels. The ratio of intensity between the faintest and loudest sound the human ear can hear is a trillion to one. In music alone, the range of audible sounds is a million to one.

Another major characteristic of sound is its *timbre*—the quality of a voice or instrument that distinguishes it from others, regardless of pitch or intensity. There is no scientific scale to measure timbre, although it is primarily a function of the wave form. Subjective terms akin to those of wine tasting ("rich," "vibrant," "dull," "stuffy," "bright") are often used to describe it. A Stradivarius violin, for example, has a clear, warm, soulful timbre compared to that of an ordinary fiddle.

⟫ The Shape of Sound

Sound has many mysterious properties. It can, for example, create physical forms and shapes that influence our day-to-day health, consciousness, and behavior. In his remarkable work, *Cymatics*, describing the science of how sound and vibration interact with matter, Hans Jenny, a Swiss engineer and doctor, has shown that intricate geometric figures can be formed by sound. For instance, Jenny has created vibrations in crystals with electrical impulses and transmitted the vibrations to a medium such as a plate or a string. He has also produced oscillating figures in liquids and gases.

The forms and shapes that can be created by sound are infinite and can be varied simply by changing the pitch, the harmonics of the tone, and the material that is vibrating. When chords are added, the results can be either beauty or chaos. A low *Om* sound, for example, produces a few concentric circles with a dot at their center, a high *EEE* many circles with wobbly edges. These forms change instantaneously when a different note or tone is sounded.

INTERLUDE
Seeing Sound

Place a large paper cup of water near a stereo speaker and notice how the vibration of the musical sounds moves the water. Or, if you have a drum head, sprinkle very fine sand on top of it and put the drum over the woofer of a speaker. Now play a sustained midrange note on a synthesizer. The sand will begin "dancing." If you prolong this sound, a pattern will begin to take shape.

At the Exploratorium in San Francisco, you can spread sawdust on vibrating metals, cymbals, or saws. By pulling a bow across the side of the cymbal, kaleidoscopic forms (or mandalas) begin to emerge.

Imagine what effect sounds can have on delicate cells, tissues, and organs. Vibrating sounds form patterns and create energy fields of resonance and movement in the surrounding space. We absorb these energies, and they subtly alter our breath, pulse, blood pressure, muscle tension, skin temperature, and other internal rhythms. Jenny's discoveries help us to understand how, like a potter shaping clay at her wheel, sound shapes and sculpts us both inside and out.

Depending on their wave forms and other characteristics, sounds can have a charging and releasing effect. In some cases, they positively charge the brain and body. At times, loud, pulsating music can energize us and mask or release pain and tension. Some of the most positively charged sounds are made by our own voices. Such sounds can relax the jaw and throat, release tension from the body, and help us break through to new levels of achievement. In Aikido and Karate, for example, sounds customarily accompany certain movements. When a martial arts practitioner utters *"Hai"* or another strong vocalization, he or she is simultaneously releasing and directing energy.

Sound can also bring about negative changes. Loud noises, such as those from a factory, train whistle, or jet engine, can deplete the body. A piercing, high, sawtooth frequency—made by a saw buzzing close to the ear—can bring immediate headaches and extreme disequilibrium. Low-frequency sounds can also invade the body, pierce the eardrum, and create stress, muscle contractions, and pain.

Once I was teaching at a hotel near the Los Angeles airport. The lobby was as stunningly beautiful as a Hollywood movie set, but as I entered, my body said, "Beware." What looked so deluxe was actually one of the most bizarre sound boxes ever created. The huge complex had been built with a four-story atrium parallel to the airport runways, and every time a jet would take off, the building became a giant amplifier of low-frequency waves.

There was more. Standing in front of a large group of students in one of the spacious seminar rooms, I felt a severe pain in my back; after two hours, I was exhausted. Rarely tired while teaching, I immediately suspected some hidden sonic influence. I had already noted the neon lights and air-conditioning noise, which contributed mild, negatively charged energy to the environment, but these didn't account for my pain. That night, I resolved to find out what was behind the wall. It didn't take long. Through a service entrance, I found five industrial-size clothes dryers turning and humming. Although I could not "hear" them, my body could feel their powerful vibrations. How many seminars in that room must have created sick and distressed presenters! And how many guests must have found themselves sonically depleted in that atrium, digesting the inaudible, low-frequency sounds of jets taking off and landing along with their cocktails and dinner?

} Noise Annoys

"One day man will have to combat noise as he once combated cholera and the plague."
—ROBERT KOCH, discoverer of the cholera bacillus

We take our hearing for granted. Yet there are many threats to the proper reception of sound, especially from noise in our environment. Complaints about discordant sounds are age-old. "I neglect God and his angels for the noise of a fly, for the rattling of a coach, for the whining of a door," confessed John Donne, the English poet. From our perspective that seems rather quaint. Today, humans are put in an even more absurd (from the Latin *surdus*, meaning "not able to hear" or "to deafen") position: automobiles, refrigerators, digital clocks, televisions, computers, telephone answering machines, and remote garage door openers emit sounds with which our brains and bodies must constantly cope. We are bombarded with hundreds of times more sonic vibratory information than our parents or grandparents could ever have imagined.

An estimated 60 million Americans have hearing loss, and a third of those losses are caused by exposure to loud sounds. Such hearing loss has many causes, from living too close to bombs and artillery in countries at war, to working at noisy occupations, to simply enjoying loud music. As baby boomers reach their fifties, society might need to prepare for an outbreak of RRAD, or Rock & Roll Affective Disorder: the decline of natural hearing ability and an increase in stress, anxiety, and fatigue brought about by a lifetime of bathing in the glory of rock and roll. Dr. Samuel Rosen, a New York specialist who has studied comparative hearing around the world, reports that in traditional African society the average sixty-year-old hears as well as or better than the average twenty-five-year-old in North America.

The American Academy of Otolaryngology estimates that more than twenty million Americans are regularly exposed to dangerous levels of sound. Children are most vulnerable. Recently, I passed a domed sports arena that held races for "monster trucks" with giant tractor wheels. As the trucks were revving up their engines and speeding down hundreds of yards of track, the low frequency sounds were so loud and hideous that most of the children in the crowd of several thousand were weeping, screaming, and holding their ears. In a scene worthy of Dickens, vendors were selling earplugs as well as popcorn and candy to the hapless youngsters. I would guess that the sounds exceeded 120 decibels; these children were literally being *injured*. Many of the adults appeared to be numb, dissociated, and unable to appreciate the dangers of the noxious fumes and ear-splitting noise.

Noise-induced hearing loss is the most common kind of hearing disability in the United States, and, in most circumstances, it's preventable. A study at a public elementary school in New York found that, in the course of four years, students whose class faced the elevated subway were eleven months behind students not directly exposed to the noise of passing trains. When the students were moved, their achievement levels returned to normal. On the other side of the country, a California study reported that 61 percent of college freshmen showed a measurable hearing loss in the high-frequency ranges caused by prolonged exposure to loud noise.

People who work with jackhammers, snowmobiles, tractors, shop tools, lawnmowers, and even vacuum cleaners are at constant risk. Some cars and electric shavers can also put hearing in jeopardy. Gunshots present an acoustical hazard. It is unfortunate that hunting associations don't sell hearing licenses, because every time someone fires a gun, he is, in effect, shooting himself in the head. The more guns he fires over the years, the less likely it is he'll be able to hear, say, someone sneaking up on him.

Rock concerts are among the worst threats, which is why, unbeknownst to fans, most rock musicians wear earplugs when they perform. (The heavy metal band Motley Crue recently agreed to sell earplugs at its performances.) Vocalists are also at risk from their own voices, which commonly reach 110, 120, and even 140 decibels, exceeding in some cases the roar of a jet engine on the tarmac. The opera star Maria Callas was once partially deafened by her own singing.

Another danger: from the boulevards of New York, Moscow, and Tokyo to the back lanes of Nairobi, Bangkok, and Rio, tens of millions of people wear stereo headphones while they jog, cycle, or work. Although headphones are convenient and affordable and have made the world's greatest music accessible to the ordinary person, they can also, according to a study at the University of Louisville School of Medicine, lead to hearing loss. During aerobic exercise, for example, your body pumps blood and oxygen into your arms and legs, leaving the delicate linings of your inner ears dangerously unprotected. Headphones, which transmit primarily low-frequency sounds (the ones that have the strongest effects on our physical functioning), can contribute to dullness of hearing, ringing in the ears, and eventually, deafness.

I am not a member of the sonic police, someone who would have you entirely eliminate headphones or any other modern technology from your life. But I caution you to use personal headphones only for short periods and at low volume when you are jogging, doing aerobic exercise, or engaging in other physical activity. (The padded headphones with better-quality reception are preferable to those put directly into the ears.) In Paris, the French Parliament recently passed a law that limits the volume on personal stereos to 100 decibels (from a previous maximum of 126), and issued a warning that loud music was creating a deaf generation.

Noise-exposure standards are now regulated by OSHA (the Occupational and Safety Health Administration, an agency of the U.S. Department of Labor) for work sites with ten employees or more. Anyone who is exposed to approximately 85 decibels daily must have an annual hearing test. For that matter, it's a good idea for all of us to have our hearing tested periodically.

Amid all the clamor of modern life, a countertrend is emerging to promote calm. In Japan, the Environmental Bureau recently designated as "sonic scenes" one hundred spots, including some that featured the gurgling of streams, the tooting of boats, the rambling of trams, the splash of waterfalls, and the chimes of churches and temples. In Hokkaido, the northern island of Japan, the bureau selected twenty-two auditory spots for its tourist map from more than 2,500 recommended by the public, and one district in Tokyo picked out ten locations that combined great aural and visual serenity.

Hospitals, one of the noisiest of environments, are also rediscovering the restorative value of quiet. Intensive care units, which are filled with the beeping of monitor alarms, the humming of motorized beds, and the pumping of ventilators, rank alongside airplane passenger cabins and factory floors as primary hazards to health and hearing. Preliminary research at the Medical College of Wisconsin in Milwaukee indicates that special noise-reduction earphones may speed up patients' healing.

❧ Hearing, Diet, and Environment

Our hearing can also be affected by what we eat and where we live. Educator and natural foods pioneer Michio Kushi tells an amusing story. In the 1960s he and his associates founded Erewhon, one of the first stores offering organic foods in bulk bins and containers, and soon were faced with an influx of mice. Not wanting to kill the mice with traps, the employees installed an alarm that broadcast ultra high-pitched sounds. The manufacturer guaranteed that the device would drive the pesky rodents from the premises. But to everyone's surprise, the mice didn't leave. They simply changed their diet. Forsaking their favorites—honey, carob, and other sweets, as well as crackers, chips, and flour products— the mice began to nibble exclusively on whole grains and seaweed. These foods apparently had the ability to neutralize the piercing effects of the siren. "These are healing foods, survival foods," Michio says. "It showed me that animals often have better intuition than humans. When confronted with a challenge to their existence, they knew immediately how to adapt."

Scientific studies have begun to confirm the important relationship between diet and hearing. Finnish researchers, for example, reported that people on a low-fat, low-cholesterol diet had better circulation to the ears and, consequently, better hearing. Based on a study of more than 1,400 persons with inner ear symptoms, researchers at the West Virginia University School of Medicine concluded that hearing improved in those who were given nutritional counseling and put on diets low in saturated fat, simple sugars, and table salt and high in whole grain cereals, vegetables, and fresh fruits. With many patients, dizziness cleared up promptly, the sensation of pressure in the ears and head was quickly relieved, and tinnitus was often less severe and, in some cases, disappeared altogether. Tomatis takes a similar approach. Although he recommends a more traditional diet, high in whole grains and fresh foods, he warns against eating acid-producing foods, yogurt, and highly processed foods, which he believes interfere with normal hearing.

Climate and environment can also affect our hearing. Tomatis once observed that the song of the cicadas seemed more and more nasal as one approached Marseille from Paris. Investigating this phenomenon, he found that the species of insects in the two regions was the same, and that the way they beat their wings together to produce their characteristic chirping was identical. What had changed, he concluded, was not their singing, but the quality of his listening. The climate and altitude modified his auditory perception.

In his travels, Tomatis has observed that the sounds that people make are conditioned by their surroundings. Forest dwellers living amid the myriad noises of the forest create polyphonic music, while inhabitants of the desert commonly play only one instrument, the drum. Mountainous cultures also develop a distinctive body of music. Because of the atmospheric pressure on their inner ear and voice, their sounds are rich in bass tones and in high frequencies. The Tibetans in the Himalayas, Inca descendants in the Andes, and people living in the Alps, Appalachias, or Urals often sing and speak with deep, guttural, and other low tones mixed with falsetto and other high-pitched sounds, echoing the unique rhythm of living amid peaks and valleys.

⟩ Hearing with the Body

You don't have to hear to listen. Several of history's most superb listeners and musicians have been deaf. Although they could not hear with their ears, they could perceive rhythmic codes and patterns through the vibrations they felt through their hands, bones, or other parts of their bodies. Helen Keller, the great educator, was both blind and deaf and learned to hear through her hands. Evelyn Glennie, a contemporary young Scottish percussion soloist with major symphonies throughout the world, learns music by hugging a stereo speaker or holding a cassette player in her lap. She tunes the timpani by feeling the vibrations in her face and feet, and, when she performs, it's usually in her bare feet, which help her to "hear" the music through the reverberations of the wooden stage. Her astonishing abilities have made the music world aware that it is possible to receive sound and perform expressively without using the traditional auditory tracts.

Glennie first learned to recognize high and low notes by putting her hands on the wall outside the school's music room. She recalls that some notes made her fingers tingle, while other notes vibrated her wrist. "I have an overall sensation of sound from many sources, whereas hearing people rely only on their ears," she reports. A few years ago, scientists from Glasgow examined Glennie and found that her brain showed no response to speech. But there was activity in response to music.

Other well-known musicians who suffer or suffered from deafness or hearing impairment (apart from Ludwig van Beethoven, who, by the time he wrote and conducted his last major works, was entirely deaf) include Brian Wilson of the Beach Boys and Bedrich Smetana, the Czech composer. Musical talent in the hearing disabled may be more common than we think. At Saint Joseph Institute for the Deaf in Bronx, New York, several students have recently shown exceptional abilities.

Boudi Foley's talent was first discovered when he was seven. The Egyptian boy's parents, both physicians, moved to the United States in the early 1990s so that their son could attend a special school for the hard of hearing. One evening, Khalil and Ahmed Foley made plans to attend a concert by the Saint Louis Symphony Orchestra. When the baby-sitter failed to show up, they took Boudi with them, expecting him to fall asleep during the performance. To their amazement, the music awakened him, and he started tapping his fingers to the beat of the symphony. Boudi's parents hired Sona Haydon, a pianist and instructor at Washington University, to work with their son. She taught him the basics of rhythm and beat by tapping on his back. Boudi now plays the piano, according to Sona, like "a prodigy," and says that he hopes to grow up and write music like Beethoven, his favorite composer.

INTERLUDE
Closing Your Eyes and Opening Your Ears

Our listening and hearing usually become more acute when we don't have visual cues. In a safe part of your home (where you don't have to worry about tripping or falling), experiment for a half hour by keeping your eyes closed and simply listening to the world around you. You may also use a blindfold, such as a scarf or towel wrapped around your eyes.

You will in all likelihood begin to feel sound coming from different appliances. Can you differentiate among them? Is the hum of your refrigerator different from that of the air conditioner or other appliances? Are you aware of birdsong or other sounds from outside your home?

People with mild hearing disorders are often accused of not paying attention, which can lead to anger and frustration on both sides. Stress, anxiety, and fatigue may also arise as hearing declines. Depression, midlife crises, or especially severe menopausal symptoms can be the result of the isolation that occurs from losing, ever so slightly, the high range of auditory stimulation.

When the loss is minor, certain frequency bands may be impossible to hear, but the sound will still seem intact. For example, if you take out the bass, you can still understand the talk on an AM radio; with an equalizer, you can remove middle frequencies and still hear music. But it is very difficult to understand what is said if you take out the higher frequencies. Unfortunately, many people don't realize that their hearing has gradually disintegrated until the loss is quite severe.

Hearing loss can affect the voice as well as the ear. This discovery dates back to the late forties, when, as a young physician, Tomatis often found himself treating the musician friends of his opera-singer father. Medical dogma had long held that the voice was primarily controlled by the larynx; to relax it in cases of vocal disorders, the standard prescription was strychnine, a potentially lethal drug. But Tomatis discovered a cybernetic loop, which suggested that the voice was primarily controlled by the ear.

As a case history, Tomatis used the great Italian tenor Enrico Caruso. Before 1902, Caruso's voice had not been especially rich, but after that time, it became especially beautiful. Caruso himself never commented on the change, but based on his studies on listening disorders Tomatis suspected that the singer had had an accident that partially blocked his eustachian tubes, and that Caruso subsequently heard "high-frequency sounds rich in harmonics as opposed to low fundamental sounds." Tracking down the singer's medical history, Tomatis found that Caruso had had a surgical operation in Spain in 1902 on the right side of his face, which evidently damaged his

Eustachian tubes and caused partial deafness and the loss of low-frequency sounds. I believe this seeming handicap, more than all Caruso's training and hard work, is a vital key to his greatness.

"Caruso sang so remarkably well only because he could no longer hear except in the [high frequency] singing range," Tomatis concluded. He listened primarily through bone conduction, which "transformed him into the greatest vocalist in the world." Later, Tomatis tracked down friends of the virtuoso, who confirmed that he was deaf in the lower frequencies in the right ear, and said that he always asked them to walk on his left side.

≀ The Art of Listening

"First of all you must use your ears to take some of the burden from your eyes. We have been using our eyes to judge the world since the time we were born. We talk to others and to ourselves mainly about what we see. A warrior always listens to the sounds of the world."
—CARLOS CASTANEDA, *JOURNEY TO IXTLAN*

How we perceive and process the sounds of nature, music, and the human voice is at least as important as the inherent quality of the sounds themselves. The same sound that magically empowers one person can scare another nearly to death. And yet this most basic of abilities—teaching a child to listen, to pay attention to inflection, and to put sounds and speech into context—has been largely neglected by modern society.

It is strange that in a culture so preoccupied with intelligence, our aptitudes are measured largely in terms of our reading, writing, and computer literacy. College boards, professional licensing exams, and job placement interviews almost exclusively emphasize linear, left-brained thinking. Of course we must develop such skills, as they are essential in the modern world. But they may not be as basic as the skills of listening and speaking. In fact, if we are deficient in listening (as opposed to hearing), we may be unable to progress to more sophisticated learning skills. In interactions with other people, most of our time is actually spent listening. According to a survey, listening absorbs an average of 55 percent of our daily communication time, while speaking occupies 23 percent, reading 13 percent, and writing just 9 percent.

Listening properly—to the full spectrum of sounds in the world around us—allows us to be fully present, in the moment. Developing proper listening is a key theme of this book and a secret to accessing the Mozart Effect.

The difference between listening and hearing cannot be overemphasized. Compared to hearing, which is the ability to receive auditory information through the ears, skin, and bones, listening is the ability to filter, selectively focus on, remember, and respond to sound. Besides receiving sound and transmitting it to the brain, our stereophonic ears give us awesome skills, including the ability to perceive distance and spatial relationships. This is nothing short of miraculous. In a crowded and noisy restaurant, you can somehow pick out the words and whispers of a friend or lover—yet, in the same restaurant, a portable cassette deck records a symphony of dishes and conversations. Listening is active, while hearing is passive. Often we hear, but we don't listen. We can take in entire conversations, newscasts, and background music without paying attention to the information presented. Faulty listening is the underlying cause of many difficulties in personal, family, and business relationships. How many times have we said or been told, "You're not listening to me"?

INTERLUDE
How Well Do You Listen?

Put this book down and list on a piece of paper the things that you hear around you. Do this without concentrating too hard; the point is to be quick and casual.

Then spend five minutes *really* listening. Close your eyes, exhale, and open the "lens" of your ear.

Jot down what you heard in those five minutes. How

has the list changed? Do you hear dissonant sounds more clearly? Are you aware of the sound of a refrigerator, air conditioner, space heater, or other "background noise" in the room? Can you sense any sounds within your body? Your ears are like periscopes, able to focus on distant or near sounds.

Our ability to listen can be affected by our day-to-day health and state of mind, and can, in turn, have an effect on those states. Sometimes the mere memory of sound can produce the Mozart Effect. Once Oliver Sacks, the celebrated neurologist and author, was hospitalized after a climbing accident in Norway with neural damage and partial paralysis. He had "forgotten" how to walk, and was afraid of losing his "motor identity." To speed orthopedic recovery during his weeks of hospitalization, Sacks chose to listen to a violin concerto by Felix Mendelssohn. Awakened by the music one morning, he rose from his bed and walked across the room to turn down the tape. To his amazement, he discovered that the recorder wasn't on. Then he realized that he was walking for the first time since his accident. By listening to the music in his mind he had been transported. The imagined sounds served as a leg for him to stand on.

⁊ Gymnastics for the Ear

"I do not treat children. I awaken them."
—ALFRED TOMATIS, M.D.

Shortly after the end of World War II, Tomatis came to realize that hearing loss often had psychological roots. The insight came when he studied older workers in an aircraft factory facing dismissal because of hearing loss caused by exposure to loud noise. When the workers were required to take audiometric tests to see whether they could keep their jobs, they performed equal to or better than the required standard. "Their desire for a good salary lent them wings as far as their ears were concerned," he noted wryly.

Through the same selective process by which it listens, the ear can also exclude sounds. A child traumatized by an enraged or screaming adult, for instance, learns to survive by shutting out those noises and listening to his or her own inner voices. Tomatis has even suggested that severely abused children who develop multiple personalities have created inner voices to protect them from the sounds of abusive adults.

This ability to exclude sounds can be a positive thing. After all, the perfect ear is not supersensitive, receptive to every noise. Rather, the perfect ear is discriminating, able to adapt in a millisecond from a passive acceptance to an active, directed consciousness that is precise and focused on sound information and language. As Tomatis points out, oversensitivity can be a curse.

To help us retune our hearing and achieve the proper balance, Tomatis has developed a device that he calls the Electronic Ear. This technology improves listening and the discrimination of sounds by exposing the listener to a continuum of sounds that have been filtered to exclude low frequencies. Over the years it has been used by educators and clinical practitioners, and as an adjunct to psychotherapy for people recovering from early childhood trauma, sexual abuse, and depression. Artists and singers seeking to overcome creative blocks or vocal limitations have also used it.

Tomatis explains that it is possible to correct a listening or learning problem by stimulating the muscles of the middle ear, where the distinction between listening and hearing begins. The Tomatis Method relies on filtered high-frequency recordings of Mozart, Gregorian chant, and the spoken voice. The sounds are not musical or appealing; they are sound, not music. To hear these filtered midrange and high-treble pitches, the *stapedius muscle* must exert control over the three small bones in the middle ear. As the Electronic Ear exercises and conditions this muscle, the physical ability to listen gradually improves.

Each listener's program is individually tailored, with most lasting from twenty to forty days and entailing about two hours a day of listening therapy. Most begin with a passive phase, in which a series of filtered musical sounds enables the ear to begin to adapt to new types of sonic stimulation. Then the natural human voice is gradually introduced, using carefully chosen high frequencies and with lower frequencies filtered out. If an individual requires long-term reeducation, there may be three- or four-week breaks between programs to allow the client time to adjust and integrate what he or she has learned.

As their listening improves, clients participate more actively. In this phase, they speak, read out loud, sing, and chant, while the Electronic Ear plays back the enhanced sound of their own voices. Through this feedback mechanism, they learn to respond naturally to the world of sound and, in some cases, spontaneously develop normal speech and articulation. Tomatis likens this process to a gymnastics of listening, a kind of Olympic training to strengthen the muscle of the inner ear.

Take Gretchen, a middle-aged German homemaker who arrived at the Tomatis Center in Paris with a depressive condition. Often clients in her state would be played a filtered version of the voice of their own mothers, but Gretchen's mother was no longer alive, so she listened to filtered Mozart tapes. "In the beginning, the high frequency sound was awful," she recalls, "but then something opened up within me. I began to feel my life was much more enjoyable. My awareness increased tremendously."

On the other side of the world, Sato, a thirty-year-old professional photographer, went to the Tomatis Center in Tokyo, suffering from what she called "sound autism," or social inhibition and the overreliance on visual stimulation and cues—a syndrome often connected with watching too much television or working in front of a computer. This manifested itself in extreme shyness, as well as stiff shoulders and eye fatigue. "During the session, I was embraced by the happiest sound through Mozart. It woke me up," she says. Over the next seven days, her physical problems disappeared, she recalled long buried childhood memories, and her social isolation gave way to a new feeling of connection to other people.

INTERLUDE
Sonic Vitamin C

Alfred Tomatis observes that the most stimulating and charging aspects of sound are in the high-frequency range. We may not want to move or dance to this kind of sound, but Tomatis believes that the higher frequencies, even in small doses, help activate our brains and increase attentiveness; it's a sort of sonic Vitamin C.

To create this effect, turn down the bass volume and, if you have a graphic equalizer, the midrange, on your sound system and bring up the treble. Music with violins will help you obtain the most "nutritious" results, but even the high hiss of a cassette (which you can create by turning up the treble on your receiver) can be helpful for a few minutes each day. Frequencies from 2,000 through 8,000 hertz produce the greatest charge. Your right ear should be directed toward the speaker.

You may wish to try this exercise using pieces from *Music for the Mozart Effect, Vol. 1—Strengthen the Mind: Music for Intelligence and Learning.*

I remember my first visit to the Tomatis Center in Paris in the mid-1980s, on a beautiful spring day. As I climbed the regal stairways of an imposing building overlooking Parc Monçeau, I saw more than forty people reclining or sitting in comfortable chairs at booths, wearing large headphones. Some were relaxing or thinking, others were reading, holding microphones with their right hands, and paying close attention to their own voices filtered through the Electronic Ear. In another room, I saw several children, not more than eight years old, who were severely handicapped, wearing headphones cushioned by pillows. They were making sounds, and seemed surprisingly attentive. Because art therapy has been integrated with the Tomatis Method, many patients—children and adults alike—were drawing pictures, painting, or sculpting. The staff consisted of about fifteen cheerful, efficient professionals in white smocks. Some were working with clients on Gregorian chant, teaching them to open the voice. Others served as speech or listening therapists, giving personal consultations and going over listening profiles with clients of all ages. At that time there were over twenty large, reel-to-reel tape recorders playing different programs for different stages in the Tomatis Method. In the waiting room, I met a nun with a bright smile on her face who told me she had come for her "Tomatis cocktail," a refreshing period of rest and recharging in the middle of her strenuous teaching week.

Many singers, actors, and musicians have made the pilgrimage to the Center. Nearly deaf, the French actor Philip Bardi came to the Center as a last resort. "Without exaggerating, I think I could only hear about 70 percent of the volume of my own voice," he told French television. "I had lost nearly 40 percent of the sounds of the outside world." Beyond hearing loss, Bardi experienced whistling in his ears for four to five hours a day, and for another three to four hours, his ears were completely blocked. He felt as if his head were underwater. He could hear noises, but not distinct words. "I slept nearly fifteen hours a night," he said, "and was still tired and began to lose my memory. I could never hear the birds, and contact with the outer world was a handicap. I no longer wanted to be around people."

Doctors felt he had a progressive type of incurable deafness. Skeptical, the actor began a three-year program of reeducating his ears at the Tomatis Center. One day, after a couple of hours of listening to Mozart with the Electronic Ear, he heard a sound he didn't recognize as he walked home. It was the chirping of birds. On the phone, he no longer had to ask people to repeat themselves. As his vitality returned, he started to participate in sports. After three years of treatment, he resumed a normal life. To hear the world and the singing of birds again constituted a miraculous rebirth.

♩ Right Ear, Left Ear

As the right and left hemispheres of the brain operate differently, so do each of our ears. I began to notice this while helping to review, in cooperation with the Sound Listening Center in Phoenix, Arizona, hundreds of listening evaluations of people in a four-month study measuring the ability to discriminate between sounds at different pitches through air and bone conduction.

When clear and bright vowel sounds were received through the right ear, the listener's voice often grew stronger, his or her posture became more erect, and stress was reduced, whereas the same sound directed into the left ear would sometimes distort the listener's pitch and cause less attentiveness. However, the left ear perceived emotions and lower tones just as well as the right ear. The right ear is dominant because it relays auditory impulses more quickly to the speech centers in the brain than does the left ear. Nerve impulses from the right ear travel directly to the left brain, where the speech centers are located, whereas nerve impulses from the left ear make a longer journey through the right brain, which does not have corresponding speech centers, and then back to the left brain. The result is a delayed response, measured in milliseconds, and a subtle loss in attentiveness and vocalization.

These findings have many practical applications. Situating yourself so that a speaker is slightly to your right in a conversation or meeting, or holding the telephone to your right ear, can improve your listening, focus, and retention of the information presented. In a classroom, simply changing a child's location so that the teacher or sound source is to her right can dramatically improve listening and performance. Placing your home or office stereo system with the speakers to the right side can produce a similar effect.

INTERLUDE
Hear, Hear

It's easy to observe the difference between hearing and listening with this simple (and amusing) exercise. Sit close to two friends and tell stories to one another simultaneously. The idea, in other words, is for each person to tell a story and try to listen to two friends tell their stories at the same time. Do this for five minutes.

If you sit in a triangle, you will hear one friend in one ear and one in the other. Notice which story is easier to concentrate on and remember. Can you listen to both of them, or is it easier to listen just to one on a particular side?

Another variation is to have two friends sit on each side of you, about a foot away from each of your ears, and sing the first six or eight notes of different tunes in each of your ears simultaneously. Is it easier for you to recognize one melody than the other? Which ear is the better listener?

This exercise drives home the importance of being able to discriminate among sounds. It also helps you to determine your dominant listening ear.

In listening tests, Tomatis has discovered that when specific auditory frequencies are filtered out, the listener's voice changes. Depending on the frequency of the weak areas of auditory perception, the voice eventually becomes more melodic, attractive, nasal, or muffled. By preventing a singer from hearing with the right ear, he found that the voice immediately becomes "thick and loses color, fullness, and accuracy." He found that he could even cause someone to lose his or her voice or ability to play music altogether. In an experiment, he caused the famous violinist Zino Francescati to lose his inner ear discrimination, and his Stradivarius suddenly turned into "a common piece of wood." Francescati played out of tune and without his usual verve.

Tomatis inspires us to listen more actively to the full spectrum of sounds in the world around us. He tells a story that illustrates the universal powers of music. "Once I traveled with my son, Paul, and his son to the south of France for the holidays. Each night at five or six o'clock, I put on some music to listen to, usually Mozart. And each evening, as I sat outside and listened, a great bullfrog came to the left side of my leg and stayed for the whole selection. This happened every night for one month. When we put on the music, the large black frog would come and dine with us." By stationing itself on his left, Tomatis noted, the bullfrog was directing its right side to the music—a peculiar confirmation of Tomatis's basic theory of right-ear dominance. He smiled and told me, "This was the most amazing Mozart Effect I'd ever seen in my life."

⟩ Listening and Posture

"The more I study listening, the more convinced I am that those who know how to listen are the exceptions."
—ALFRED TOMATIS, M.D.

I first met Tomatis in Toronto in the early eighties. A tall, imposing figure, completely bald, with horn-rimmed glasses, he passed a wonderful afternoon with me discussing classical music, opera singers, and my beloved music teacher, Nadia Boulanger, who had lived near the Tomatis Center in Paris. (Every year, tens of thousands of people participate in listening development programs at over two hundred Tomatis Centers throughout the world.)

Among other things, I questioned him about the nature of the ear, the function of the brain, the relation of the ear to the development of handwriting. I was charmed by his incredible ease and knowledge, and I was astonished when he showed me how to tune a voice just by making a clear vowel sound such as OUU in one ear one pitch at a time. Although he bluntly corrected my posture (which he feels is directly related to listening capacity), I sensed warmth beneath his brusqueness.

Finally, I summoned the nerve to ask him a question that would show either my extreme confusion about his philosophy or my brilliant intuition. "Dr. Tomatis," I said, "do you mean to imply that it is the ear that grows the brain?" With no hesitation—and to my relief—he asserted that the cells and organs within the ear create the impulses of movement, a response that evolved as our ear did from the earliest form of a jellyfish all the way to human consciousness.

Beginning in the 1950s, Tomatis worked to create a new paradigm of the ear's development by looking at the vestibular system,

which gives us our ability to balance and regulates muscle movement. From the very first vertebrate life, he discovered, the ear
has been used not only for auditory purposes but also to regulate
movement. As the ear evolves from fish to reptile, from birds to
human beings, we see a progressive development of the organs in
the inner ear that aid in establishing motion, laterality, and verticality. Although this evolutionary process is extremely complex—
something like the move from the Victrola's large, primitive speaker
to the small, sophisticated transistors of a Walkman—it has been
critical to the evolution of the human into a being able to move
forward, backward, up and down, and side to side at will.

The ear choreographs the body's dance of balance, rhythm, and
movement. From the simple motions of the jellyfish through the
complex activities of homo sapiens, the ear is the gyroscope, the
CPU, the orchestra conductor of the entire nervous system. The ear
integrates the information conveyed by sound, organizes language,
and gives us our ability to sense the horizontal and the vertical.
Listening well creates a range of positive effects, including improved vocal control, more energy, a better disposition, and even
improved handwriting and posture. Disorders or weakness in the
vestibular function may result in speech impediments, poor motor
coordination, and difficulties in standing, sitting, crawling, or
walking.

Through the medulla, or brainstem, the auditory nerve connects
with all the muscles of the body. Hence, muscle tone, equilibrium,
and flexibility are also directly influenced by sound. The ear's vestibular function influences the eye muscles, affecting vision and
facial movements, and it also affects chewing and taste. Through
the vagus nerve, the inner ear connects with the larynx, heart,
lungs, stomach, liver, bladder, kidneys, and small and large intestines. This suggests that auditory vibrations from the eardrum interact with parasympathetic nerves to regulate, control, and "sculpt"
all the major organs of the body.

Tomatis views the ear as the key organ in humanity's development of a vertical posture, which first set our species apart from
early mammals. Sitting or standing upright, with the head, neck,
and spine erect, allows maximum control over the listening process,
and stimulates the brain to full consciousness. It enables the entire
body to become, in Tomatis's words, "a receptive antenna vibrating

in unison with the sound source, whether it be musical or linguistic."

"The ear is not a differentiated piece of skin. The skin is a differentiated piece of ear," Tomatis boldly asserts. Following the labyrinthine thread of sound through the ear and central nervous system—and comprehending the way in which the inner ear affects jaw movement and our ability to turn, bend, and situate ourselves in space—is central to an understanding of human development. It's also the key to understanding how we can utilize the Mozart Effect.

No wonder Tomatis gave me a hard time about my posture.

Besides verticality and right/left orientation, other aspects of posture can have a dramatic effect on listening. Daniel Meyer, an acupuncturist in Texas, suggests that during routine examinations, patients sit with eyes closed in a relaxing, high, firm chair, allowing the legs to hang freely and the head to find a balanced, comfortable position on the shoulders. Once the listening posture is found, the face becomes fuller and more relaxed, as if buoyed by helium. After a few minutes of this relaxed posture, the patient often feels a greater connection to his or her own body, along with a new receptivity to the doctor or caregiver. Both therapist and client are ready for meaningful communication.

INTERLUDE

Comprehensive Listening Exercise

1. Give yourself a relaxed afternoon or evening to explore a piece of music. Choose one about seven to ten minutes in length. I suggest something classical that features a solo instrument and ensemble: Mozart's *Eine Kleine Nachtmusik;* Granados's *Intermezzo to the Opera* for Cello and Orchestra; Fauré's *Pavane;* Beethoven's first movement of the *"Moonlight" Sonata;* or the slow movement of a violin concerto by Dvorak, Brahms, or Mozart. You could also try one of my compilations, *Music for the Mozart Effect, Vol. 2—Heal the Body: Music for Rest and Relaxation.*

2. Darken your listening room and make yourself comfortable on a reclining chair or couch. Have a pen and paper close by. Close your eyes and listen to one movement.

3. Let your mind go where it will; you can even daydream.

4. After the movement is complete, write down your impressions. How did your body feel when the piece began? What did you notice about your body as the music progressed? Did any images enter your mind? Did you feel any emotions? Did you remember particular events in your life? Or did you simply "space out"?

5. Now bring up the lights and replay the same music. This time, sit up in a comfortable chair and gaze at a spot on the wall in front of you. As the music plays, keep your eyes focused on that one area.

6. When the music is complete, write down your experiences. How did they differ from when you first listened to the piece? What did you find most interesting about sitting up with your eyes open? Did you find anything annoying about it?

7. Now play the music for a third time. If it's an orchestral or violin piece, stand. If it's a piano work, sit on the edge of a straight chair. As the music starts, imagine you're either the soloist or the conductor of the piece. Conduct the piece or play it on the imaginary instrument with feeling, skill, and whatever interpretive facility you can muster. (Play it realistically; don't "camp" it up.) Close your eyes if you wish. Be sure to move your body and arms intuitively.

8. Now write down your impressions again after the music has stopped. What did you learn about music? Did you learn anything about the instrument?

9. Close your eyes and spend a few minutes being aware of your body. Does it feel different from the way it did when you began this exercise? Do you notice any changes in breathing, heartbeat, or temperature? Is your mood brighter, sadder, more even? Are you more relaxed, more focused, more active?

Although there are no "right" answers, I think you will be surprised at how light, posture, and other variables subtly affect your listening.

The concert hall offers another venue for flexible listening, but not, perhaps, in its present incarnation. Many have prophesied doom for symphony orchestras, arguing that we have created musical museums rather than living auditoriums (true "rooms for listening" from the root *audio*). The War Memorial Opera House in San Francisco always posed a special challenge. Once, during a Pavarotti concert, a matron sitting next to me proclaimed, "Music may tame the savage breast, but even Pavarotti can't make these goddamned chairs endurable." During a performance of Wagner at the War Memorial, a young man lamented, "If I could oxygenate my brain during each of Wagner's interludes, this would be a truly transcendent experience. But my $90 ticket does not, evidently, come with air." In 1996, the War Memorial closed its doors for a major renovation (necessitated in part by the last major earthquake in San Francisco) that promises its tony patrons comfortable chairs and oxygen for the next millennium.

My friend Valerie has stopped subscribing to a local concert series because she found that for the same price she could afford to buy new compact disks and set up her home listening environment in an entirely different way. Valerie prefers lying down with the lights dimmed for some of the music. She finds that when listening in certain horizontal postures, she begins to sense a mythic, archetypal dimension that she doesn't perceive when sitting erect in a concert hall. For other selections, she likes to move energetically as the music is played. Valerie's choice is, of course, debatable: live performance has a charm and power all its own. But it could be that concert halls in the twenty-first century will be different from the ones today, designed to allow individual listeners to find their own unique means of receiving the wisdom and power of the music.

For fifteen years, I've experimented with postures that allow the listener to enter into heightened states of perception and to find greater unity with the music. The best audiences, I've found, are those that have the opportunity to move in some way before they sit down to listen. Dancing or moving for five to seven minutes before a chamber music concert energizes the ear and brain—and so the rest of the body listens better.

♩ The Sound of One Hand Clapping

"The strange beating together of hands has no meaning, and to me it is very disturbing. . . . It destroys the mood my colleagues and I have been trying to create with our music."
—LEOPOLD STOKOWSKI

The ritual of applause is an aural abomination, at least in the concert hall. The powers of music, which build up in the body and reach a peak at the end of a performance, are immediately dissipated by clapping. When great music takes me to a state of transcendence—as does Beethoven's *Ninth Symphony*, a Palestrina motet, or Paul Winter's *Missa Gaia*—I prefer to stay where I am and not to be bombarded by a tidal wave of noise. Most often, friends find me applauding at concerts only when I wish to help erase what I've just heard from memory as quickly as possible.

In the Far East, clapping is used precisely in this way. Meditators are taught to clap to dispel illusions and to purify the atmosphere. The deepest listening is antithetical to applause, enabling the fragrance and nectar of sound to tickle the skin and massage the soul. Some communities today, including a few churches and concert halls, have substituted for clapping the waving of the hands to express appreciation.

Clapping has its uses; it's a good way to integrate the left and right brains, as the hands meet in the midline of the body, creating harmony between rational and aesthetic awareness. To the shaman, clapping was a way to set boundaries between one state of mind and another. But we need to find new ways to show appreciation for the music we have just enjoyed without dispersing those magical sounds. Perhaps the sound of one hand clapping is the truest of all applause.

⟩ Two Harps in Unison

The power of listening should not be underestimated. To listen is to vibrate together with another human being. In the *Tao Te Ching*, Lao Tzu likens two people in harmony to two harps playing in unison. When we listen to a good speaker or singer, we begin to breathe more deeply, our muscles relax, and our endorphins flow, adding to contentment and serenity. On the other hand, a poor speaker or singer causes us to strain and to tighten the larynx. The body contracts as it attempts to shield itself from irritating or displeasing sounds.

This process begins from the earliest age. Scientists have recently reported that babies perceive musical sounds in the same way that adults do, preferring harmonious tones to harsh, or dissonant, ones. In one study, researchers exposed thirty-two infants, all four months of age, to short selections from unfamiliar European folk songs. Consonant and dissonant versions of the same tunes were played; while listening to the more harmonious melodies, the babies' focus improved, they wiggled less, and they exhibited less fussiness. A large number of the infants whined or turned away from the speaker when the dissonant versions were played.

In another study, researchers at the State University of New York at Buffalo found that by four and a half months, babies prefer listening to Mozart minuets that have short pauses between compositional segments in what musicians regard as a "natural" flow, as opposed to pauses inserted elsewhere in the same music. Says one of the researchers, Carol L. Krumhansl, a psychologist at Cornell University, these findings point to the primacy of listening and build on other work showing "the innate basis for musical perception."

In the East, "Original Mind" signifies observing the world fresh, with the purity and innocence of a child. Whether or not we are lucky enough to have access to a Tomatis Center or a state-of-the-art concert hall, the first step in listening well is to listen with childlike wonder. As Gandhi, one of history's most patient listeners, reminds us, "If we have listening ears, God speaks to us in our own language, whatever that language is."

CHAPTER 3

Sound Healing

THE HEALING PROPERTIES OF
SOUND AND MUSIC

"When I hear music, I fear no danger.
I am invulnerable. I see no foe.
I am related to the earliest times, and to the latest."
—THOREAU, JOURNAL, 1857

It was the beginning of Act One of a live broadcast of Rossini's *The Barber of Seville* from the Metropolitan Opera House in New York. Lorna was driving home on a rainy afternoon when a truck rear-ended her just before the woman playing Rosina was to sing.

"The impact was sudden and stunning," recalled the self-possessed New Jersey professional. "But even as I entered a world of shock and pain, I found a world of bliss and order. I listened to the whole aria and the next fifteen minutes of the opera as ambulance people and firemen tried to free me from the wreckage of my car." State emergency crews later told Lorna that she had been unconscious until she was strapped in a cot in the ambulance, but she remembered listening to Rosina's voice throughout the ordeal. "My spirit stayed with my body," she says. "The music kept me alive. I was able to listen and stay conscious, alert, and at peace with the music. I never thought I was injured because the music was so alive. I just kept listening, listening. From the beginning of that aria, I knew I had to finish the opera of my life."

I have encountered many stories like Lorna's. And I have asked myself: Is music actually healing us, pulling us through crises, reorchestrating our abilities? By developing our listening skills, are we able to awaken our spirits and activate our immune systems, thereby restoring our injured bodies and scattered minds? The Mozart Effect is not a panacea, but it holds a key with which each of us can open ourselves up, to hear the world more efficiently—and to heal.

♪ Orchestrating Your Life

People understand and approach healing in many ways. For me, healing is the art of balancing the mind and body, the feelings and the spirit. It is best achieved with an everyday routine that keeps all sides of oneself properly nourished and in harmony. But not everyone has the same needs, and yours may be vastly different from mine.

For me to have a healthy day, I have to be stimulated intellectually. I can go a week without venturing outside and taking a walk, because I listen to music while lying down and do "exercise" in my mind. I do need to play the piano, the organ, or to conduct for half an hour a day, as well as romp with my dog, Chauncey. I like to spend another hour or two in my office, even if it's only to do trivial things. I enjoy artistic stimulation, so I listen to music or go to a film or the theater for a few hours. I release energy through vocal activity—toning, chanting, teaching, or simply talking on the phone. And every day I spend a few quiet moments in a small meditation room in my house. All these activities charge my brain and are a part of my daily healing ritual.

Most days, of course, hold unforeseen challenges: unexpected visitors, missed deadlines, a flood of phone messages, an overdrawn credit card, a car that won't start, a sudden storm, a bad cold. Although I may not like these nuisances and interruptions, they keep me alert and teach me the art of living. By keeping my balance in a world of constant change, I have learned to be the real conductor of my life, not a fated player.

Healing is in the culmination of every moment and the anticipation of every moment to come, with all its pain and shadow, pleasure and joy.

Music is my principal healing tool and is almost always in reach. Yesterday afternoon, for example, I had been interviewing a prominent researcher in connection with this book for three hours, and I felt tired. I said, "Excuse me, would you mind if I play some music for a few minutes?" And so I put on a new recording of Handel's *Messiah* called *A Soulful Celebration,* performed by Quincy Jones and Stevie Wonder, and immediately the room was filled with joy. The music changed the whole atmosphere for me—and for my guest. When we returned to the interview, I felt more present, in the moment, and clear. Music can catapult the mind, body, and heart into the present more quickly than any modality I know.

⨍ Becoming Whole

"Music is your own experience, your thoughts, your wisdom. If you don't live it, it won't come out of your horn."
—CHARLIE PARKER

To heal not only means to become present, it means to become *whole,* in harmony and in balance. Although holistic therapies are based on this concept, it seems abstract. How, you may ask, can we become more whole than we already are?

It is easier to define wholeness in musical terms. To do this, we must go beyond the contemporary model of the body as a well-oiled machine conforming to manufactured specs, and think of it instead as an orchestra receiving and producing a symphony of sounds, chemicals, electrical charges, colors, and images. When we are in good health, the instruments in our orchestra perform fluidly and in tune. When we are sick or ailing, one or more instrument is flat or sharp, unstrung, deficient in tone. Part of our body may be in harmony and part out of tune, or each section of the ensemble may be playing its part well—except that the whole is out of sync. Imagine all the instruments of the body playing at their loudest— that's the worst of all possible sounds. But the opposite extreme— absolute silence—suggests a body without life.

Bringing a body into balance requires observing the orchestra in its entirety and assessing it accurately—its current condition and past experience, its inherent strengths, its potential for improvement. And the real genius of healing lies in teaching the body, mind, and heart to discover and play their own music—not the score that has been dictated by social norms.

It's important to point out that healing is not always synonymous with curing. Although relieving a disease or eliminating pain may be the ultimate goal, the immediate one is learning to integrate our conscious and unconscious life—an ongoing process and an end in itself. During a voluntary internship at Parkland Hospital in Dallas in the mid-eighties, I observed a patient with AIDS becoming more and more whole as his body grew weaker. The love he received, the peace he felt, the radiance he expressed were extraordinary. I have another vivid memory from the late sixties, when I worked as a volunteer in a tuberculosis hospital in Haiti. The environment was treacherous, the care far beneath any standard I could imagine. Visiting a rural clinic where the only medicine available was aspirin, where one nurse supplied water to more than a hundred patients, I observed people singing and humming. One patient was Marie Geneviève. Only a few days from death, she hummed constantly to herself. When I asked her why she replied, "As long as I sing, I am well."

In *Anatomy of an Illness*, Norman Cousins describes his visit to Pablo Casals at his home in Puerto Rico shortly before Casals's ninetieth birthday. The renowned cellist suffered from rheumatoid arthritis, emphysema, and other ailments, including swollen hands and clenched fingers. But as a stooped Casals labored to seat himself at the piano, Cousins witnessed an astounding transformation.

> I was not prepared for the miracle that was about to happen. The fingers slowly unlocked and reached toward the keys like the buds of a plant toward the sunlight. His back straightened. He seemed to breathe more freely. Now his

fingers settled on the keys. Then came the opening bars of Bach's *Well-Tempered Clavier,* played with great sensitivity and control. . . . He hummed as he played, then said that Bach spoke to him here—and he placed his hand on his heart.

Plunging into a Brahms concerto, Casals's fingers, "now agile and powerful, raced across the keyboard with dazzling speed. His entire body seemed fused with the music; it was no longer stiff and shrunken but supple and graceful and completely freed of its arthritic coils." After finishing, Casals went into breakfast, standing erect, without any trace of the infirmities he had displayed a short time before.

For many like Casals, music is the key to transcending the pains of the moment. From Zen monasteries to intensive care units, accounts abound of men and women who experienced the remission of a disease or disorder as the result of some sound or melody, who went from agony to *satori*—bliss, sudden enlightenment, rebirth.

⟩ How Music Affects Us: A Medley

"Music sets up a certain vibration which unquestionably results in a physical reaction. Eventually the proper vibration for every person will be found and utilized."
—GEORGE GERSHWIN

Most of us enjoy listening to music without being fully aware of its impact. Sometimes it's stimulating, at other times *over-stimulating*—even invasive. Whatever our response, music produces mental and physical effects. To come to understand how to heal with music, we have to look more deeply at what it actually does. Once we have this knowledge, we can—no matter what our level of musicality—learn to change our "sound channels" as effortlessly as we would our television channels so as to produce the specific effects we want. Here are some of music's possible therapeutic uses:

Music masks unpleasant sounds and feelings. In the dentist's office, for example, the sounds that reverberate in the jaw and other bones create enormous chaos. Quiet Baroque music can disguise or even neutralize the penetrating sounds of the dentist's drill. (The popular music you often hear in a dentist's waiting room will not necessarily be calming when you're sitting in the chair and waiting for that drill to descend.)

The voice alone can massage away painful sounds. Recently, while having a tooth filled, I instinctively began to hum and found I needed little anesthesia. The dentist, alas, was not too agreeable. "The sounds you're making are not appropriate for other patients," he complained. "Your music isn't appropriate for *any* patient," I countered. So much for that dentist. Another I went to was more musically sophisticated, encouraging me to use sounds to mask his drilling. Happily, it seems that he, and not his colleague, represents the wave of the future. Dental professionals are increasingly aware of the effects of tone on bone conduction and on the power of tone to dispel the turmoil created by the harsh sounds and vibrations of their instruments. Obviously, you can apply the same principles to repel or override invasive noise in other situations, whether you're in traffic, at home, or on the job.

Music can slow down and equalize brain waves. It has been demonstrated repeatedly: brain waves can be modified by both music and self-generated sounds. Ordinary consciousness consists of *beta waves*, which vibrate from 14 to 20 hertz. Beta waves occur when we focus on daily activities in the external world, as well as when we experience strong negative emotions. Heightened awareness and calm are characterized by *alpha waves,* which cycle from 8 to 13 hertz. Periods of peak creativity, meditation, and sleep are characterized by *theta waves,* from 4 to 7 hertz, and deep sleep, deep meditation, and unconsciousness produce *delta waves,* ranging from .5 to 3 hertz. The slower the brain waves, the more relaxed, contended, and peaceful we feel.

Like meditation, yoga, biofeedback, and other practices designed to unify mind and body, music with a pulse of about 60 beats per minute—including certain Baroque, New Age, and ambient selec-tions—can shift consciousness from the beta toward the alpha range, enhancing alertness and general well-being. Shamanic drum-ming can take the listener into the theta range, resulting in altered states of consciousness and even, perhaps, a perception of other dimensions.

Playing music at home, in the office, or at school can help to create a dynamic balance between the more logical left and the more intuitive right hemisphere—an interplay thought to be the basis of creativity.

If you are daydreaming or find yourself in an emotional, unfo-cused mood, a little Mozart or Baroque music in the background for ten to fifteen minutes can help to steady your conscious aware-ness and increase your mental organization.

If, on the other hand, you are very analytical and find it hard to improvise, romantic, jazz, and New Age music can produce the opposite effect, shifting awareness from your left to right hemi-sphere, and "loosening you up."

Performer-composer Kay Gardner describes an experience she had while caring for her father, who was in the advanced stages of both Alzheimer's and Parkinson's disease. While listening to the piece "Crystal Meditations" on *Essence,* an album I composed for piano and synthesizer, she discovered that the music pulses at both alpha and theta rhythms simultaneously. After putting it on, Kay sat next to her father and tried to communicate. It was rare for him to be lucid for more than twenty seconds at a time (he would often stare or hallucinate), but after the music had been playing for about five minutes, she began a conversation about his health and his future. "Somehow, almost miraculously, we were able to communi-cate for about ten or twelve minutes," she writes in *Sounding the Inner Landscape.* "It truly was a blessing to have been able to have this conversation with him . . . before he died." My music had, if only for a short time, restored order to Kay's father's brain waves. I cannot imagine anything more gratifying to a composer than to have made an encounter like this possible.

Music affects respiration. Breathing is rhythmic. Unless we are bounding up stairs or lying down, we usually take from twenty-five to thirty-five breaths a minute. A deeper, slower rate of breathing is optimal, contributing to calmness, control of the emotions, deeper thinking, and better metabolism. Shallow, fast breathing can lead to superficial and scattered thinking, impulsive behavior, and a tendency to make mistakes and suffer accidents.

As it turns out, listening to fast, loud music after a steady diet of slower music can produce the latter effects. "My objections to Wagner's music are physiological," Nietzsche once observed. "I breathe with difficulty as soon as Wagner's music begins to act upon me." By slowing the tempo of music or by listening to music with longer, slower sounds, one can usually deepen and slow the breath, allowing the mind to calm down. Gregorian chant, New Age, and ambient music commonly produce this effect.

Music affects the heartbeat, pulse rate, and blood pressure. The human heartbeat is particularly attuned to sound and music. The heart rate responds to musical variables such as frequency, tempo, and volume and tends to speed up or slow down to match the rhythm of a sound. The faster the music, the faster the heart will beat; the slower the music, the slower the heart beats, all within a moderate range. As with breathing rates, a lower heartbeat creates less physical tension and stress, calms the mind, and helps the body heal itself. Music is a natural pacemaker.

Although music with a strong beat can activate and energize us, a Louisiana State University study revealed the "dark side" of rock music. Researchers found that listening to hard-driving rock music increased the heart rates and lowered the quality of workouts in a group of twenty-four young adults. In contrast, easy-listening or softer music lowered heart rates and allowed for longer training sessions. In another study, on the effects of rock music, researchers at Temple University found that university students exposed to recordings by the Beatles, Jimi Hendrix, the Rolling Stones, Led Zeppelin, and other similar bands breathed faster, showed reduced skin resistance to stimuli, and had an increased heart rate compared to those exposed to random background noise. (The Rolling Stones' "Honky Tonk Women" generally produced the strongest responses, and the Beatles' "Sergeant Pepper's Lonely Hearts Club Band" *Reprise* the least.)

Clearly, music can affect the heartbeat, but the converse is also true: our heartbeat can determine our musical preferences. In a third recent study, female undergraduates using Walt Disney's "It's a Small World" as a stimulus tended to prefer tempos similar to those of their own resting heart rates.

Poetry, which shares many tonalities and rhythms with music, can also strengthen the heart, expand the lungs, and energize the internal organs. Alex Jack, a holistic health care teacher at the Kushi Institute in Becket, Massachusetts, believes that, like Mozart in the world of tone, Shakespeare wrote in a cadence that optimally unifies mind and body. In *Diet for a Strong Heart,* Jack explains that iambic pentameter, the form Shakespeare favored, speaks directly to our hearts. "This pattern of alternating stresses imitates the human heartbeat, the rhythmic expansion of diastole and contraction of systole. When recited out loud, iambic pentameter closely parallels the actual rate of the beating heart . . . 65 to 75 beats per minute. . . . For example, when his mother accuses him of madness, Hamlet replies in a way that perfectly unifies form and content: 'My pulse as yours doth temperately keep time/And makes as healthful music.' " Like Mozart's music, which is enjoyed worldwide, people in all cultures intuitively respond to performances of Shakespeare's plays, even though many have difficulty following Elizabethan English. Perhaps it is no wonder that music historians and critics commonly refer to Mozart as "the Shakespeare of opera."

Music can also change blood pressure. Dr. Shirley Thompson, an associate professor of epidemiology at the University of South Carolina School of Public Health, reports that excessive noise may raise blood pressure by as much as 10 percent. Although the mechanism is not fully understood, such noise may trigger the body's fight-or-flight mechanism, which causes adrenaline and norepinephrine, two strong hormones, to be released, speeding up the heart and straining the blood vessels.

In a 1989 study, medical researchers reported that my album, *Essence: Crystal Meditations,* with an average beat of 55 hertz, and Daniel Kobialka's *Timeless Lullaby,* with a frequency of 44 hertz, significantly reduced systolic blood pressure in all nine subjects. Other experiments using a variety of musical styles suggest that systolic and diastolic blood pressure can both be lowered as much as five points (mm/Hg) per listening session, and heart rates can be reduced by four to five beats per minute. By playing tapes of such music every morning and evening, people with high blood pressure can train themselves to keep their blood pressure down.

Music reduces muscle tension and improves body movement and coordination. As we saw in Chapter 2, through the autonomic nervous system, the auditory nerve connects the inner ear with all the muscles in the body. Consequently, muscle strength, flexibility, and tone are influenced by sound and vibration. In a study at Colorado State University in 1991, twenty-four undergraduate women were asked to swing their arms and hit a target pad on completion of the downswing. Researchers found that when the young women coordinated their movements with the beat of a synthesizer rather than following their own internal rhythms, they had significantly more control over their bicep and tricep muscles. And, in a study of seventy university students enrolled in an aerobics class, researchers reported that music increased the subjects' strength and improved their ability to pace their movements, all while enhancing their mood and motivation. Also, the rate and the precision of the movement tended to match the rhythm and tempo of the music.

In Norway, in the 1980s, educator Olav Skille began using music as therapy for children with severe physical and mental disabilities. He devised a "musical bath," a special environment in which youngsters could be immersed in sound, and found that a range of New Age, ambient, classical, and popular music could reduce muscle tension and relax the children. Known as vibroacoustic therapy, Skille's method has spread to other parts of Europe. In a study of patients suffering from severe spastic conditions, researchers found that vibroacoustic training increased the range of movement in participants' spines, arms, hips, and legs. In general, music in the lower frequencies—between 40 and 66 hertz—resonates in the lower back region, pelvis, thighs, and legs. As the frequencies of the music increase, effects are felt more in the upper chest, neck, and head.

Similarly, in recovery wards and rehabilitation clinics, music is widely used to restructure and "repattern" repetitive movements following accidents and illnesses.

INTERLUDE

Orchestrating a Workout

The rise of aerobic exercise coincided with the early years of disco, and it's easy to see why. It was disco's strong beat that paced the aerobicizers' movements.

Whether it accompanies vigorous dancing or a simple morning walk, music will help to carry your body through exercise, increasing your stamina and—not incidentally—making the time more pleasant. Here is a ten-minute sonic workout I think you'll enjoy.

1. For three or four minutes, play music while you do yoga or stretching exercises. (Spanish guitar music is excellent for this purpose.) Improvise your movements and allow them to flow naturally.

2. Now dance and move to some more active, stimulating music, for example, the music of Riverdance.

3. Finally, lie down and listen to a second, slower movement of a Mozart symphony or string quartet. Slower music allows the body to center itself, feel refreshed, and cool down.

Creating your own workout tapes with your favorite music will allow you to orchestrate your own well-being.

Music affects body temperature. The creaking of a door, the howling of the wind, and other eerie noises can send chills up our spine and put goose bumps on our flesh. Hollywood soundtracks are notorious for exploiting these effects, as well as for dubbing in dissonant music to accompany scenes of uncertainty, danger, and doom on the big screen.

All sounds and music exert a subtle influence on our body temperature and hence on our ability to adapt to changes in heat and cold. Transcendent music can flood us with warmth. Loud music with a strong beat can raise our body heat a few degrees, while soft music with a weak beat can lower it. Music does this by influencing blood circulation, pulse rate, breathing, and sweating. As Igor Stravinsky observed, "The percussion and the bass . . . function as the central heating system." On a cold winter day, listening to warm friendly music—especially music with a strong beat—will help you warm up, while in the dog days of summer, detached, abstract music can cool you off.

Music can increase endorphin levels. Endorphins, the brain's own "opiates," have been the subject of much recent biomedical research, and several recent studies suggest that endorphins can lessen pain and induce a "natural high." At the Addiction Research Center in Stanford, California, scientist Avram Goldstein found that half of his subjects experienced euphoria while listening to music. The healing chemicals created by the joy and emotional richness in music (movie soundtracks, religious music, marching bands, and drumming ensembles) enable the body to create its own anesthetic and enhance the immune function. He also found that injections of naloxone, an opiate blocker, disrupted the heightened sensation of listening to music. He theorized that "musical thrills"—the exhilaration produced by listening to certain music—were the result of endorphin release by the pituitary gland, the upshot of electrical activity spreading in a region of the brain connected to both the limbic and autonomic control centers.

The *Journal of the American Medical Association* reported in 1996 on the results of a music therapy study in Austin, Texas, which found that half of the expectant mothers who listened to music during childbirth did not require anesthesia. "Music stimulation increases endorphin release and this decreases the need for medication. It also provides a distraction from pain and relieves anxiety," a researcher explained.

Briefly, in addition to countering stress and pain, natural highs or peak experiences may at times elevate the levels of T-cells, the lymphocytes that boost natural immunity to disease. T-cell decline is associated with AIDS/HIV infection, leukemia, herpes, mononucleosis, measles, and other disorders. In the future, the study of music's ability to regulate endorphin levels promises to have far-reaching applications in healing.

Music can regulate stress-related hormones. Anesthesiologists report that the level of stress hormones in the blood declines significantly in those listening to relaxing, ambient music—in some cases replacing the need for medication. These hormones include adrenocorticotrophic (ACTH), prolactic, and human growth (HGH) hormone. Political leaders, trial lawyers, surgeons, moms, and other people who operate under great stress intuitively sense the powers of music to calm and relax. "I cannot listen to music too often," Lenin confessed after listening to a soothing Beethoven sonata. "It makes me want to say kind, stupid things, and pat the heads of people."

Music and sound can boost the immune function. If the body proves successful at resisting disease, it is because the system works in harmony; the blood, lymph, and other fluids circulate properly; and the liver, spleen, and kidneys maintain their overall integrity. Current research in immunology suggests that insufficient oxygen in the blood may be a major cause of immune deficiency and degenerative disease.

Here's where the Mozart Effect comes in. Certain types of music—as well as singing, chant, and various forms of vocalization—can actually oxygenate the cells. Buddha Gerace, a voice researcher in Lake Montezuma, Arizona, has developed vocal exercises that can increase the lymphatic circulation to as high as three times the normal rate. In fifty years of teaching voice, Gerace has witnessed many remarkable changes, and he credits his exercises with helping actor Henry Fonda boost his immune function and recover from vocal troubles during the Broadway production of *Mister Roberts*.

In a study at Michigan State University, researchers reported in 1993 that listening to music for only fifteen minutes could increase levels of interleukin-1 (IL-1) in the blood from 12.5 to 14 percent. Interleukins are a family of proteins associated with blood and platelet production, lymphocyte stimulation, and cellular protection against AIDS, cancer, and other diseases. In the study, experimental subjects were asked to select and listen to music from one of four categories—New Age (selections by David Lantz, Eric Tingsan, and Nancy Rumbel), mild jazz (Kenny G.), classical (Mozart), and impressionist (Ravel)—while control subjects were merely provided with magazines.

The experimental subjects listening to music of their choice also showed decreased levels of cortisol (up to 25 percent less), which is a steroid hormone associated with the adrenal complex. Unnaturally high levels of cortisol can paradoxically lead to a cortisol insufficiency (in the way that high blood sugar levels ultimately exhaust insulin production), which in turn leads to a decline in immune response. Injections of hydrocortisone are used for a wide variety of inflammatory diseases, allergies, rheumatoid arthritis, colitis, and eczema. The scientists concluded that preferred music "may elicit a profound positive emotional experience that can trigger the release of hormones which can contribute to a lessening of those factors which enhance the disease process."

Music changes our perception of space. As the Irvine research on the Mozart Effect demonstrated, certain music can improve the brain's ability to perceive the physical world, form mental images, and recognize variations among objects. In other words, music can affect the way we experience the space around us. Slow music contains more space within the tones than fast music. When we feel pressed for time, find ourselves in gridlock on the highway, or otherwise feel confined, Mozart's chamber music or ambient music like Steven Halpern's *Spectrum Suite* can give us more room to navigate or relax. In this sense, music is sonic wallpaper. It can make our environment feel lighter, more spacious, and more elegant, or it can make our space feel more orderly, efficient, and active. In a hospital recovery room, music can help reduce feelings of restriction and confinement.

Music changes our perception of time. We can choose music to slow us down or to speed us up. Brisk, repetitive, or marching music can quicken our pace. Music of a classical and Baroque nature provokes more ordered behavior. Highly romantic or New Age music helps soften a stressful atmosphere. In some cases, this music can even make time seem to stand still. On the other hand, in a hospital or a clinical setting, where the minutes can seem like hours, bright, up-tempo music can make time seem to pass more quickly.

INTERLUDE
Sonic Relativity

Do you recall the optical illusion in which lines of equal length look shorter or longer depending on which way the little arrows attached to the lines are pointing? Music can create temporal illusions that change our perception of time. Here's one that Einstein, an enthusiastic violinist, would surely have enjoyed.

Find a listening partner. Ask him or her to sit, eyes closed, and listen to the two following exercises.

Using a watch with a second hand, sing an *ahhhh* sound for five seconds. Then take a breath, and sing a lower *ahhhh* sound for another five seconds. Finally, lower the note once again and sing for another five seconds. (If you like, you can follow the familiar pitches of the opening three notes of "Three Blind Mice.") Do not, in any case, exceed fifteen seconds.

Ask your partner to open his or her eyes, stretch for a moment, then sit with eyes closed again, while you whistle the first fifteen seconds of a popular song such as "The Entertainer," "76 Trombones," or even "Jingle Bells."

Now ask your partner which of these fifteen-second exercises seemed longer. To some, the first will feel longer because there is more space and breath within it; to others, the second will feel longer because it conveys so much more sonic information (variety of notes, number of notes, and number of phases.)

Sound and music subtly affect our sense of time and space and can be used to speed us up, slow us down, or modify our environment.

Music can strengthen memory and learning. We have seen that when we exercise, music can extend our stamina. The same is true when we study. Playing light, easily paced music (for example, Mozart or Vivaldi) in the background helps some people to concentrate for longer periods; others it may distract. Listening to Baroque music while studying can enhance one's ability to memorize spellings, poetry, and foreign words. Dr. Georgi Lozanov's method of using music to enhance memory is perhaps the most well-known, and we will consider it in the chapter on education.

Music can boost productivity. Research into health and memory in work environments has radically changed the way music is used in the workplace. The University of Washington reported that in a study of ninety people copyediting a manuscript, accuracy in the group listening to light classical music for ninety minutes increased by 21.3 percent. By contrast, the skills of those listening to a popular commercial radio format improved by only 2.4 percent. Meanwhile, those subjects editing in silence were 8.3 percent less accurate than those working alongside the usual office noise. AT&T and Du-Pont have cut training time in half with creative music programs. Equitable Life Insurance increased the output of transcribers by 17 percent after introducing music to the office for six weeks, and Mississippi Power & Light raised efficiency in the billing department by 18.6 percent after instituting a nine-month office listening program.

Music enhances romance and sexuality. Music can inspire passion—or extinguish it. A friend once told me about an evening when she wished to seduce her boyfriend over dinner. The candles, flowers, food, and drinks were all in place. At the last minute she pulled an album from the shelf that she felt would be perfect: Beethoven's "Moonlight" Sonata. "What could be more romantic?" she thought, conjuring up images of couples strolling arm-in-arm through the moonlit streets of Paris or Vienna. The doorbell rang, she pushed the "play" button, and, for the next ten minutes, the evening was flawless. What she didn't realized was that only the first movement of the "Moonlight" Sonata actually evokes moonlight. Then the music turns light, fast, active, and she and her boyfriend felt as if they were dashing through their meal. Unfortunately, the tempo didn't carry them into the bedroom. The next sonata on her cassette was the "Pathetique," and what followed was . . . pathetic.

It didn't dawn on my friend to change the music. A better choice might have been the soundtrack to *Out of Africa,* which creates a more leisurely emotional environment.

Music stimulates digestion. Researchers at Johns Hopkins have found that rock music causes people to eat faster and to eat a larger volume of food, while classical music—especially slow string music—makes them eat more slowly and consume less. Taking a cue from these and other market studies, fast-food chains pipe in music that tends to be bright and briskly paced, encouraging customers to fly through their (whopping) meals and out the door—their exits underscored by the ringing of cash registers.

Swanky restaurants feature more sophisticated sounds. I recall the opening of a fine Boulder establishment, which specialized in nouvelle cuisine. Three friends accompanied me to a richly decorative setting full of contemporary art with bright, contrasting colors. We sat down. We perused the enticing menus. But something, I sensed, was wrong—this was not going to be a night out. It was the music: high-powered jazz, a good match for the décor, but not for fellowship, food, and conversation. My friends and I could barely hear each other over the dissonant sounds, and the tempos made us eat too fast. The food was extraordinary, the sound environment a disaster. At the end of the meal, I mentioned this (politely) to the owner, who was shocked, insulted. Why, she had modeled this restaurant on one of the most successful establishments in Greenwich Village. "The music," she said, "is the vital personality of our restaurant. It cannot be changed."

"The prices will keep the students out," I said. "And the sound will keep out the people who can afford the food."

She was out of business within six months.

Lorenzo, an Italian restaurateur I know, is more musically savvy. He has two seatings per evening, at 6:00 and 8:00 P.M., and he works with a harpist, violinist, and pianist to pace each course. "We never want our customers to feel rushed," he says—and then adds, confidentially: "When it's time to leave, I can always add a Strauss waltz to move their conversations out of the restaurant."

Music fosters endurance. Since the birth of culture and civilization, people have worked to the accompaniment of songs on farms and in fields, in ships and on horseback, in marketplaces and around the hearth. Music in such settings fosters stamina and endurance. Think of "I've Been Working on the Railroad," which was sung while people laid the tracks across America. The use of strong beats—about 90 per minute—gives strength, especially if combined with physical exercise, such as walking or dancing. Or even cycling. A recent, musically paced transcontinental bicycle race between Santa Monica, California, and New York City set a world's record of nine days, twenty-three hours, and fifteen minutes. One cyclist reported that listening to cassette tapes featuring instrumental music designed to synchronize cardiovascular and muscular activity increased his long-distance cycling performance by 25 percent. Similar "synchronized high-performance music" tapes are now available for jogging, skiing, and other activities that require stamina and that have their own cadence and rhythm. (Remember, such tapes must be played quietly during exercise to avoid injury to the ear.)

Music enhances unconscious receptivity to symbolism. Film directors are extremely aware of how important the soundtrack is to the success of their movies: At times, the sound can create and maintain the tension of a film better than what's happening on the screen, invoking archetypal symbols and appealing to the viewer's unconscious. In the same way, new, experimental therapies have used relaxation combined with music to tap into the unconscious and release traumas that have long been locked within the body. In Chapter 6, we will look at the most promising therapies in this field.

Music can generate a sense of safety and well-being. "Safe" music is not necessarily beautiful, slow, or romantic. It is simply music that provides a haven for the listener. The popular music of each generation not only gives voice to its collective concerns, but also creates a sonic sanctuary. My parents' and grandparents' generations found safety in the lofty hymns they knew by heart: Through graceful song and prayer they were able to endure the Great Depression, the world wars, and many other hardships. During the Vietnam era, the songs of Simon and Garfunkel, Joan Baez, Judy Collins, and Bob Dylan were written and performed in a spirit of confrontation and protest, yet for millions of young people, this music created a safe way to feel and communicate their complex concerns and fears. Today's youth also use music as a refuge. Through volume, high energy, and forbidden lyrics, contemporary hip hop, rap, punk, and grunge insulate young people in a world that seems to them overly materialistic and hypocritical.

*   *   *

These examples show us the power of music to take us back to self-generated healing systems—and to help us connect to deeper rhythms of life. Over the last fifty years, our society has become dependent on specialists. We have been conditioned to go to the doctor when we feel a pain or an unfamiliar sensation, and we expect him or her to diagnose our condition and tell us what to take or do. As we begin to integrate mind and body and to participate fully in the wellness process, we become more self-reliant. Drawing on our newfound musical wisdom, we may find that the older medical models can be applied more efficiently and creatively.

⟩ Beyond Amadeus

We all have our favorite music and are charmed by its effects. Rather than identifying subspecies of the Mozart Effect—such as the Brahms Effect, the Gershwin Effect, the Sinatra Effect, the Ray Charles Effect, the Grateful Dead Effect, or the Madonna Effect—I will briefly outline some of the broad influences of different types of music.

Please note that, within each genre, there are a variety of styles. Some are active and potent, while others are passive and relaxing. For example, hot jazz may get your blood circulating, set your pulse racing, and send your hormones into overdrive, while cool jazz may lower your blood pressure, put your brain into alpha mode, and mellow you out. The following tendencies are general and can be significantly modified by the listener's condition, diet, environment, and posture:

- Gregorian Chant uses the rhythms of natural breathing to create a sense of relaxed spaciousness. It is excellent for quiet study and mediation and can reduce stress.
- Slower Baroque music (Bach, Handel, Vivaldi, Corelli) imparts a sense of stability, order, predictability, and safety and creates a mentally stimulating environment for study or work.

- Classical music (Haydn and Mozart) has clarity, elegance, and transparency. It can improve concentration, memory, and spatial perception.

- Romantic music (Schubert, Schumann, Tchaikovsky, Chopin, and Liszt) emphasizes expression and feeling, often invoking themes of individualism, nationalism, or mysticism. It is best used to enhance sympathy, compassion, and love.

- Impressionist music (Debussy, Fauré, and Ravel) is based on free-flowing musical moods and impressions, and evokes dreamlike images. A quarter hour of musical daydreaming followed by a few minutes of stretching can unlock your creative impulses and put you in touch with your unconscious.

- Jazz, the blues, Dixieland, soul, calypso, reggae, and other music and dance forms that came out of the expressive African heritage can uplift and inspire, release deep joy and sadness, convey wit and irony, and affirm our common humanity.

- Salsa, rhumba, maranga, macarena, and other forms of South American music have a lively rhythm and beat that can set the heart racing, increase respiration, and get the whole body moving. Samba, however, has the rare ability to soothe and awaken at the same time.

- Big band, pop and top-40, and country-western can inspire light to moderate movement, engage the emotions, and create a sense of well-being.

- Rock music by such artists as Elvis Presley, the Rolling Stones, or Michael Jackson can stir the passions, stimulate active movement, release tension, mask pain, and reduce the effect of other loud, unpleasant sounds in the environment. It can also create tension, dissonance, stress, and pain in the body when we are not in the mood to be energetically entertained.

- Ambient, attitudinal, or New Age music with no dominant rhythm (for example, the music of Seven Halpern or Brian Eno) elongates our sense of space and time and can induce a state of relaxed alertness.

- Heavy metal, punk, rap, hip hop, and grunge can excite the nervous system, leading to dynamic behavior and self-

expression. It can also signal to others (especially adults living in the same house as their musically assaultive teens),
the depth and intensity of the younger generation's inner
turmoil and need for release.

- Religious and sacred music, including shamanic drumming,
church hymns, gospel music, and spirituals, can ground us in
the moment and lead to feelings of deep peace and spiritual
awareness. It can also be remarkably useful in helping us to
transcend—and release—our pain.

⸙ Pulse, Pace, and Pattern

Music has a pulse, as does everything that lives. Pulsa-
tion means flow, the steady current of energy coursing through
and around us. Our circulatory system is an intricate network of
surge and release, activity and rest. Finding the pulse of music
opens—or paces—the pulse of the listener.

Not only music but language itself is rhythmic. Record your
voice as you speak on the telephone, and you will find that there
are phrases—musical sentences—within which you can sense the
pulse and pace of an underlying rhythm. You are actually reading
the words of this book at a certain pace and rhythm. Turn on your
classical station for a moment, reread this full page, and notice
whether you are reading faster or slower. Then switch the channel
to a station playing popular music, and notice how your ability to
receive the sound or information has changed. As you read this page
aloud, you'll notice how the pace or pattern changes once again.
You will discover that your voice—and the way you convey spoken
information—is truly musical.

Although we do not become perfectly synchronized with music
merely by listening to it, the pulse of the music does influence the
tempo of our thinking and behavior. At a dance, for instance, the
music will stimulate body movement, and different styles of music
will cause us to move in different ways. However, while driving a
car and listening to the radio or tape deck, the body won't harmonize to the same degree. We're thinking about driving, so our con-

sciousness is divided. If music is playing in the background while we are talking to a friend, it has much less effect than it does when we're attending a concert.

Nevertheless, whether we focus on it or not, the pulse of music subtly defines the boundaries of our physical, mental, and social environments, influencing how strongly, harmoniously, and fluidly life moves within and around us.

Closely associated with pulse is pace. Fast or slow, the pace of sound can determine whether we feel healthy, rushed, relaxed, sluggish, out in front, or completely left behind. Music that doesn't have a standard, organized beat may invigorate us for a time, but could annoy us over the long run. The pace of sound affects our inner metronome, our ability to coordinate our physical and mental functions.

Music creates multiple patterns simultaneously. The structure and design of its tones affect our body and our movement, while its changing harmonies and chords can sway our emotions. The lyrics, or stories, that ride in on a piece of music can take us back in time to losses or joys. This is why we love listening to the songs of our youth or early adult years; the music evokes rich and personal memories.

Music can be delicate and quiet, but never sedentary. Even a tone that extends for hours at a time, unvarying, carries a pulsing wave that affects our mind and body at many levels. What we bring to each sound is also of vital importance. In terms of healing, the Mozart Effect extends far beyond the sound itself or the quality of the performance or recording. You, the listener, determine the final impact: You are an active conductor and participant in the process of orchestrating health.

Your cassettes, compact discs, and audio components give you unprecedented control over how you organize the pace and rhythm of your day. The music you play when you wake up on a workday is probably vastly different from the music that you enjoy on a leisurely weekend or vacation. By paying close attention to the pulse, pace, and pattern of music, you can create a sonic diet to keep you energized, refreshed, and relaxed throughout the changing seasons and cycles of your life.

Nature also responds to the Mozart Effect. Some of the most intriguing research in the field of healing with sound has explored the use of music to enhance plant growth. Dan Carlson is a pioneer in what is called sonic bloom. In 1960, when serving in the U.S. Army in Korea, he witnessed the horrors of food shortages and observed what people would eat when they ran out of staple crops. First, they'd eat the fruit or the full plant containing the seed; then the stalks or vines; and, finally, the roots. Within a couple of years, there was no food.

Carlson went back to his home in Minnesota and contemplated ways to improve plant growth, not only by enriching soil, but also by strengthening the mouthlike openings in leaf structures. He thought it might be possible for plants to select what they needed to grow best rather than being force-fed (as the apostles of new chemical soil supplements preached). He began to experiment with the idea that sound would prompt plants to open up their pores, enabling them to absorb more nutrients. First, he considered the times of the day when plant pores were most open, and discovered that plants grew best in the early morning when the birds were singing. Then it hit him. Perhaps certain types of music or nonmelodic sounds would stimulate plant growth.

Carlson devised cassette tapes that contained nonmusical sounds (that is, sounds that we don't consider true melody). He found a specialist in Minneapolis, Michael Holtz, who confirmed that certain music has vibrations and frequencies in common with birdsong. One of the first types of music he found to which plants seemed to respond is played by the sitar, the traditional stringed instrument from India. The sound of the sitar is not for all Western ears, but plants can't seem to get enough of it.

Meanwhile, Dorothy Retallack, a graduate student at Temple Beull College in Denver, also began to experiment with plants and music. She constructed five small greenhouses and placed corn, squash, marigolds, zinnias, and petunias inside. The greenhouses were all the same size and received the same lighting, water, and soil. For several months, she played different types of music to plants in four of the chambers. (As a control, the fifth had no sounds piped in.) One group of plants got Bach, the second Indian classical music, the third loud rock, and the last county-western. She found that Bach and Indian music stirred the growth of the plants dramatically. The flowers were more abundant, and the vines even grew toward the speakers. In the rock & roll greenhouse, all was not well: There were many fewer flowers, and the plants didn't seem to want to grow. In the country-western greenhouse, to Retallack's surprise, she found that the plants developed almost identically to those in the house where there was no music at all.

⟨ The Drum of Life

Music can have a healing effect on families and communities as well as on individuals and plants. Although every musical instrument can be used to this end, percussive instruments, especially drums, have traditionally been used to energize or influence groups of people. From the most spontaneous Zulu tribal drumming circle to Ron Snyder's Da-Drum, an ensemble from the Dallas Symphony, percussion is the pulse of an instrumental piece or song. Early in the 1990s, Mickey Hart, longtime drummer for the Grateful Dead, wrote *Drumming at the Edge of Magic,* which revealed the importance of drumming in the history of culture and civilization. Soon a grassroots movement, Rhythm for Life, developed to support creative drumming and percussion activities throughout the country.

Many lives have been transformed by the improvisational musical events sponsored by Rhythm for Life. One belonged to Louise, the grandmother of six boys. Louise had practically raised her grandchildren, as both of their parents worked, and now lived with her extended family. Music was a part of their home and church life, but not always in ways Louise enjoyed. At times, in fact, she felt cursed, because three of her grandchildren wanted to be drummers, and she was forced to endure years of throbbing, often painful sounds blasting from the basement of her home.

The house seemed to have arhythmia from three in the afternoon until ten at night.

One night, the oldest son, Rick, asked his grandmother if she'd like to go out with him to hear some drumming. Tolerant, kind, and loving as she was, Louise dreaded the thought of partaking in some ear-splitting extravaganza. But she was so amazed to be invited that she accepted: It couldn't be worse than it already was at home.

Rick took his grandmother to a large gymnasium where elders, children, and people of every age in between came together, all with stick, mallet, or conga in hand. Louise knew she could never play such things; she began to dread her entrance into the gym, feeling like a condemned soul on the threshold of the underworld.

Inside, Rick handed her a light frame drum with a long handle (it looked like a tennis racquet) and said, "Here G'ma. Here's a Remo for you. Bet it's going to be your friend."

Louise was horrified. "I think this is going to be too loud for me tonight," she said.

"That's why I gave you the drum," said Rick. "Whenever it gets too loud, just hit it and it will soften the sounds, G'ma. I think you'll like it."

Soon, many people gathered in the middle of the gymnasium with instruments that Louise had never seen. They all looked normal, just like the folks at her church. . . . And then the pulse started, and Louise found herself in a world she'd never entered before— even with all of the sounds coming out of her basement all those years. Afterward, she told me that banging on that simple frame drum amidst all that pulsing, she *became* the beat. She also became fifty-five years younger in a mere thirty minutes. Knowing there was no right way or wrong way to drum felt liberating: "I never knew that I could never make a mistake before," she said. "And I didn't know I was a musician!"

Now, a couple of times a week, Louise joins her grandsons in the cellar, playing backup percussion. Incidentally, she has also introduced them to the *quieter* aspects of sound.

A strong sense of group identity—and of belonging—is created through events like the ones sponsored by Rhythm for Life. All over the country percussion groups of mixed ages meet regularly: seniors drumming to Lawrence Welk, Glenn Miller, and other music of their generation; young people jamming to the sounds of Gloria Estefan, Boyz II Men, and Hootie and the Blowfish. Making music quickly forges strong bonds, allowing people to come together for a few precious beats of eternal time.

CHAPTER 4

Sound Voice

YOUR ORIGINAL HEALING INSTRUMENT

"While the mate was getting the hammer, Ahab without speaking was slowly rubbing the gold piece against the skirts of his jacket, as if to heighten its luster, and without using any words was meanwhile lowly humming to himself, producing a sound so strangely muffled and inarticulate that it seemed the mechanical humming of the wheels of his vitality in him."
—HERMAN MELVILLE, *MOBY DICK*

The human voice is a remarkable instrument of healing, our most accessible sonic tool. The slightest utterance massages muscle tissue in the upper body and causes it to vibrate from within. Every movement of the body, in turn, affects the way we inhale and exhale, and so has an impact on our voice. Yet we rarely pay attention to our own voice—at least, until we use it in an unfamiliar way—say, by learning a new language, one of the few times when we are not distracted by the meaning of the sounds.

The foundation of the voice is breath. We take in breath, transport it from our lungs to the depths of our cells, and discharge it back into the world. In many religions, breath implies spirit. The Hebrew word *ruach* means not only the divine spirit of Genesis hovering over the earth, but also the breath of God. Similar dual meanings can be found in many languages. As we discover ways to invoke the spirit through the voice, we notice patterns emerging in our breath, the movements of our body, and—if we are exquisitely sensitive—our brain waves. I suggest that you think of your breath like this: as the *prana,* the *ki,* the life force on which the voice rides. With each breath, you take in the same air that was once breathed by Buddha, Jesus, Shakespeare, and, yes, even Mozart.

The word *voice* comes from the French *voix* and the Latin *vox.* English words such as *vocal, vowel, vouch,* and *provoke* share the same root. "Vocation," a related word, comes from *vocare* (to call), and originally signified a musical, or at least a rhythmic, calling. It's no coincidence that such calling, especially in the form of a *chant,* plays a prominent role in world religions. At the Wailing Wall in Jerusalem, the fervent recitation and the bobbing of the head by devout Jews elevates them to the realm of the spiritual. Muslims, in facing Mecca and praying five times a day, chant from the Holy Koran. Followers of Tibetan Buddhism recite mantras as they twirl prayer wheels. Even secular America has its mantras, such as "Hold that line!" and "Go team, go!," which echo through sports stadiums and arenas, energizing millions of sports fans.

In this chapter we will look at the extraordinary effects of self-generated sounds such as tones, chants, mantras, and raps, which not only bring us closer to the divine spirit, but also, on a more mundane and practical level, offer ways to relieve pain, control day-to-day tension, and increase vitality.

≀ The Primal Voice

The birth cry marks the commencement of life. Thereafter, from its first coos and moans, the baby expresses its being and consciousness through its voice. "Express" is putting it mildly. A baby can bawl and whine for hours, and its cries convey the incredible power that it knows to be its *self.* Utterance then becomes the pathway to self-knowledge, self-naming, and self-respect—as well as self-hatred. The voice, in many ways, is the most exposed "organ" of the body.

Although usually shrill to adult ears, the infant's cries, shrieks, and babbles release stress, express emotion, and constitute an essential stage in development. To encourage vocalization, it is vital for parents (and siblings) to play games like pat-a-cake with babies and toddlers. Gurgles and goos, oohs and ahs, communicate not only the joy the baby feels, but also help the baby to realize, long before he or she can coordinate his or her body or thinking, that the voice is the basic tool for relating to the world.

With the first satisfied coo, the infant begins to acquire its earliest consonant. From *ma* and *ba* to *ga* and *da*, the vocal chords grow from a tiny 3 millimeters to 5.5 millimeters by the time the child is one year old. And by the time he or she is a teenager, the vocal cords will have expanded to nearly 10 millimeters. Breathing also changes with age. Because of the very small opening of the larynx, an infant must breathe nearly one hundred times per minute to get enough oxygen in the first weeks after birth. Respiration slows as the child matures, and by the late teens has stabilized to between thirty and forty breaths a minute.

The child soon learns to comprehend the meaning of words by attending to the order of sounds and shifts in tones and noting the feelings conveyed by each. The melodic variation that the voice exhibits in language is called *prosody*. Innovative educators pay enormous attention to the development of vocal and musical skills in the child, since it is generally true that the more exposure to music, poetry, and reading out loud in childhood and infancy, the richer the voice will be.

As we develop our linguistic and cognitive abilities, we tend in modern society to dismiss as unimportant the primal sounds so natural in childhood. I have long been distressed that we give such small consideration to the loss of the boy's familiar "childhood" voice when he passes through puberty to manhood. With his initiation into adulthood, the youth must not only give up the feelings of childhood but also, in the most potent vibratory sense, the voice of childhood. Girls do not usually pass through such sonic obstacles. Their speech and persona do not alter as radically until menopause, when the female voice often drops noticeably.

The popularity of modern therapies devoted to reexperiencing one's birth, making primal screams, and discovering the inner child appear to be connected with recovering the spontaneous, intuitive voice and vocal freedom that we enjoyed in infancy and childhood. We all need to be heard. Once we know that we are heard, we begin to mature by developing ideas that will hold listeners' attention. In our modern society where teenagers often feel that they have not been heard, the loud screams of punk, heavy metal, and other forms of popular music may help release the pent-up emotions of a dysfunctional childhood, or simply the tensions of adolescence. Similarly, when we are hurt, we invariably find that there is a sound that our body wants to make. Often the end of suffering or the release of pain is accompanied and accelerated by the sounds we make with our voice. These sounds of suffering, in turn, can bring pain to empathic listeners.

One exercise I use in the classroom involves asking groups of students to make nonsense sounds. I call this "secular glossolalia"—speaking in tongues—because it is a form of babbling that lets them express emotion. The exercise is easy. At the beginning, I point to something a student is wearing and make up a funny word, such as "tingledrop" for earring. Each person has to pass the tingeledrop along and give it a new name. Then students are asked to invent new names for other items, such as a chair, the sky, or a piano.

In the next phase, the group is broken down into pairs and one person in each pair is asked to describe to the other something stressful. The only rule is that students may not speak in English or in any language they know fluently. Many remain tongue-tied until I give them a vocabulary of phonemes that taps into their intuitive right brain and emotional midbrain. Babbling in a singsong fashion, we say "bippity, boppity boo," "hippity, hoppity, hoo," "flip, flap, flop, flup," bouncing nonsense syllables back and forth. Then I ask them to spend about ten minutes improvising more nonsense syllables, using this new "language" to unburden themselves to their fellow students.

The role of the listener is just that—to listen, and to serve as a compassionate presence. The listener makes no comment, only nodding or gesturing while the babbler expresses his or her innermost feelings. There is no verbal therapy or interpretation, simply healing with sound. After both people have had the chance to speak in this new tongue, they discuss privately in English the emotions they felt. Over and over, students comment that this process has a greater cleansing and therapeutic effect than all the talk in the world. Even without meaningful syllables, the voice can release tension and anxiety, leaving the students feeling remarkably improved.

Finally, the group spends an hour using calls, rhymes, shouts, and raps in order to further develop vocal skills without the encumbrance of language. Afterward, when a student returns to plain English to describe the day that has passed, his or her voice is always richer, more colorful, and more vibrant.

⟩ I Tone, Therefore I Am

"Three times my husband erased the recording on the answering machine and tried again to get Dara, our six-year-old, to greet callers and instruct them to leave a message. Each time she said: 'Please leave your tone at the end of your message.' Finally he gave up and recorded her voice with its inverted message.

"The greeting has been on our answering machine for more than a year, and continues to attract return messages from callers, even some from those who have misdialed. People tell us how Dara's words have touched their hearts. Dara's grandfather pointed to the reason: We do leave a tone by the sound of our voice and the feel of our actions, an impression that may be remembered long after our messages are forgotten."
—GUIDEPOST

As adults, many of us have lost touch with our voice as an expressive tool. We aren't as unselfconscious or spontaneous as we were as children. But if we only try, we can do amazing things with our vocal equipment.

In the mid-eighties, when I was living in Richardson, Texas, I spent a period of time systematically exploring different sounds. My "laboratory" was a small, extremely packed music room that held a Erard grand piano, two synthesizers, more than sixty Oriental bells, three German metallaphones, an English upright piano, and two octaves of bamboo instruments from Thailand. One day I turned down the lights, put a blindfold over my eyes and earplugs in my ears, and began experimenting with self-generated sounds.

The point of this self-imposed blindness and deafness was to see if I could touch some dimension of myself that would understand sound as Helen Keller had. I noticed that by putting my hands on different parts of my body, I could *feel* my voice. Higher sounds vibrated in certain places in my skull, while certain vowels opened up my chest cavity and massaged my throat. My hands became seismomitors, sensing the subtle variations between, say, a 2 and a 2.5 earthquake. It was not singing, and I was not concerned with the breath or the diaphragm. I was engaged in some kind of sonic Zen meditation.

This exercise went on throughout the afternoon and until late in the evening. It must have lasted twelve hours. Exhausted, I went to sleep, but decided to keep the blinders on and earplugs in. I felt like a giant tortoise that had retreated into its shell, and what followed was extraordinary. The loss of sight and hearing—which would have been a nightmare had my senses been damaged by some accident—became an unexpected gift. I actually began to dream of my *sonus* (sound), that part of me that underlies my personality. I could perceive a distant roar inside the cells of my body—as if, previously, external sounds, light, and other sensory stimulation had obscured my awareness of this inner sound.

When I woke up, I held a tone for perhaps five minutes. I then moved on to the most simple Gregorian chant, followed by a South Indian hymn, at the same time contemplating what I had learned over months of sounding in different postures with my eyes open and closed. Humming while lying down with my eyes closed had an effect altogether different from sitting with my eyes open and a fixed gaze. My inner landscape changed when I moved, compared to when I remained still and made sounds. I realized that to enter the world of sustained vowel sounds—to begin toning—is to enter nonordinary time, controlled by the vibrating plates of shifting inner continents.

I did not coin the word *toning*. Meaning *to make sound with an elongated vowel for an extended period*, it dates back at least to the fourteenth century. "Tuning and toning each Word, each Syllable, and Letter to their due Cadence," wrote Jonathan Swift in 1711. And, in 1973, Laurel Elizabeth Keyes wrote a simple and intuitive book called *Toning: The Creative Power of the Voice,* which reintroduced the word into the modern vocabulary.

Our paths crossed a few years after publication of her book, although Keyes's method did not make a deep impression at the time. In the summer of 1978, I was in Denver interviewing for a position with a large church music organization when one of my friends insisted that I meet a remarkable woman who healed people with the voice. I was curious, but not particularly excited. I entered a modest home and was welcomed by a short, lively woman who had spent her life working in the field of comparative religion. In 1963, Keyes founded the Order of Fransisters and Brothers, a lay order following the injunction of the well-known prayer of Saint Francis: "Lord, make me an instrument of thy peace."

From the moment she met me at the door, Laurel's incredible warmth and love were palpable. Toning, she explained, was an ancient method of healing that she hoped would, because of advances in science, come to be recognized and applied with fresh understanding. It did not, she said emphatically, depend on faith. "Anyone can use toning, just as we use electricity," she explained. "There are natural channels in the energy in our body, and if we recognize and learn to flow with them, they will keep us healthy." Laurel asked me to make sounds and, at her prompting, my voice glided upward and downward so that she could feel the energy in my body. (I remember finding it peculiar that, listening to my voice, she would stand directly in front of me and then move from one side to the other. Now I use this manner of listening myself; it allows me to hear a speaker's voice clearly with each of my ears.)

Keyes's book recounts many stories of people healed—seemingly by miracle—with tone. Although my success with toning has been more modest, I have witnessed thousands of people relax into their voices, become more centered in their bodies, release fear and other emotions, and free themselves from physical pain. Over the past eight years, I have seen many people apply toning in practical ways, from relaxing before a dreaded test to eliminating the symptoms of tinnitus or migraine headaches. Toning can release psychological stress before surgery, lower the blood pressure and respiratory rate of cardiac patients, and reduce tension in those undergoing MRIs and CAT scans. Toning has also been effective in relieving insomnia and other sleep disorders.

All forms of vocalization, including singing, chanting, yodeling, humming, reciting prose or poetry, or simply talking, can be therapeutic. But I have found that nothing rivals toning. Other methods, especially singing and speaking, move the vibratory epicenters so quickly that there is little time for sounds to resonate and take hold. Toning oxygenates the body, deepens breathing, relaxes the muscles, and stimulates energy flow. When performed by a voice rich in timbre, toning will massage and tune up the entire body.

Celia Mantrozos, a professional musician, teacher, and performer, came to me for intensive vocal training in 1990. Only a few days later, on the way home, she fainted at the Denver airport and was taken to the hospital, where doctors discovered a hemangioma, a nonmalignant type of brain tumor, in the right temporal lobe. Well enough to be transported to a hospital closer to her home, Celia underwent a five-hour operation in Dallas to remove the tumor.

Unlike other patients, she did not appear to be experiencing discomfort after surgery. In fact, the neurological ward had never had such a peaceful craniotomy patient. To what, a nurse asked Celia, did she attribute her remarkable calm? Celia recalled that, as soon as she had regained consciousness, she had hummed continuously. "I tone and chant," she said, to the surprise of the nurse and her doctor, "and that keeps my brain intact." Celia declined medication for pain, claiming not to have any. Finally, she agreed to take Advil, but only to reduce the swelling. The proud surgeon released her from the hospital a few days later, amazed at her recovery.

Walking to work several years ago, Betty Brenneman, an accomplished string player and teacher of special education in Racine, Wisconsin, slipped on ice and broke her right ankle. She was in the middle of a park and knew that it could easily be ten or fifteen minutes before help arrived. She had been toning for six months and developing an awareness of where different sounds resonated in her body. As excruciating pain shot through her fallen body, Betty experimented with her voice, gliding it up and down to find the sound that would release her pain. Feeling a response in her ankle, she tried various vowel sounds, and discovered that long O worked best.

"In twenty seconds, I felt no pain!" she recalls. "I noticed the transcendent beauty of the park. Wondering if the pain would return if I stopped singing, I stopped, and it returned with a vengeance! I immediately resumed toning, and in about fifteen to twenty seconds, the pain stopped. I frequently sang to my ankle as it healed, and it made a big difference."

INTERLUDE

Sounding Away Pain

The voice can be used as a masking device for severe pain. Sit or stand in a comfortable position, or, if you are bedridden, position yourself so that your throat and neck are relaxed.

Now close your eyes and locate the source of your physical discomfort. Make an *ah* or an *ou* sound (the most soothing) and visualize the pain in your body being released through your voice. The *ou* sound is pronounced like the *ou* in the word *soup*.

If the pain is acute you may want to make a high *ee* sound. The *ee* and *ay* sounds release sharp pains and can help you to let go of inner anger and torment. (Be sure to let anyone nearby know that you are experimenting with sound and not to be alarmed.)

It takes a few minutes of toning before the pain begins to change its shape. Never strain the voice, and rest between each minute or two of sounding. Often sounds can trigger an endorphin release that will mask the pain for a short time. Pain that has emotional origins may also be released, which will enable the body to heal more effectively.

Remember, there is no one sound that works for everybody or produces exactly the same effects. Experiment, and find the unique tone or tones that work for you.

Toning can also stabilize the emotions. Janis Page of Denver was in the grip of fear and anger. From her studies in Chinese medicine, she knew that those emotions were correlated with liver and kidney imbalance, so she directed her tones into those organs. Lying down with her eyes open, she began to feel a strong, deep pulsing energy moving through her entire body as she made vowel sounds. It was especially strong near the middle of her body, where the liver and kidney are situated. When she stopped toning, Janis remained on her back and felt the pulsing continue for several minutes, gradually diminishing in intensity. By the time it had faded, she felt herself balanced and at peace, her fear and anger gone.

Humming, a quiet form of toning, is especially effective in relieving disorders in the voice box itself. Singing teachers and others whose work involves putting special demands on their voice may develop nodules, polyps, lesions, and abnormal folds in the throat and larynx. Humming an *m* sound, says Jean Westerman Gregg, president of the National Association of Teachers of Singing, is responsible for some astonishing restorations of normal functioning. "I am continually amazed at the healing power of the larynx itself when excessive pressure is removed and gentle vibration is used as a restorative technique," she has written. As an example, she cites the case of a public school music teacher who was found to have a blood-filled polyp in her larynx. The woman was pregnant and did not wish to have surgery until after delivery. Taking matters into her own hands, she began to hum every day. When after six months she gave birth to a little girl, doctors found that her larynx had returned to normal, and she no longer needed surgery. Gregg encourages singing teachers to experiment with humming, but to do so carefully and gently, being guided by intuition. The vibratory sensation, she says, should be allowed to go where it will, without an attempt to "place" it.

INTERLUDE
A Five-Day Toning Class

One of the simplest ways to calm your mind, stabilize the rhythms in your body, and improve your voice is through toning or humming. Did you know that Mozart hummed when he composed? In a letter explaining his method, he wrote: "When I am, as it were, completely myself, entirely alone, and of good cheer . . . my ideas flow best and most abundantly. *Whence* and *how* they come, I know not; nor can I force them. Those ideas that please me I retain in memory, and am accustomed, as I have been told, to hum them to myself."

As described in this chapter, toning involves making elongated vowel sounds and serves to balance brain waves, improve respiration, deepen the breath, reduce the heart rate, and impart a general sense of well-being. If you practice these exercises for five minutes each day, you will be on your way to discovering the positive effects of tone.

Day 1—*Hum*

Sit comfortably in a chair, close your eyes, and spend five minutes humming—not a melody, but a pitch that feels comfortable. Relax your jaw and feel the energy of the hum within your body. Bring the palms of your hands to your cheeks and notice how much vibration is occurring within your jaw. This five-minute massage will release stress and help you to relax.

Day 2—*Ahhhh*

The *ah* sound immediately evokes a relaxation response. You produce it naturally when you yawn, and it can help you both wake up and go to sleep. If you feel a great deal of stress and tension, take a few minutes to relax your jaw and make a quiet *ah*. There is no need to sing. Just allow the sound to move gently through your breath. After a minute or so, you will notice that your breaths are much longer and that you feel more relaxed. In your office or at school, where toning may disturb others, you can simply close your eyes, breathe out, and think the *ah*. Although this is not quite as effective, it is still useful.

Day 3—*Ee*

This is the most stimulating of all vowel sounds. It can awaken the mind and body, functioning as a kind of sonic caffeine. When you feel drowsy while driving or are sluggish in the afternoon, three to five minutes of a rich, high *ee* sound will stimulate the brain, activate the body, and keep you alert.

Day 4—*Oh*

The *oh* and *om* sounds are considered the richest of all by many people who tone or chant. Make the *oh* sound. If you put your hand on your head, cheek, and chest, you will notice that the *oh* vibrates most of the upper parts of the body. Five minutes of the *oh* can change the skin temperature, muscle tension, brain waves, and breath and heart rates. It is a great tool for an instant tune-up.

Day 5—Experimental

Start at the lowest part of your voice, and let it glide upward, like a very slow elevator. Make vowel sounds that are relaxing and that arise effortlessly from the jaw or throat. Allow the voice to resonate throughout the body. Now explore the ways in which you can massage parts of your skull, throat, and chest with long vowel sounds. Let your hands trace the upper parts of your body very slowly, and you will see which vowels emit the strongest, most stress-releasing energy.

In the 1940s and 1950s, some of the greatest innovations in voice therapy were made by Dr. Paul J. Moses, a clinical professor of speech and voice in the Division of Otolaryngology at the Stanford University School of Medicine. He considered the voice the primary expression of individuality and believed that by listening to it, neurotic patterns could be analyzed, observed, and at times treated. Like tree rings, the tone, inflection, intensity, and other objective characteristics of the voice offered clear indications of each person's life history, he asserted.

Through a series of recorded interviews, Moses was able to make a complete medical diagnosis of each of his patients. Based on the range and symmetry of the individual's vocal line, the prevalent key or tone to the voice, the way the voice expressed melody and rhythm, along with loudness, precision, accents, and other variables, he constructed a comprehensive physical and psychological profile. As an experiment, he once analyzed the personality of an adolescent boy by listening only to a recording of the boy's voice. His results compared favorably with a Rorschach test and the report of a psychiatrist who had analyzed the boy in person. "Vocal dynamics truthfully reflect psychodynamics," he concluded. "Each emotion has its vocal expression." Moses's pioneer work in treating schizophrenia with the voice has been the subject of recent medical studies, as we shall see in the Postlude to this book.

Over the last decade, I have developed my own approach to vocal therapy, one that builds on the insights of Moses and Tomatis. In every person's tone and breath lies the key to understanding temperament, and to diagnosing many types of physical and psychological disorders. Unlike the singing voice, the toning voice has not usually been rehearsed or trained to enhance or mask certain distinctive characteristics.

Vocal scans, for example, can be a revelatory tool in the evaluation of personality. A scan is a light and natural ascent or descent in pitch. It is smooth and fluid rather than rough or in steps—like a pianist moving up and down the keyboard in what is known as a *glissando*. The spontaneous physical gestures that accompany a vowel scan offer vital clues to a person's nature. Some people launch into the scan carelessly, with no preparation, while others start and stop a number of times, pausing to reflect and fidget. It is remarkable how all this tends to mirror their basic personality traits. By listening to the rhythm of the voice, its strength, the amount of breath it holds, and which vowel sounds are made in which registers (for example, the chest or head), precise conclusions can be drawn regarding an individual's personality and general health.

As Sherlock Holmes could tell almost everything about someone from a solitary hair or a callused finger, a skilled listening therapist should be able to diagnose the broad outlines of a person's past, present, and probable future from a single tone, which I believe to be a hologram of the entire body. Actually, most of us do a more limited version of this on the telephone every day without realizing it. At the first utterance of a friend or family member, we know intuitively whether everything is going smoothly or if there is some cause for alarm.

Often, I hear within the voice emotions that are blocked, the result of traumas that have been "forgotten"—or repressed. Kay, a forty-seven-year-old homemaker from Pennsylvania, came to my class with a large cyst on the right side of her right breast. Although I could not see it and did not know about it when I heard her voice, I could detect a large "break" in her scan. When I stood on her left side, there was no break in her voice; when I stood on her right side, there was no voice in her middle range.

I asked Kay if she was experiencing anything peculiar in the right side of her chest. As tears filled her eyes, she told me about her cyst. I asked her to close her eyes and scan again thinking of that area of her body. Within two minutes, she began to sweat and moan. Finally, she screamed, "Don't take it away! Don't take it away! Don't take it away!"

I sat with her and held her hand for ten minutes while she rocked, hummed, and cried. I encouraged her to breathe deeply and hum very quietly. Finally, she opened her eyes and said, "Only my aunt knew I had a baby when I was fourteen. I wanted to keep it, I wanted to feed it, and all I remember is holding his head to my right breast for only a minute. Then he was gone." Within a day, her aunt told Kay never to think of the baby again, to go back to school and resume her life as if nothing had happened. She shut down all memories and feelings about the baby. Kay went on to say that she had since married, had two children, and made a good life for herself.

I suggested that she sit and imagine nursing her lost son, humming lullabies to him. A therapist who was present invited Kay to process this work with her, if she wished.

Within three months, her cyst had completely disappeared.

❧ The Voices of Venus and Mars

"How'd you figure out where they [the boots worn during the murder] were?"

"Well, that's just it. I was loading the dishwasher, you know, humming a little tune, and boom, I just knew."

—SUE GRAFTON, M IS FOR MALICE

In his absorbing book, *The Singing Cure,* Paul Newham, founder of the International Association for Voice and Movement Therapy in London, explores the therapeutic differences between speaking and singing. Whereas Sigmund Freud pioneered the "talking cure," in which patients' free associations offered a "royal road" to the unconscious mind, Newham argues that the singing voice offers a more direct route to the unconscious. "The whole purpose of psychoanalysis is to disable the controlling domination of the conscious, particularly the superego, to see what emerges when the language of the unconscious is allowed to speak," he explains. "Freud did that through language, through free association. I think that it's one stage further to strip away verbality itself and to allow the voice to speak directly [through song]."

On a recent visit to London, I met with Newham to discuss his current work, especially his research into the voice and women's health. He told me that many women experience the voice as a point of convergence between the thoughts and the feelings, almost like a bottleneck. Thoughts descend from the head and converge in the voice before they are articulated, while feelings are primarily experienced as rising up from below the voice, with love and passion coming from the heart and grief and sadness from the stomach.

For women, Newham argues, sound has strong biological associations. By opening the back of the throat to its widest point, women may on some level feel that everything in their abdomen is going to come up and out through the mouth. Look, for example, at a woman who has had a hysterectomy. Often, says Newham, she will keep her vocal tract narrow and experience herself as having a "lovely voice." Because the vocal tract is so constricted, the woman feels no connection with the lower part of the body—which is fine by her. But when the pharyngeal space widens (as when, for example, she sings full-throttle), the woman suddenly feels as if she's gulping or vomiting. The result of this opening up is that the woman experiences the "emptiness" below more directly. But with voice work, designed to keep the vocal tract open, she can overcome her feelings of emptiness and regain her preoperative feelings about her body.

In Boca Raton, Florida, Irene Kessler, Ph.D., has been working with women with eating disorders for eight years. In a group of compulsive eaters, bulimics, and bulimarexics, she has introduced Newham's system of voice movement therapy, along with journal keeping, drawing, and other expressive arts. "These women have all been in therapy previously, but are still having problems with food, body image, and weight," says Kessler. "For all of them, food is the main focus of their day. They are unable to find out why they remain depressed and unhappy, although they function pretty well in their daily lives."

The initial phase of therapy called for the women to take part in movement exercises. Singing and toning were gradually added, which made participants more relaxed. Their willingness to interact and enjoy their voices markedly increased, and soon afterward they were able to begin individual vocal work. As Irene massaged their necks and shoulders, the women's voices began to open up. "It was obvious at the start that there was a lot of difficulty maintaining the sounds," says Kessler. "They choked off, stopped in mid-sound. At the same time, feelings were held back: 'I know I had one tear, but then it stopped,' they'd say. They were able to express themselves through their voices, but they didn't connect the sound to their bodies; their feelings were nonspecific. At the same time, the exercises brought a sense of relief, of being clean inside, and after making sounds they became very calm."

After about ten weekly two-hour group meetings, significant changes began to occur for the women. They were able to speak more freely of their emotions, and their interest in creative pursuits revived. At the same time, their eating habits improved, and they expressed renewed interest in cooking healthy food, resisting overwork, and exercising. A year later, the members of the group continue to benefit from a tremendous change in self-esteem, emotional balance, and physical health.

Men, too, have vocal issues specific to their sex. The change in a boy's voice at puberty is more profound than that of a girl. A boy's voice may drop as much as a whole octave in the musical scale, whereas a girl's may drop only a second or a third. Over the years, I have found that men are able to explore childhood traumas through making higher sounds and tones. I've met dozens of men who, while singing or chanting in a higher register, remembered the intuitive and vulnerable side of themselves that they left behind in childhood. Occasionally, a man may relive major experiences from his early teens. Jason, a man in his thirties, sat next to me in a workshop directed by James Hillman and Michael Mead. In an exercise designed to evoke early childhood memories, Jason felt stuck. Then, as if struck by lightning, his voice became soft and light. He recalled his mother and sister telling him of his grandfather's death. He began to weep and then remembered his father telling him never to cry again. Later that month, his voice dropped.

Another approach to voice therapy was pioneered by Alfred Wolfsohn, a German-born singing teacher whose work remains on the cutting edge of healing. Plagued by the sounds of artillery and human agony that he had heard in the trenches as a soldier in World War I, Wolfsohn cured himself of aural hallucinations by singing the terrible sounds that haunted him, thereby exorcising the demons of fear and guilt. Discovering that he was able to express a wide spectrum of sounds—of joy and bliss as well as terror and suffering—Wolfsohn went on to develop a therapeutic method based on opening the voice. Fleeing Nazi Germany for London, Wolfsohn opened a small research center, where he taught his students and clients to break their own, individual "sound barriers" and make a full range of spontaneous noises, including those of animals, birds, and even machines.

Interestingly, Wolfsohn strongly opposed the classical singing tradition that divided the vocal range by gender: soprano and alto for women; tenor, baritone, and bass for men. Building on Jung's concept of the *anima* and *animus*—the feminine side of a man and the masculine side of a woman—Wolfsohn taught that by extending the vocal range through singing exercises, one could contact the opposite sex within oneself, thereby integrating the psyche and healing a variety of psychological and physical conditions.

In 1955, to demonstrate the range of the human voice, Wolfsohn created a showcase for one of his pupils, Jenny Johnson, whom scientists and medical doctors confirmed had developed a range of between eight and nine octaves. Johnson was able to sing all the parts in Mozart's *The Magic Flute,* from the high soprano of the Queen of the Night to the deep bass of the sorcerer Sarastro.

In the course of his long, productive life, Wolfsohn showed that the personality could be deepened and enriched by opening the voice. "The truth is that the natural human voice, freed from all artificial restrictions, is able to embrace all these categories and registers—indeed, it is able to go much further," he concluded.

⟩ The Power of Gregorian Chant

Hear, O my son, the words of the Lord, and incline thy heart's ear.
—THE RULE OF SAINT BENEDICT, OPENING WORDS

One of the most amazing stories of healing in the annals of sound and music is the case of the melancholy monks. In the late 1960s, Dr. Alfred Tomatis was summoned to investigate a strange malaise that had descended upon a Benedictine monastery in the South of France. It was shortly after Vatican II that the brothers had become listless, fatigued, and mildly depressed. Although the monks were anxious about a series of theological reforms, dietary changes, and new routines, their physical symptoms had no clear cause. As such, their condition had stumped several leading European specialists, and nothing seemed able to restore the devout brothers and their abbey to the joyful, active daily round they had once enjoyed.

After arriving on the scene and finding seventy of the ninety monks "slumped in their cells like wet dishrags," Tomatis offered his diagnosis. The cause of this despondency, he declared, was not physiological, but audiological. The monks' enervated state was the result of eliminating several hours of Gregorian chant from their daily routine.

Previously, the whole community would come together eight or nine times a day to chant for ten to twenty minutes at a stretch. The long, resonant tones—the glorious *ooooo*'s and serene *eeeee*'s in "Gloria in Excelsis Deo" especially—allowed a feeling of release and supplied a common focus. Most visitors would have found the chanting exhausting, but for the monks it was a way of keeping their internal motors primed. It slowed down their breathing, lowered their blood pressure, and elevated their mood—and their productivity. They weren't conscious of the physiological benefits of their chanting, but they had clearly become accustomed to it.

Tomatis told the abbot that he would like to put the men back on a diet of Gregorian chant. He did, and the effect was dramatic. Within six months, the monks were once again vigorous and healthy. They needed less sleep, and they went back to their appointed tasks with renewed enthusiasm.

Other than the fall of the Berlin Wall and the dissolution of the Soviet Union, the greatest unanticipated event of our time, in my view, has been the phenomenal popularity of Gregorian chant. In the early nineties, the unadorned recording of music more than a thousand years old by the Benedictine monks of Santo Domingo de Silos in Spain rose to the top of *Billboard's* classical *and* pop music charts in Europe and the United States. More than four million copies of this album, featuring long lines in the Latin originally sung and spoken in the Dark Ages, now enliven the musical libraries of people in forty-two countries.

I believe that the resurgence of Gregorian chant and other sacred music signals that the modern psyche is ready for recharging through the regenerative power of sound. When we hear this beautiful music, we're put in touch with the soaring architecture of monasteries, chapels, and cathedrals, with their heightened sense of space and prolonged sense of time.

Gregorian chant originated as a form of plainsong in the Roman Catholic church under the auspices of Pope Gregory the Great. Born at the end of the sixth century, Gregory is depicted in early Christian art receiving the gift of chant from a dove, representing the Holy Spirit, who sits on his shoulder and sings into his ear. Traditionally, monks would travel to Rome to spend a decade studying chant in a Scola Cantorum, a school for singing. Before returning to the monastery to instruct his community, a monk would have mastered several hundred chants based on passages or themes in the Bible, especially the Psalms.

Monastic communities met many times a day to sing, pray, and meditate on the word of God in intervals called the sacred hours, or offices. The year, too, was divided into intervals. The ecclesiastical calendar, with its fixed and moveable feasts, became a sort of symphony heralding the seasons and tonalities of the liturgical year. Church architecture contributed a further tonal element, since the proportions of most medieval cathedrals corresponded to harmonic ratios.

By the ninth century, chants were being notated through lines on parchment, with small squares and rectangles providing the singer with a guide for breath and pitch. Originally there was no part singing, and, in the first millennium, virtually no musical instrumentation. By the year 1000, the chant had split in two, with one group holding a drone or moving in parallel voice to the chanting melody. The era of the chant lasted through the late Middle Ages and into the Renaissance, when folk music in the forms of dance and madrigals spread through Europe, and when an elegant music known as *counterpoint* became the basic expression of the church. Although Gregorian chant was never completely lost, it dwindled in popularity until its revival at the beginning of the twentieth century.

Gregorian chant is profoundly different from modern forms of music. For one thing, it lacks the timing of either classical or rock music—the steady, foot-tapping beat that allows us to organize our movements to the sound. Rather, the rhythm is organic, based on the natural flow of the text, breathing, and tonal patterns of prolonged vowel sounds. Also, there are no accompanists, no rich string sections. True Gregorian chant is monophonic, meaning that everyone sings the same line. There may also be a call and response among cantor, priest, and chorus. (Beware of Gregorian chant recordings that have organ accompaniment or singing in harmony. These are not authentic representations of the early styles.)

Because it is so restful and inviting, Gregorian chant provides a positive environment in the office, home, or car. There are not many notes, nor is there a strong melody moving toward a firm conclusion, only light inflections of a simple motif. The lengthy, often single-note phrases suggest long exhalations. Each time a vowel is drawn out, it gradually changes shape, like incense wafting in the air. Incredibly, some syllables can be extended for dozens of notes. Think of the long sounds in "Gloria in Excelsis Deo" or the delicious tones in "Alleluia"—the limousine of sacred chants—which can be stretched out for minutes and repeated for hours. You don't have to be a monk to luxuriate in the tranquillity of a chant's long vowels.

INTERLUDE
Alleluia

Gregorian chanting inspires even, relaxed breathing. The chants themselves have either a repetitive pattern (in the form of words or short melodies) or a smooth, long pattern with few words. By using only three notes and repeating the same phrase many times, we can sense inside our bodies the effects of chanting.

Alleluia, a sacred word in many traditions, means praise. Use this as your mantra, or substitute a word that holds meaning for you. "Om," "shalom," and "peace" are possibilities. Short prayers that have personal meaning can also be used.

Let's take "alleluia" as an example. Begin by slowly repeating the word *Al-le-lu-u-u-u-ia* and allow the first three notes or syllables to be sounded on the same pitch. Then, on the middle three notes, slowly move up to a higher pitch. Finally, lower the tone before you return to the last syllable on the original pitch. Here is a diagram that may help:

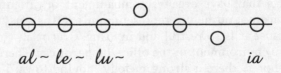

al ~ le ~ lu ~   ia

Whatever word you use, sing it over and over as described above. After three to four minutes, the mind, body, and breath will "entrain," and the word's inner meaning will emerge. Allow the melodies to swell and, as they repeat, to weave their significance into your breath and body.

Music historians have remarked on the unique pleasures of chant's anonymity. "It is as if there is no actual singer, and yet the music itself is full of presence," Katharine Le Mée writes in *Chant: The Origins, Form, Practice, and Healing Power of Gregorian Chant.* "Time seems to stop and the darting mind falls still and attentive, arrested from its worldly concerns and preoccupations. . . . Like fire, each line has its own brightness and energy, a force that is called forth, raised, and then surrendered. Like water, the music rises and falls in a gentle wave of love that bathes, cleanses, and caresses our spirits, leaving us buoyed up and restored."

Church Latin is filled with pure vowel sounds, unlike the complex diphthongs of English (or the tripthongs of Texan English, which I grew up with). Chanting extends the vowel sounds, which reverberate in the skin and bones, and the vibrations stimulate the frontal lobes in the brain. To chant along with a tape or to make up your own Gregorian chantlike sounds is akin to having a brain massage.

Much of the aesthetic power of chants arises from the architecture of the Norman and Gothic cathedrals in which they are often sung. The immense rock floors, high stone walls, and lofty, arched ceilings create an extraordinary acoustical phenomenon, with sung notes that can reverberate for as long as seven seconds. These disembodied echoes seem to come from both everywhere and nowhere.

Nevertheless, chanting can be successfully done outdoors, under a ceiling of clouds and stars. Native American chanting, which usually takes place on the open prairie or under the night sky, features a strong drumbeat below the melody, with prayer or invocation above it. This kind of chanting can make the landscape—the plains, the hills, the mountains, the desert, and the stars—come alive.

♪ Chant as a Living Art

Chanting is more of a living art than ever, and not only among Native Americans. One of the most ardent modern practitioners of chant is Charlotte Miller, director of Peregrina, the Women's Chant Choir at All Saints Episcopal Church in Phoenix. Miller has dedicated twenty years to exploring the healing aspects of chant—ever since one night in the Hawaii Opera Theater when she noticed that the pain of her arthritis disappeared when she sang or chanted. In her quest to put us back in touch with our own sacred sound, she has managed to skillfully meld Gregorian, Sanskrit, and Vedic chanting. In addition to her work with the choir, Miller holds seminars and works with individuals to help them heal themselves with chant.

The music of Taizé offers an even more dramatic example of how chant is being adapted to our modern, multicultural world. Taizé is a community in France, not far from the ecclesiastical hub where the great abbey of Cluny stood, that was started in the 1960s by a small group of Protestants and Catholics, who sought to create an ecumenical place for youth to explore the great spiritual questions of life. From this community has emerged some of the most powerful living and healing music on the planet.

Recently, I made my third visit to the Sisters of Mercy Convent and Retreat Center in Burlingame, near San Francisco, where every month Sister Suzanne directs an evening of Taizé chant in their large and splendid chapel. Half an hour before the music began, I noticed a young girl about fourteen who had brought her teddy bear and sleeping bag, resting just outside the door. I was reminded of the medieval churches, where people would sleep near the highly ornamented portals of the greatest cathedrals ever built, merely to be close to the comforting energy of sound, incense, and prayer. I asked the girl why she didn't go into the chapel and she replied, "I am not a Catholic, but I am very spiritual. I don't know why, but I feel protected and loved by the sounds of the music. I'm a little afraid to go in, and I'm afraid to live in the outside world. I try to come every month, but I don't want my friends to know. It makes me feel there is something holy here on this earth."

A few minutes later, Sister Suzanne and a group of string players gathered around a dimly lit keyboard and began to play humble music with simple, sweet, and highly repetitive melodies: "Come and fill our hearts with your peace. You alone, O Lord, are holy. Come and fill our hearts with your peace. Praise to the Living God."

The flickering candles, the beautiful icon of Mary, and the Gothic arches were soon bathed in these words, and the congregation, which now crowded all the hallways and aisles, every pew, and every inch of the floor, must have numbered five hundred. For nearly three hours, texts like "Dona nobis pachem"—Give us peace—"Sing to our God, all my being" were recited dozens of times, the musicians seeming to penetrate more deeply into the soul of the prayer with each passing moment. The effect was of a seamless fabric of voice and sound: the instruments played a variation on each refrain, and a soloist offered an occasional descant or verse. For hours, young and old, people of every race and creed, gathered to pray.

The music of Taizé bridges the sacred and the secular. Combining the reverence of chant with the accessibility of vernacular instruments such as the flute and guitar, and with texts that include as many as six or seven languages in one song, Taizé signals the emergence of a new planetary music. It is a truly universal liturgy, unusually hospitable to cross-cultural worship. Verses are sung in the languages of those attending—English, French, Spanish, or Swahili; the congregation sings the response in Latin. It can be heard in Methodist, Baptist, and Presbyterian churches, in the Scottish New Age community of Findhorn, by those who make the pilgrimage to Lourdes, and even in the Vatican.

It's no wonder. For two or three hours, those who attend feel immersed in a highly charged energy field of healing and grace. The world of the voice and the voice of the world are becoming one.

⟩ Overtone Singing

Perhaps you have heard Tibetan monks singing two or three pitches at once, or producing chords that span octaves. Unlike the high-frequency tenor chants of Gregorian monks, Tibetans make low-frequency, guttural sounds that bear little resemblance to what we in the West regard as music. But this unusual form of chanting—known as *overtone singing*—can be exhilarating.

In the early 1980s, the Gyuto monks of Dharmsala, India, brought their sacred music to the West, performing at the Cathedral of Saint John the Divine in New York City and elsewhere. The very deep, elongated sounds of their singing inspired contemporary musicians such as Pauline Oliveros, John Cage, and Philip Glass to adapt them for compositions of their own. In an interview, Khen Rinpoche, Abbot of the Gyuto Tantric College, explained one of the techniques traditionally used to master this skill: "There is a particular exercise of going to the side of a loud waterfall and practicing until a state is reached where [the monks] can clearly hear their own voice amidst the roar of the water," he explained.

Overtone singing is not unique to Tibet. The vocal musics of India, the Philippines, and China have their share of such styles. And Tuva, a city in western Mongolia, hosts an overtone competition each spring. Kathy Brown, a Canadian popular singer and one of my most innovative students, was invited to be one of the judges in this competition in 1995. "Originally, they wanted the dozen or so foreign performers to compete against the Tuvans, but as we flatly refused, they interspersed us throughout the program so as to provide (comic) relief," Brown told me. "Judging was a daunting task, but well worth it for the memorable sight of the grand prize winner riding off into the sunset on his new horse in his new national costume."

Overtones are not as mysterious as they sound. Even in the United States, barbershop singing (first developed in the late nineteenth century) relies on similar principles to achieve a certain richness of timbre. But you don't have to join a barbershop quartet or go scream your head off at Niagara Falls to develop this ability. We create overtones in all of our vowels. Sing the second line of "Old MacDonald Had a Farm," *eee-eye-eee-eye-oh*, prolonging the vowel sounds as much as possible, and you may be able to hear how overtones are produced. To do this, you have to change vowel sounds gradually, using very little air and paying close attention to the placement of the tongue in the mouth. The position of the tongue changes the "color" of the sound. Try making an *eee* sound with a big smile on your face. Then change the sound to *ah*, keeping your jaw in the same position and continuing to smile. Notice how your tongue moves.

Jonathan Goldman, founder of the Sound Healers Association, believes that vocal harmonics calm the body and clear the mind more efficiently than any other form of sound.

⟩ Spiritual Doo-Wops

One of the most widespread forms of vocalization today is the *mantra*, or short chant, consisting of a single syllable or phrase repeated over and over. The Sanskrit mantra *Om*, chanted daily by millions of businessmen and truck drivers, housewives and athletes, as well as holy people and religious devotees, is popular not only in India but throughout the world. By making this ancient *Om* sound as slowly as possible, it is believed, you become one with all creation.

This remarkable syllable, usually spelled phonetically as *om* in the West, is better represented by three letters, *Aum,* as it is in the East. The sound of the first letter, *A*—pronounced *Ah*—represents the beginning of the breath, the inhalation, as well as the creation of sound. The *u* sound—pronounced as a long *o* gliding into a short *u*—is the full, elongated body of the sound. You could call it the middle of the word or the heart of the sound. It holds the vowel and the extended breath until the final *m*. The humming *m*—pronounced *mmmmm*—is the dying part of the cycle and represents the stage of dissolution in the full spiral of life, breath, and sound. The three parts represent the triune aspects of God in Hinduism: Brahma, the Creator, is manifest in the A; Vishnu, the Preserver, in the U; and Shiva, the Destroyer, in the M. Thus, one simple sound, like all sounds, represents birth, maintenance, and completion. The Judeo-Christian tradition has its own version of AUM—Amen.

After "Push 'em back, push 'em back, way back," one of the most popular mantras in North America today is *Om Namah Shivaya*. This chant—each syllable of which resonates in a different region of the mind and body—appeals to God to vanquish the limitations and illusions of human consciousness and to open a perfect pathway to the divine. Those who practice it for long periods report that it makes them more attentive and helps them to transcend the difficulties of life through the compassionate embrace of God. In Hinduism, the *bija,* or "seed," is the vowel sound that creates and carries energy from the invisible world, and that serves as the embryo of each tone. The power of this essential tone can purify the mind and body. The more you chant, the more energy you accumulate, and the more powerful will be the results. Another popular mantra is the *zhikr,* a repetitive prayer traditionally performed by the Sufis in the Middle East.

There is something very pleasing about the repetition of syllables and the making of nonsense sounds. Thus, chanting can be effective whether the words have meaning or not—whether one repeats *Om mani padme hum* in the Tibetan Buddhist canon or *shaboom, shaboom, ya, da, da, da, da, da, da, shaboom, shaboom* in the sacred Motown tradition! Doo-wops were repetitive chants inserted into pop songs in the fifties and early sixties, and I like to think of them as laying the groundwork for baby boomers' subsequent investigation of *spiritual* doo-wops.

⸙ The Tao of Rap

In exploring the power of the voice, we should not neglect a vital new form of chant that has entered popular culture: rap. Although this music has gotten a lot of bad press for being violent, aggressive, and invasive, its way of speaking in rhythm and rhyme links it to poetry. Rap developed as a vocal martial art to protect people in the streets from the dehumanization of their world. Yes, it often seems emotionless, and at times it's indelicate. But as a form of self-therapy, it is highly effective. Rap enables the left brain to talk to the body, especially the deeper systems that govern instinctual response and survival.

Chain Saw, one of rap's originators, and a member of DaChamba, a Chicago-based rap group, describes what he views as authentic rap: "Rap in its beginnings was real back then. Nobody was talking about nothing they didn't live or breathe." To him, "real" means city streets and violence, and this is his way of testifying: "It is real. I need to speak about it, I need to sing about it."

The members of DaChamba are concerned that people are now rapping just for the money, without the same passion and urgency. "You cannot make this music without being from the ghetto," continues Chain Saw. "As long as it's a real message, we will find ways to communicate. Kids rap, mamas rap, there's nothing to be scared of, unless you're afraid of hearing the truth of what life in the city is about. If you know your own body's history and you know what's happened to your parents and friends, then you have a right to rap. If you're just out to be angry and show how mainstream offensive you can be, it's not really rap."

Story and belief translated into song is humanity's common currency and has connected us for thousands of years. I cannot consider these new forms of music invalid in the healing process. Although I am outraged by music that is lewd or misogynistic—especially when it seems to be using profanity just for a thrill—I understand the need of every child and youth in America to be heard. In the arduous universe of poverty and drugs, rap is a vocal form that has evolved *organically*. It reflects the poverty and violence that permeates the lives of many young people in cities, and that is rapidly approaching critical mass.

Rap doesn't only speak to the young and alienated but also to those who are language-impaired, to stroke sufferers and accident victims. Even when the disabled are not able to understand the plainly spoken word, they may be able to grasp words that are expressed in rhyme and rhythm. One reason for this is that the brain processes speech that is expressed in rhythm and rhyme differently from regular speech. Thus, the very same rap that a beleaguered parent views as a curse could be a godsend to someone with aphasia.

INTERLUDE

Rap and Unwrap

Speaking in a poetic rhythm while walking, working, or dancing has been part of every culture. Rap, our own urban form
of chant, has emerged as a vivid way to organize thoughts
into a street-smart rhythmic pattern. What seems challenging
to the left brain is actually quite easy once you feel the
rhythm within your body. A seventh grade girl in Chicago
made up the following rap to express her feelings:

> *REALLY BAD*
> *THAT'S THE WAY I FEEL.*
> *CAN'T THEY SEE*
> *I GOT A BAD, BAD DEAL.*
> *IF THEY WOULD ONLY LISTEN*
> *TO WHAT I WANT TO SAY,*
> *I WOULDN'T FEEL BAD*
> *EACH AND EVERY DAY.*

While commuting to and from work, imagine putting
your thoughts into rhythm. Begin to tap with your hand in
groups of four beats, accenting the first, and talk as you tap.
Within a few minutes, you may notice how easy it is to
speak to the beat—in other words, rap! Unwrap your
thoughts, then let them be spoken in rhythm. For example:

> *TODAY I WAS TIRED.*
> *TODAY I WAS BORED.*
> *TODAY I WAS STUCK*
> *AND FEELING LIKE MUCK.*
> *I STARTED TO RAP*
> *I STARTED TO MOVE*
> *IN ONLY FIVE SECONDS*
> *I WAS IN A NEW GROOVE.*

It might take some practice to find the rapper within you. But if you choose a private place, no one has to hear you during this experiment. Just keep talking and babbling. If you are not sure what to say, make up your own language, but let your tongue and heart express whatever you're feeling. Rap cleanses the mental palate, and you don't even need an ear-splitting boom box as an accessory!

‹ Paradise Regained

Shyness, shame, and other psychological blocks can get in the way of "good" vocalization and interfere with putting the Mozart Effect into practice. Julie was one of the shyest young women I have taught. She had a light, whimsical voice, a feathery voice, and her greatest fear was of speaking in front of a group. Even ordinary conversation with friends and associates was difficult for her. I would not be surprised if at some time in her life Julie had been told to "sit down and be quiet" and "be nice and listen." Though she was an attractive and gifted fashion designer and professional chef, she was unable to reach out to the world, incapable of expressing her feelings and (often brilliant) thoughts.

Through a class in music and healing, I was able to bring Julie's voice into a different tonality and to build her self-confidence. I did that by asking her to make vowel sounds out loud—*a, e, i, o, u*—and to create sounds that represented fear, joy, and relaxation. In the very first class, within minutes, she began to release her inhibitions. For weeks, she created sounds every night as she served as chef at a restaurant. Julie experienced an emotional release that was much stronger than she had been able to express in words. In the weeks that followed, she began to invent her own new language—"spoken English."

Within two months, Julie was able to stand in front of a group and to speak with friends, and her presentation was clear and concise. Those years of suffering, of not feeling strong enough to communicate with the outer world, were rapidly overshadowed. Within three months, timidity and fear gave way to pride and self-esteem. Julie was a new woman—the woman she had known herself to be inside, but who had never shone forth before. She went on to get a good job as a professional designer and became known for her marketing skills—the ultimate test of communication.

One of the most dramatic cases of overcoming a speech block involved Gérard Depardieu, the French actor who seems to show up in every French film exported to the United States. Now we hear him speak with a mellifluous voice, but, in the mid-1960s, Depardieu was a tongue-tied young man still struggling to become an actor. Coming from a background of family difficulties, educational failures, and personal sorrows, Depardieu could not express himself. He could hardly speak, and the more he tried, the worse his stammering became.

A drama teacher directed him to the Tomatis Center in Paris, where he met with Tomatis himself. The doctor found that Depardieu's listening was severely damaged. His right ear was unable to control incoming sound, which meant that his own voice, even at a whisper, sounded very loud. In addition to inhibiting his voice, the faulty ear affected neural functions related to memory and concentration. Tomatis diagnosed the cause of Depardieu's voice and memory problems as deeper emotional problems underlying his physiological difficulties and told him that he could help relieve his speech problems. Depardieu asked whether the treatment would involve surgery, medication, or speech therapy. Tomatis responded, "For the next several weeks, I want you to come here every day for two hours and listen to Mozart."

"Mozart?" Depardieu asked, surprised.

"Mozart," Tomatis declared.

The next day Depardieu returned to the Tomatis Center to don headphones and listen to Mozart. The violin concerto was modified by the Electronic Ear, and with minimal filtering it sounded like ordinary music. At other times, it was so distorted that the high-pitched sounds were hardly recognizable, seeming like scratches on a broken record. Though puzzled and skeptical, Depardieu continued the treatment. After only a few more sessions, he began to experience positive changes in his daily routine. His appetite improved, he slept better, and he found himself with more energy. Soon he was looking forward to the sessions. After several months,

Depardieu returned to acting school with new poise and confidence, and went on, of course, to become one of the consummate actors of his generation, beloved for his creative intelligence, dominant but gentle presence, and distinctive voice, rich with tone and musicality.

"Before Tomatis, I could not complete any of my sentences," he said, looking back. "It was he who helped give continuity to my thoughts, and it was he who gave me the power to synthesize and understand what I was thinking."

Tomatis shrugs off the novelty of his work. He sees an age-old application of this wisdom in the Gospel account of how Jesus cured the stammerer:

> They brought to Jesus a man who was deaf and had an impediment in his speech, with the request that he would lay his hand on him. He took the man aside, away from the crowd, put his fingers into his ears, spat, and touched his tongue. Then, looking up to heaven, he sighed, and said to him, *"Ephphata,"* which means "Be opened." With that his ears were opened, and at the same time the impediment was removed and he spoke plainly. (Mark 7:32-35)

"Jesus knew the power of listening," observes Tomatis, a devout Catholic. To him, Jesus embodied the Word—the logos, the perfect sound. And Jesus's admonition—"He that hath an ear, let him hear"—shows a deep understanding of the role of the ear and the voice in unifying mind, body, and spirit.

INTERLUDE

Listening to Your Own Voice

Stand, close your eyes, and pay attention to your breathing for a couple of minutes. Loosen your jaw and keep your lips together. Then, with your eyes closed, hum very lightly on each exhaled breath. Slowly move your head to one side and then the other, forward and backward, and notice how the way you listen to the sound is changed by your posture.

Now lie comfortably on the floor. Take a moment to stretch your hands and feet. Now explore the sound of your voice in a horizontal position. Hum for five minutes with your eyes closed and five minutes with them open. You may find that the sounds feel different depending on whether your eyes are open or closed.

Depending on your posture, you may notice a significant difference in how your voice vibrates inside your body.

Your voice changes quality in nearly every room of your house or apartment. It is not that your voice is actually different; the acoustics of the room modify the way it sounds.

Listen to your voice in four different places: the kitchen; the shower or bathroom; the closet where you keep clothes; and the garage (if you have one). In the bathroom and garage, sounds generally seem louder because there are no carpets or drapes, and less material to absorb them. In the clothes closet, on the other hand, sound is readily absorbed.

Listening to the ways your voice is modified by different acoustic environments can improve your self-awareness and ability to communicate with others.

Many people suffer from the same symptoms that nearly kept Depardieu from becoming an actor. They lack confidence in their voices, although the voice is as much a part of one's self-image as one's face or body. (In polls, public speaking is consistently ranked as a major fear, right up there with anxiety about moving and dread of going to the dentist.) As children, some people might have had voices that were judged too quiet or too loud. Someone—a father or mother, a grandparent, or an early teacher—might have said, "Speak up, I can't hear you" or "Shut the hell up." All too common are stories of a child's spirit being wounded by criticism of his or her voice, by adults who fail to understand how interchangeable that voice is with the child's conception of him- or herself.

Such experiences can lead a child to feel deeply rejected, "out of tune," not good enough to be listened to—which in turn can gener-ate a lot of repressed anger. I look at such censure as a kind of banishment from Eden. In a society that worships rock stars, school and church choirs, country-western singers, Hollywood and Broad-way crooners, opera divas, and other vocalists, being told, in effect, that we cannot carry a tune can constitute the end of innocence. Thereafter, a child may subliminally regard him- or herself as a fallen angel, condemned to a life of speaking in prose. Studies report that, when told they couldn't carry a tune, over half of the people surveyed believe it. What would you think if I told you that, in high school, Elvis Presley was told by his music teacher that he couldn't sing? Fortunately, Presley was confident enough to bring his guitar to class, sing a popular song, and persuade her otherwise.

In teaching several thousand students over the years, I have not found a single one who cannot match a sound or the harmony of a sound within a few minutes. Any voice can be tuned; all that is required is that someone make pure vowel sounds in each of the person's ears.

But forget about that for a moment. Even people who can't sing can benefit hugely from doing so. In a study of "untuned" singers, researcher Marvin Greenberg identified ten elementary school stu-dents, all males, who could not sing in tune or match pitch and made arrangements for them to join an elite school chorus. After eleven weeks of rehearsals, the boys' self-esteem and self-image im-proved, even though they continued to sing off-key. I wouldn't necessarily suggest that this group of "melodically challenged" males dash off and cut a CD, but they should certainly be encour-aged to sing as often and as unashamedly as they please.

As we grow up, the world conditions us to use our voices in increasingly limited ways. You may remember in elementary school a choral director asking you to sing the solo, or being cast in a play—both experiences that lent power to your voice. Think how wonderful it felt to use your voice freely—to relax your jaw, express what has not been expressed, overcome your fears, and release frus-trations that may have been building up for hours, weeks, or years. Now take a moment to consider your voice today, both speaking and singing. (They are worlds apart: some of the most powerful speaking voices are totally inhibited when it comes to singing, and I have known many brilliant opera singers and recording artists

who speak in an almost apologetic manner.) Whether you're studying pop or choral music, aspiring to be the next Pavorotti or Bette
Midler, or just humming in your shower, focus on what along the
way has held your voice back or made it stronger.

This will be the first step to creating your own Mozart Effect.

CHAPTER 5

Sound Medicine

USING MUSIC FOR THERAPY AND REHABILITATION

Canst thou not minister to a mind diseased.
Pluck from the memory a rooted sorrow.
Raze out the written troubles of the brain,
And with some sweet oblivious antidote,
Cleanse the full bosom of that perilous stuff
Which weights upon the heart . . .
—MACBETH, REFLECTING ON MUSIC,
IN *MACBETH*, SHAKESPEARE

As we enter the new millennium, we move from an era in which physicians diagnose and prescribe and patients mechanically obey into one in which we all share responsibility for our health and well-being. As patients, we can use music and self-generated tones to help us become more sensitive to our own rhythms and cycles. Meanwhile, thousands of doctors, nurses, shamans, and mind/body therapists around the world are putting the Mozart Effect into action.

American medicine first experimented with the therapeutic use of music during the nineteenth and early twentieth centuries. As early as 1804, Edwin Atlee, drawing on the work of philosopher Jean-Jacques Rousseau, Declaration of Independence signer and physician Benjamin Rush, and other Enlightenment thinkers, wrote

An Inaugural Essay on the Influence of Music in the Cure of Diseases, in which he hoped to show that music "has a powerful influence upon the mind, and consequently on the body." In the 1870s, a unique series of therapeutic concerts debuted at Blackwell's Island, New York City's facility for the insane. The sessions, featuring the Ninth Regiment Band, vocalists from the New York Musicians Guild, and distinguished pianist John Nelson Pattison, were hosted with much fanfare by New York City's Charities Commissioner and monitored by medical doctors and civic officials. In the 1890s, mental health reformer George Alder Blumer hired immigrants to perform live music for patients at Utica State Hospital, the first established music program in an American medical facility. And in 1899, James L. Corning, a neurologist, carried out the first controlled study using music to treat patients. In a paper entitled "The Use of Musical Vibrations Before and During Sleep," he reported that the music of Wagner and other Romantic composers could reduce morbid thoughts and enhance waking images and emotions.

The first mention of music therapy by the American Medical Association came in 1914, with a letter in its professional journal by Dr. Evan O'Neill Kane, who reported using a phonograph for "calming and distracting patients" during surgery. Several years later, Eva Vescelius, founder of the National Therapeutic Society of New York City, predicted, "When the therapeutic value of music is understood and appreciated, it will be considered as necessary in the treatment of disease as air, water, and food." She foresaw a time when every hospital, prison, and asylum would house a department of music and be funded accordingly. In 1918, Columbia University offered the first course in "Musicotherapy," taught by Margaret Anderton, a British musician who had worked with soldiers wounded in World War I; in 1929, Duke University Hospital became the first facility of its kind to offer recorded music to patients via radios or wall-mounted speakers on children's and infants' wards. In the 1930s and 1940s, the use of music and sound to mask or reduce pain in dental and surgical procedures proliferated. The University of Chicago funded several large-scale investigations, including the anesthetic use of music prior to surgery for peptic ulcer, a condition that did not respond well to conventional medication.

Modern music therapy developed in the late 1940s, growing out of the use of music to treat combat fatigue among soldiers following

World War II. Although the Army Surgeon General, the Chief of the Navy's Bureau of Medicine and Surgery, and the Veterans Administration Chief of Medical Services ruled that music could not be classified as a therapy alongside penicillin, quinine, or radiation, it certainly had its place in the army's roster of remedies. E. Thayer Gaston, who taught in the music education department at the University of Kansas, established the first music therapy intern and training sites in the United States at the University of Kansas and the Menninger Clinic in Topeka. In the postwar era, hospitals, clinics, and nursing homes invited local musicians to perform. Patients at the Memphis Home for Incurables might have been otherwise miserable, but they were among the first in the country to hear a young Elvis Presley on guitar.

One of the first organized uses of music for healing in America was made by Dr. John H. Kellogg, the flamboyant popularizer of cornflakes and the director of the country's first health spa. His sanitarium in Battle Creek, Michigan, touted the therapeutic value of music and imagery—and, like so many health-care and spiritual-care professionals today, he had neither the time nor the curiosity to find out why it worked. He just saw that it did and opted to employ it in the name of healing.

In the past fifteen years, I have lectured to more than a quarter of a million people who want to improve some aspect of their lives with music. Many come on faith, but many don't: they want to know *why* it works. No one can answer that question fully, but there are several principles on which music therapists and other professionals in the field rely.

The first and most important is *entrainment*, which means being "in step" or "in sync" with music. When we dance, we are like hobos who jump on the freight train of the beat. Swept along, our bodies automatically adjust to the pace, pulse, and rhythm of the sound; the music evokes an organized pattern of responses. The emotional pulse of great concert music entrains an entire audience. The beat of disco music entrains a group doing aerobic exercises. Naturally, every piece of music does not fully entrain the body. Drums that beat 120 times per minute will not increase the heart rate by the same amount. But they can increase the heartbeat somewhat—and then, paradoxically, after five or six minutes, deeply calm the body.

INTERLUDE
You Got Rhythm

The heart is the greatest drummer. When we beat a drum, we activate muscle, breathing, heartbeat, and brain wave patterns that create a remarkable feedback loop. Ten minutes of drumming every day releases tension, resets the mind and body's inner clock, and serves as both a stimulant and a sedative.

You do not need a drum set or any sophisticated tools for this exercise. A simple, one-sided, vibrating vessel will work. I have seen retirement centers use plastic waste baskets and sticks to create surprisingly serviceable sounds.

If you're unsure of your drumming ability, remember that *you cannot make a mistake*. Allow a beat to begin. Even though it sounds monotonous at first, stick with it: it will arouse your interest after a few minutes. Rhythm will grow out of your movements and the sound.

Sit comfortably in a chair, holding your make-shift drum and mallet. Close your eyes and locate the heartbeat within your body. Now pick up the stick, and gently find a drumbeat to match your heart. Continue for a few minutes and then see if you can double the beat so that it's twice as fast as your heart. Then, after three minutes, return to a beat that matches your basic heartbeat and notice whether it has become faster or slower. Then reduce the number of your drumbeats to match every other beat of your heart.

After doing this exercise a couple of times, it gets easy, and you can experiment with many rhythmic variations. It takes about ten minutes for a complete drum tune-up, but its revitalizing and calming effects will persist throughout the day.

A good music therapist often entrains with a client—that is, he or she makes the same leap and matches the new rhythm, move-

ments, and breath, thus creating a reassuring continuum. Entrainment can lead to a profound encounter between a therapist and a
client (not to mention a musician and a listener). In general, the
stronger party sets the tone. But, like the law of gravity, entrainment involves a mutual attraction and reciprocal response. The
therapist strives to move at the pace of the patient with the aim of
eventually drawing him or her into a more balanced rhythm.

When listening to mood music, we become subtly entrained to the
sonic environment. This is often preferable to silence, particularly for
people in pain, because silence can enhance their awareness of discomfort. Light background music can relieve stress and anxiety, simply—as
the following expressions suggest—by enabling us to "strike a sympathetic chord," "harmonize," or become "attuned to our surroundings."
Entrainment explains how brain waves, heart rhythms, respiration,
emotional tone, timing, pacing, and other organic rhythms can
change subtly according to the music we listen to.

Just as one can develop a tolerance for certain medications, one
can become habituated to music. Thus, listening to the same auditory stimulation repeatedly—even the most magnificent composition—can interfere with entrainment. Luckily, the *iso principle* (from
"isomorphic," the Greek root word for "same form") has emerged
as an essential tool in music therapy to prevent this sonic numbing.
Through a gradual change of pace in rhythm, speech, or emotional
content, a steady entrainment is achieved that brings a patient from
one physical or emotional state into another.

Ravel's "Bolero" demonstrates the iso principle. From slow and
quiet to wild and frenzied, the music builds not only in speed, but
also in emotional expressiveness, and the listener's mood is apt to
change accordingly. "The Sorcerer's Apprentice" by Dukas and even
the traditional Lord's Prayer sung throughout the world in Protes-
tant churches—moving from the simple and humble "Our Father"
to the pulsating and exuberant "Kingdom, Power, and the Glory"—
exemplify this approach. In music reflecting the iso principle, there
is never an abrupt change, surprise, or hiatus.

Diversion, the third principle employed by many music therapists, involves using music to deflect attention from pain and discomfort. This is, perhaps, common sense: You play bright, happy
music when you're down in the doldrums, for instance. Diversion,

however, doesn't last long and doesn't work to change fundamentally the mind/body relationship. Nevertheless, by taking your body in a new (and mildly unexpected) direction, diversion can produce a temporary therapeutic effect.

Over the last half century, music therapy has made tremendous strides as a rigorous scientific discipline. By 1964, the *Journal of Music Therapy* offered clear-sighted, peer-reviewed research from music therapists on such topics as "The Effect of Sedative Music on Electromyographic Biofeedback Assisted Relaxation Training of Spastic Cerebral Palsied Adults." Several groups have also helped the profession grow into an accredited behavioral science. In 1998 the National Association of Musical Therapists (NAMT) and the American Association of Music Therapists (AAMT) will merge into an expanded organization called the American Music Therapy Association (AMTA). Spurred on by these organizations, awareness of the therapeutic value of music is spreading *con brio* through the medical profession.

In the United States today, more than five thousand music therapists work in hospitals, rehabilitation units, health-care and educational facilities, clinics, nursing homes, prisons, schools, day-care centers, and homes. More than half work with the mentally ill, developmentally disabled, and the elderly. The rest treat those suffering from chronic disease (especially Alzheimer's and AIDS), physical disabilities, sexual abuse trauma, autism, hearing- and speech-impairment, substance abuse, and learning disabilities. Seventy American colleges and universities offer undergraduate or graduate degrees in music therapy.

One encouraging sign of its growing acceptance: Under certain conditions, music therapy is now considered a reimbursable service under Medicare's hospitalization policies. (If you've ever tried to get reimbursed for nonmainstream or "fringe" medical treatment, you will know how significant such recognition is.)

❧ Medical Awakenings

The power of music to integrate and cure . . . is quite fundamental.
[It is the] profoundest nonchemical medication.
—OLIVER SACKS, *AWAKENINGS*

At the Institute for Music and Neurologic Function at Beth Abraham Family of Health Services in the Bronx, the site of one of the nation's most vital and innovative music therapy programs, miracles happen daily. Recalls Oliver Sacks, one of the founding members of the Institute, "When I first came to Beth Abraham in 1966, there was already a music therapist here and a vivid sense of how music could help certain neurological patients. I wrote of this in *Awakenings,* and when a film director came to make the documentary of our patients in 1973 his first question was, 'Where is the music therapist? She seems to be the most important person around here.'"

In 1991, Sacks testified before the U.S. Senate Special Committee on Aging on the therapeutic powers of music in treating neurological disorders. In his testimony, he described Rosalie, a patient with Parkinson's disease at Beth Abraham, who remained transfixed, completely motionless, for most of the day, usually with one finger on her glasses. "But she can play the piano beautifully, and for hours—and when she plays her Parkinsonism disappears, and all is ease and fluency and freedom and normality," Sacks told the enthralled panel. "Music liberates her from her Parkinsonism for a time—and not only music, but the imagining of music. Rosalie knows all Chopin by heart, and one has only to say 'Opus 49!' to her for her whole body and posture and expression to change." Sacks went on to describe how her EEG—usually registering comalike stillness—and her motor activity became completely normal, even when the music was just playing in her mind!

Stories like this are typical at Beth Abraham. "It seems that memory is always preserved, but it cannot always be retrieved," Music Therapy Director Concetta M. Tomaino explains. "Music holds a key to gaining access to the system of memory retrieval." Therapists at the Institute speculate that music could aid in the reversal or prevention of certain types of deafness. "It is possible," they write, "that music contributes to the recovery of neural function in several ways: by promoting nerve cell regeneration, by directing the establishment of new neural connections and pathways, and by shortening the time to recovery of function." Scientists have known that compensatory mechanisms can be triggered by loss of neurologic function. Parts of the brain that have lain dormant can "take over," in whole or part, the damaged function. Known as *neural plasticity,* this phenomenon may be jump-started or kicked into higher gear by music and sound, as well as by certain types of exercise and language. Beth Abraham is currently researching ways by which stroke victims can recover brain function and behavioral activities with the help of music therapy.

Another exciting exploration stems from the new Brain Electric Source Analysis (BESA) technique, which scientists are using in conjunction with Magnetic Resonance Imagery (MRI) to investigate the neurological basis of music perception. BESA is able to map the distribution of music-related activities in the brains of patients with dementia and other neurological disorders. Scientists hope to learn whether music's rhythmic patterns could contribute to permanent changes in hearing—and whether those benefits could even extend to touch, movement, perception, and other sensory, motor, and cognitive functions.

Recently, the Institute reported that scientists were able, for the first time, to induce the regeneration of auditory hair cells in human beings. Loss of the cilia, the tiny hairs in the inner ear that detect sound, has been thought—until now—to be irreversible. All of this bodes well for the next millennium. The combination of new technology and radically new ways of thinking about music could mean that, within a decade, our current understanding of the auditory system will be happily obsolete.

Music in the Operating Room

Linda Rodgers, a clinical social worker and classically trained musician from Katonah, New York, has dedicated her professional life to developing ways for patients to control their responses to surgery. Her interest in the field dates back to her childhood tonsillectomy. For the rest of her life, Rodgers would recall the unpleasant details—"everything," she says, "from the moment my mother woke me early in the morning, saying I wasn't going to school that day but to the hospital . . . to the moment I saw another little girl in the admitting room wearing a pink organdy party dress and convinced she was going to a party . . . to the moment I woke up after surgery expecting to dive into bowls of glorious ice cream, as I'd been promised, only to realize that I had a horrid sore throat and I was about to get sick to my stomach." Recollections like these set the stage for lasting anxiety about surgery, hospitals, doctors, nurses—everyone on the scene.

In 1982, after graduating from Hunter College School of Social Work, Rodgers went to work at Mount Sinai Hospital in New York and obtained permission to watch open heart surgery. Besides the startling cacophony of sounds in the operating room, she was surprised to hear the music of Frank Sinatra piped in over two loudspeakers. Although the surgeon told her that he enjoyed Sinatra's upbeat lyrics, the song made Rodgers feel dreadful. She had first heard it in the mid-1950s when her father had surgery for cancer of the jaw, and the song took her instantly back to that terrifying moment. "Had I been the patient on the operating room table, how could anyone possibly have known my own very personal reaction?" she wondered.

The experience led Rodgers to investigate patients' ability to hear under anesthesia. She soon uncovered a wealth of research indicating that they do continue to hear, even when rendered unconscious. One of the classic experiments involved an anesthetized cat whose EEG channels all dramatically responded to the barking of a dog. "The auditory pathway, unlike all other sensory systems, has an extra relay," Rodgers explains. "Auditory fibers are not affected by anesthetics, so they continue to transmit sound. Simply stated: *We never stop hearing!*"

In a 1993 lecture Rodgers discussed the role of music therapy in the operating room. She pointed out that music is an emotional experience, and that its effects are intensely personal. The ideal music for this setting, she discovered, is *anxiolytic*—designed to reduce anxiety. Developed by the department of anesthesiology at a hospital in Lüdenscheid, Germany, in the mid-1970s, anxiolytic music avoids lyrics, singing, and anything else that can trigger harmful memories or associations. The idea is to provide a free-flowing river of sound, allowing listeners to relax and let the music envelop them.

To further protect against patients inadvertently hearing harmful noise or tasteless conversation (such as "This old bag won't make it") during surgery, she recommends that audiotapes selected by each patient be played before, during, and after surgery on cassette players with earphones. Rodgers has developed a set of soothing color-coded tapes that hang on the IV near the bedpost, so the patient can always be sure which selection is being played. "As patients learn how to control their anxiety and pain more effectively," Rodgers concluded, "it is reasonable to expect a more rapid recovery from surgery with fewer complications, reduced number of days in the hospital, and a more positive response to coping with future medical problems." Nowadays, this treatment is more mainstream than ever.

In 1997, President Bill Clinton tore a tendon and required extensive surgery, which he chose to undergo without general anesthesia. The President instructed his surgeons to fill the operating room with country-western music—the kind that pulled him through his tough Arkansas youth in such high spirits.

As it happens, Linda Rodgers, like Mozart, was steeped in music from infancy. Her father was Richard Rodgers, who composed Broadway musicals that inspired and entertained generations, including Oklahoma!, Carousel, The King and I, and The Sound of Music.

INTERLUDE
Tuning Up for Surgery

A recovery room or intensive care unit is extremely noisy; it is not, ironically, a health-producing atmosphere. Following surgery and heavy medication, you may awake in an uncomfortable, dream-like state, made more anxious by the din. Listening to music can serve as a guide in these circumstances, allowing you to awake after the operation in a safe, familiar auditory environment.

If you know that you will be hospitalized, spend a few days beforehand rehearsing for your recovery. Find an album of slow and beautiful baroque or classical music. Each day before the procedure, listen to the album while lying down with your eyes closed. Tell yourself that you are well, you are healing, that the operation is over, and that you are now in a safe environment. The music will mask the noise and help to reassure you.

Many hospitals now provide music systems for recovery, surgery, and preparation. Check beforehand and, if not, bring your own portable cassette or CD player, ideally one that plays music continuously. Ask the nurse or nurse's aide to turn it on when you are brought into the recovery room, so that it can be playing when you are awake. Linda Rodgers' surgical audiotape series consists of three tapes: Pre-Op, Intra-Op, and Post-Op. The three-tape set can be ordered for $30.00 from Surgical Audiotape Series, 70 Maple Ave., Katonah, NY 10536. Or you can use my own compilation, *Music for the Mozart Effect, Vol. II—Heal the Body: Music for Rest and Relaxation*.

Popular music, fast music, and vocal music do not work as well in this environment because of their emotional content and dynamic beat. Music for recovery need not be your favorite music. But it should be transparent and calming.

❧ Musical Prescriptions

"The doctor had said they should try playing music to her. . . .
She could hear the tinny sound of the Mozart spilling from Grace's
earphones and she found a rhythm in the music and worked to
it, manipulating the wrist now."
—NICHOLAS EVANS, *THE HORSE WHISPERER*

Beth Abraham and Mount Sinai represent hundreds of hospitals, clinics, and universities around the world that actively support and promote music therapy.

- At Charing Cross Hospital in London, patients can listen to classical music while undergoing local anesthesia prior to surgery. *New Scientist* reported that those who elect this form of music therapy suffer fewer complications and recover more quickly. "Some of them are in a world of their own with the headphones on," one anesthetist observed. "They hardly notice all the noise [of sawing and drilling] we make during hip replacements."
- In a study published in 1995 in the *Journal of the American Medical Association*, researchers at the State University of New York at Buffalo scrutinized the impact of music on fifty male surgeons, aged thirty-one to sixty-one. The doctors worked while listening to music each had selected—their preferences spanning forty-six classical compositions, two jazz pieces, and two Irish folk songs, the latter complete with drums and tin whistles. Researchers concluded that under these (exceedingly pleasant) conditions the surgeons had lower blood pressure and a slower heart rate and could perform mental tasks more quickly and more accurately.
- At Saint Luke's Hospital in Chesterfield, Missouri, music therapy is provided in such areas as physical rehabilitation, respiratory ICU, breast cancer support groups, stroke recovery, labor and delivery, psychiatry, and general medical.
- At Saint Mary's Hospital in Green Bay, Wisconsin, nurses use music to enhance the healing environment, and cassette players and headphones are available in all patient areas.

- Dr. Paul Robertson, visiting professor of music and psychiatry at Kingston University in Ontario, Canada, cites studies showing that patients exposed to fifteen minutes of soothing music require only 50 percent of recommended doses of sedatives and anesthetic drugs for often very painful operations.

- At the University of Massachusetts Medical Center in Worcester, the music of harpist Georgia Kelly has been prescribed in lieu of tranquilizers and painkillers for cancer patients and other seriously ill patients.

- The University of Louisville School of Medicine sponsors the innovative Arts in Medicine Program in cooperation with the Department of Psychiatry and Behavior Sciences. Since 1990, the musical division has been coordinated by Alice H. Cash, Ph.D., a keyboard artist, musicologist, and clinical social worker who has pioneered the use of chant and toning with a variety of clients and the use of music with Alzheimer's patients. Meanwhile, a number of the hospital's surgeons are famous for toting boom boxes into the operating room.

The Multisensory Sound Lab at the Department of Communication Sciences and Disorders of the University of Oklahoma (one of several such facilities in the country) offers new hope to deaf and hearing-impaired children. The Oval Window Lab, developed by Norman Lederman of Boulder, Colorado, consists of a sound-sensitive floor big enough to accommodate fifteen children—and give them quite a show. The audio system amplifies sound (transposing it as much as two octaves to magnify the effects) and transforms it into vibrations that can be felt through the body and also seen through a variety of visual, tactile, and auditory displays—colorful line sequences, kaleidoscopic patterns, and a Luma light tower that is exquisitely sensitive to different frequencies.

What does all this accomplish? Researchers have found the Sound Lab useful in improving auditory discrimination, control of the voice, and development of speech.

A 1994 article in the *Journal of the Academy of Rehabilitative Audiology* profiled a typical client, a two-year-old girl who had moderate to severe hearing loss and did not talk. Accompanied by her mother and a clinician, she was seated on the sound floor and given binaural hearing aids that transmitted sounds alternatively between left and right ears. Surrounding lights were lowered to enhance the effect of the Luma, and sound stimuli—including the mother's voice, an electronic bass drumbeat, and a battery-powered toy cow that "mooed"—were introduced.

Upon hearing the sounds through her hearing aids, the little girl promptly lay on the floor with her palms down in front of the Luma. The sound appeared to increase her sensation of floor vibration. Within 20 minutes, she responded consistently to her mother's voice and the cow's moo without visual or "vibrotactile" feedback. She also learned to point at the unlit Luma when sound was presented and the multisensory stimulation turned off. For the first time in her life, she was learning how to hear.

≀ The Legend of the Ur-Song

Evidence suggests that dance, utterance, and song preceded speech, which means that music is humanity's original language. Researchers have found that about two-thirds of the cilia—the thousands of minute hairs in the inner ear that lie on a flat plane like piano keys and respond to different frequencies of sound—resonate only at the higher "musical" frequencies (3,000 to 20,000 hertz), indicating that, at one time, human beings probably communicated primarily with song or tone. The world's oldest musical instrument, a bone flute dating at 43,000 to 82,000 years, was unearthed in the mid-1990s in Slovenia.

In the West, myth and legend suggest that even before the Tower of Babel there existed a universal alphabet composed of tones and rhythms. The speculation is that this Ur-song consisted of a series of two or three notes and pitches that everyone in the world could understand. It is easy to imagine such a melodic tongue when we hear parents summoning their children from a distance, calling out names like "Do-ri," "Bob-bi," or "Su-zi," the second syllable dropping in pitch. In the 1970s, conductor and composer Leonard Bernstein and Harvard educator Howard Gardner investigated the Ur-song and found that practically every ear in the world recognizes a three-note motif similar to the beginning of "Ring Around the Rosie" or "This Old Man."

The roots of shamanic and indigenous music reach back to the dawn of civilization, when the sound of the drum, rattle, and other primitive instruments would bring communities together, launch the crop plantings and harvests, usher in the seasons, and march tribes into battle. Music would celebrate birth, marriage, the initiation of each person into the life of the community, and, finally, deaths. The shaman—an extremely broad term for an ancient healer—invoked great spirits to heal and protect individuals as well as tribes and families. Sounds were the medium through which prayer, invocation, and exorcism took place. It was felt that music and sound magically allowed the powers above and below to come together. The shaman was the bridge between the worlds, able to call down, call up, cast out, and subdue the denizens of heaven and earth.

In ancient healing systems, the spiritual world governed. Spirits were held responsible for causing—and resolving—the great problems of life. So ancient healers—unlike modern doctors, who simply diagnose and dispense medication—sought to bridge the ordinary and the higher consciousness, most often through the use of talismans, music, and sound. Ceremonies and rituals—such as Navajo "singings," which weave together sandpainting and chant—brought art, music, and other healing therapies together in one seamless whole.

Healing was a high drama consisting of three elements: the shaman or practitioner, the patient, and the invisible (the spirit) that does the work between the worlds. The ancients realized how important it was for the ill or diseased person, as well as the family and community, to be a part of the cure. By activating unconscious symbols that were shared by the entire society and embodied in its myths, they incorporated cultural images, totems, power objects, and dreams into the healing process. Music was employed by the priest- or priestess-practitioner to assist the afflicted in integrating mind and body and focusing on the origin and cause of the condition. This current of sound could help to quicken a person's will and speed up recovery of both physical and or mental health.

This is true in modern Christian healing services as well as in the most ancient aboriginal rites. When I was in college, my aunt would pray for me in "tongues." This was her way of contacting the spirit. The sound and cadence of a television evangelist is similar to the rhythmic patterns evoked by shamans in indigenous societies. Whether in Tulsa, Johannesburg, or Bali, these tongues open a spiritual doorway to their unique beliefs.

{ Indigenous Music Today

"The night before the circumcision, there was a ceremony near our huts with singing and dancing. Women came from the nearby villages, and we danced to their singing and clapping. As the music became faster and louder, our dance turned more frenzied and we forgot for a moment what lay ahead."
—NELSON MANDELA, *LONG WALK TO FREEDOM*

From Siberian shamanism to Mexican Roman Catholic healing masses, from Native American medicine ceremonies to traditional African rituals, indigenous rites throughout the world have astonishing similarities. Whether accompanied by drums, rattles, or flutes, the voice calls down the spirits as it did tens of thousands of years ago. Singing, breathing, dancing, and moving in unison create a collective consciousness—whether in the course of a night-long drumming circle or a seven-minute convocation. In an indigenous ceremony, all participants move together into a trancelike state. Once the group is entrained, the stage is set for the healing spirits to manifest themselves.

In 1971, I visited Indonesia for the first time. Before the days of tourists, superhighways, and videocams, I accompanied several people on a three-hour ride and walk into a remote village in Bali where a local community had gathered for the initiation of two young girls following their first menstruation. I was amazed that the entire village participated in the ritual. The men were all sitting on one side and the women on the other. There was no exact time for the ceremony to begin or end.

To invoke the proper spirit, a man in white, a Hindu priest, came and sacrificed a small chicken. This was followed by the most incredible singing—powerfully rhythmic, surging songs from the men, alternating with sweetly lyrical melodies from the women. From between a pair of columns in the temple emerged two small girls (they looked no more than ten years old!) wrapped in *sarongs*— elegant, tight, batik dresses—their heads adorned with fresh flowers and their eyes shut. The girls were carried down the center of the entryway to the temple on the shoulders of priests. With their eyes closed for perhaps an hour, they danced in near perfect unison— their gestures conforming alternately to the simple, flowing movements of the women and the rapid, intricate movements of the men—as the sweet sounds of the mothers mingled with the powerful, purgative sounds of the fathers and ushered them into womanhood. Their expressive little hands told a story I could not understand, but I could see that their dance expressed the polarity between the male and female worlds, and that it symbolized the journey of an innocent young virgin to the threshold of maidenhood in the timeless language of myth and ritual.

The ceremony was not a performance for tourists, but a privileged night for a few foreign musicians and artists. I watched entranced, thrilled to be able to witness this age-old human drama unfold, but at the same time feeling deep sadness for our culture, which has lost this basic, life-giving connection. Few rituals exist today for American adolescents beyond those they have created for themselves, usually in the arenas of sports and popular music.

A few years later, on a visit to South Africa, I had a similar experience. I was riding in a Mercedes toward Elizabethtown near the coastal cities of New London and Durban when a tribal group of young boys and older men ran across the highway. I asked my escort from the South African Teachers Association to stop the car. As I watched, I realized a new superhighway had been constructed over a sacred pathway. The ancient trail ended in a hut where I was told the boys would be circumcised and prepared for their manhood as warriors. Although the members of this tribe went to school, spoke English, and labored in South Africa's gleaming modern economy, in their rites and rituals they continued to preserve the traditional nexus of the land, ancestors, and spirits. Upon reaching the hut, they immediately began chanting and singing, fathers and sons together.

In his autobiography, from which I quoted at the beginning of this section, Nelson Mandela describes a similar initiation ceremony he underwent as part of the Xhosa tribe. The promise of the modern, postapartheid South Africa that Mandela has helped to shape is that the traditional and modern will be woven together in a rich new tapestry. I can think of no more hopeful testament to this than that, in 1997, Robben Island, the prison fortress where the future president of South Africa spent eighteen years, became an arts and culture center.

ʒ   Healing with Traditional Music

As you can see, the Mozart Effect encompasses traditional and indigenous sounds as well as classical and modern ones. The popular acceptance of "world" music—one of the major trends of the 1990s—has opened doors to every part of our human heritage. Now we have access to the sound of unique instruments and arrangements from every continent, which means that musicians can serve as true missionaries of sonic healing.

World music also serves as a bridge between traditional healing and modern medicine. Skeptical Western physicians and other health-care professionals are more likely to give credence to methods with centuries of results than to newer holistic therapies. Here are a few examples.

CHINESE MUSIC THERAPY

In China, traditional music therapy is adapting itself to modern diseases and disorders. Recently, I was introduced to a series of albums entitled *Obesity; Constipation; Insomnia; Relaxation; Stress; Liver, Heart, and Lungs,* along with an orchestral piece that I have fondly nicknamed "The Kidney Bladder Suite." Most of the albums use traditional Chinese instruments and are flawlessly performed. On a recent visit to Japan, I also came across several compilations of classical and romantic music with prescriptive suggestions. For insomnia, Debussy's "Ondine" or "Scherzando" or Bach's "Goldberg Variations" are recommended. For headaches and migraines, the Japanese suggested Mendelssohn's "Spring Song," Dvorak's "Humoresque," or even a dose of George Gershwin's "An American in Paris."

Over the centuries, healing systems have evolved in Far Eastern medicine and philosophy that associate the pentatonic or five-note scale with the seasons, the organs and functions of the body, and with specific foods and tastes. The five tones also exemplify different instruments, ways of making music, and styles of performance. The Chinese music described above is pentatonic.

One of the most charismatic figures in Chinese music therapy is Kung Tai, age twenty-eight, who combines rhythm, *qi gong* exercise movements, and lyric writing. Like his Western contemporaries, Kung is bent on adapting the ancient arts of music healing to contemporary needs. In 1986, while meditating, Kung felt his body vanish and saw a golden light radiating from a lotus-shaped stage. He then heard a voice singing clear celestial music, a theme that became the basis for his work "A Leisurely Journey." In 1991, he gave his first public concert in the Beijing Music Hall to more than two thousand people. In the audience, several dramatic cases of spontaneous healing reportedly occurred. Since then, Kung has performed live from the Beijing TV Studio.

Another contemporary Chinese music therapist, Wang Hsu-Tong, has, in collaboration with Shanghai composer Wu Hsiao-Ping, begun investigating the effects of rhythm on human physiology. Dr. Wang says the purpose of his treatment is to follow nature and allow the sound to gently heal an illness. Dr. Mong Chin-Shan, a colleague, believes music holds great promise as a noninvasive treatment and is superior to drugs, which he feels should be used only as a last resort. He also finds music surprisingly effective in treating neuroses and emotionally based illnesses.

INDIAN HEALING MUSIC

Across the Himalayas, India has a long tradition of merging music and medicine. On an expedition to the subcontinent several years ago, Pat Moffitt Cook, editor of *The Open Ear*, a cross-cultural journal on music and healing based in Bainbridge Island, Washington, met with a well-known village healer called Koshalya. On greeting Cook, Koshalya motioned for her to go alone into her healing hut, which was made of painted white bricks and covered with a thatched roof. Inside, Koshalya customarily prayed to Sitla, the Hindu goddess of disease, to help her patients.

In the room, which was ten feet square with a low, six-foot ceiling, Pat Cook noticed an aluminum food dish. She picked it up and sat for several minutes "feeling the space." Suddenly, she heard a simple melody, and thought at first that someone was humming outside the hut. Then it seemed as if the melody were reverberating in the walls. Was the hut singing? Cook began to hum along, under her breath. Still holding the dish when the music stopped, she gently put it down and knew it was time to go.

Outside, she described her experience and Koshalya's face glowed. She explained that Cook had heard *the* music, the healing song. "So Sitla has called you from America," she said. "I will teach you all that I know." Koshalya wrapped her weathered hands around Cook's, and the two women gazed wordlessly at each other. Cook, who told me that at that moment she felt a profound feeling of peace, went on to join the Indian woman as a friend, student, and researcher.

Although Cook's initiation is easy to scoff at, the approach to healing that she came to learn is as old as the Vedas and Upanishads, the sacred literature of India extending back thousands of years. As in Native American vision quests and prophetic dreams, sacred music and song are believed to be a gift of the gods. According to myth, Lord Shiva created music and dance from the primordial sound and taught them to the goddess Parvati, his wife, who shared them with the other gods and goddesses. Taking pity on human beings, the god Brahma brought music to earth as the fifth Veda, the Sama Veda. Narada, meanwhile, invented the *vina,* a harplike instrument, and Bharata introduced the *ragas* in the classic *Natyosastra.* Ever since, Hindus have worshipped Saraswati, Brahma's consort, as the goddess of music, knowledge, and speech. Through the ages, distinctive genres and schools have evolved, among them the *ragas* of the Alvars in the Tamil language of South India.

A raga is a traditional composition of religious music with improvised tonal progressions, rhythmic patterns, and melodic formulas. Unlike most Western music, in which the notes are distinct,

the tones in ragas and most other Indian music tend to blend together, creating a soothing, unifying sound.

At hospitals, universities, and healing centers throughout India,
traditional Indian music is the subject of research and a tool of
therapy. In Bangalore, doctors at the National Institute of Mental
Health and Neuro Sciences recently prescribed sound therapy for a
famous mathematician who was stealing money from a small shrine
to Ganesha, the elephant-headed god of wealth, to pay for his tobacco addiction and soothe his nerves. In Madras, the Raga Research
Center has assembled an interdisciplinary team of doctors, neurolo-
gists, psychiatrists, psychologists, and musicians who experiment
with different ragas for use in music therapy. They have found two
particular ragas beneficial in treating hypertension and mental
illness.

LOST MUSICAL TREATMENTS OF THE MIDDLE EAST

Like travelers on the old Silk Road, we can trace the use of music
in healing from China and India across Central Asia to the gateway
to the West. When he was twelve years old, Rahmi Oruc Guvenc,
a Turkish music therapist, had a remarkable dream. "I saw a person
I didn't know, and he had a violin, which he held out to me and
said, 'Play.' I said, 'I don't know how. How can I play?' He said, 'No,
you will play.' So I took it and I began to play. When I woke up, I
told this story to my father, and he went that same day and found
me a violin."

After studying violin for three years, Guvenc switched to the
ud, the ancestor of the lute, the *ney*, a reed flute, the three-string
rehab, and other traditional Turkish instruments. As his grandparents had immigrated from Tatarstan to Turkey, he found himself
interested as well in the music of Central Asia. After receiving a
degree in philosophy at Istanbul University, Guvenc went on to
medical school, where he specialized in music therapy. Although
the courses were Western oriented, he found a professor who encouraged him to recover the lost musical methods of the Middle
East. Guvenc's research led him to El Farabi, Ibn Sina (known in
the West as Avicenna), and other great physicians of the medieval
world who incorporated music into their treatment. He learned that

Islamic hospitals sometimes included special music rooms, and that doctors relied on *makam* (tonality or scale) for specific disorders. Guvenc also studied the music and dance of the Sufis, the whirling dervishes, and the folk music of Tatarstan and Kazakstan.

After receiving his medical degree, Guvenc established a center for music therapy at Istanbul University where he sees patients and trains students from many nations. The discipline is rigorous, with each student required to learn to play three instruments as well as master age-old instrument-building techniques. The music therapy center presently has a staff of forty, with a branch in Vienna.

AN ARGENTINIAN MUSE

Silvia Nakkach, an Argentine native and cross-cultural musical performer and therapist, commutes from her home in San Francisco to Rio and Madrid, where, like a modern-day muse, she seeks to transform lives with the help of sounds and rhythms. Her multicultural events begin with her students—typically healers, teachers, and teacher-trainers—standing close together, slightly touching one another. Taking her cue from the mood of the group, Nakkach guides participants in an improvised welcoming prayer, a new aria, or an aboriginal call from the Amazon. "It is important to me not to follow a prepared script but to allow the music that the specific group-mind triggers to emerge," she says. Recorded drones, toning, and sonic meditations consolidate the musical trance state and "transpersonal field."

In the workshop's second phase, this state of consciousness is reinforced by the singing of ragas and by shamanic rhythm exercises. Nakkach introduces participants to ancient vocal music, Afro-Brazilian chants, Scandinavian folk psalms, modern vocal techniques, and rhythmic expressions from other cultures. In the third phase, spontaneous expression is encouraged, and members of the group share structured improvisational strategies, including visualizations with music, repetitional singing, bossa-nova or tango patterns, voice projection, poetry and lyrics building, "mesostics" word games, and choral prayers.

"Sustained listening and concentration becomes the door for self-transformation," Nakkach observes. "As a result of the process, we all witness the birth of a new-ancient form of true therapy: the emergence of the healing voice and the power of self-generated prayer."

Although she works with people from many continents, Nakkach says she finds that South Americans are particularly adaptable and in touch with their creative nature. Also because of their often intense struggle to survive, South American families are closely knit and participate more frequently in musical and artistic activities than families in wealthier, northern regions.

Nakkach's influence has extended into many areas. One of her students in Brazil leads street children of the Rio favelas in a program of prayers and indigenous chants. Nakkach's musical exercises have helped students cope with hunger, homelessness, and other features of modern urban life. Brazilian children enter the shamanic field in a few minutes, she explains, because the shaman is an archetype in their consciousness that is easily activated by rhythm and sound.

"You clap for a minute, and the gods will appear," she tells her students. "It's so simple to bring the other worlds of ecstasy through the voice and body in transformative exercises."

THE POWER OF AFRICAN-AMERICAN MUSIC

> *"Singing about your sadness unburdens your soul. But the blues hollers shouted about more than being sad. They were also delivering messages in musical code. If the master was coming, you might sing a hidden warning to the other field hands. . . . The blues could warn you what was coming. I could see the blues was about survival."*
>
> —B. B. KING, *BLUES ALL AROUND ME*

Traditional African music was dominated by the ring, a circle around which people moved and sang, danced, and shouted joyfully to the accompaniment of rhythmic drumming. In his book, *The Power of Black Music*, Samuel A. Floyd, Jr., director of the Center for Black Music Research at Columbia College in Chicago, traces the ways in which the many styles of African-American music, including gospel, jazz, the blues, soul, and rap, descended from this basic form. "For Africans," he writes, "song and dance were religious affirmation; they were urgently compelled to perform music and dance as a means of keeping in contact with their ancestors in order to 'retain their power of self-definition or perish.' For African-Americans, the spiritual was the musical vehicle within the ring for this affirmation and unity, for these songs were 'masterful repositories of an African cultural spirit' and, through the shout and its developments, they proved central to the maintenance and perpetuation of African cultural values."

In Africa, drumming evolved into a high art, and by using two drums together to tap out a Morselike binary code, skilled "talking drummers" could communicate complex information for a 60-mile radius. Fearful of revolts and uprisings, Southern plantation owners quickly prohibited native drumming when slavery came to America. Although the ring was broken and dismissed as heathen worship, African musical traditions continued in the form of field cries, hunting cries, street cries, Christian worship, minstrelsy, and other forms of vocal expression, with the banjo and fiddle replacing the drum as the principal instruments. The "cornfield hollers" that slaves perfected to communicate across fields, valleys, and hollows harkened back to the yodels of the Pygmy and Kongo peoples of the African homeland. Calls, cries, and shouts—rich in emotional expression—were used for more personal communication. Black folk songs, work songs, love songs, children's songs, hymns, and other music were spread by itinerant "music physicianers." Often escaped slaves who had fled North with only a fiddle on their backs, the physicianers served as the bards, journalists, historians, humorists, and chroniclers of the early African experience in America.

Although the circle dance eventually gave way to couple and then solo dance, elements of traditional musical forms and their healing rhythms remained. Floyd chronicles the evolution of the blues from the music of Senegambian *gewels* (griots or bards), who played for dances, performed acrobatics, told stories, and posed riddles for the audience to solve. He likens jazz improvisation to the African dance-possession events that often resulted in collective trance and spirit possession. He also discusses the Ellington Effect, the highly sensitive and nuanced awareness of jazz band leader

Duke Ellington to the "tonal personalities" of his sidemen, and his inimitable use of call-response to evoke the sounds of the "callers, criers, and 'story' tellers of the African and African-American past."

Ironically, with the loss of traditional values, notes Floyd, African culture is surviving today as much in the white as the black community. He suggests that a new planetary music is being created as European, African, and African-American traditions converge and blend. As Hale Smith, the popular composer of *Innerflexions*, puts it: "My teachers Marcell Dick, Duke, Benny Carter, Mozart—all them cats are part of [my influences]."

INTERLUDE

Hands (and Voices) Across the Water

Music from different world cultures is starting to crossbreed. Paul Winter, a jazz soprano saxophone player, often blends Russian folk songs, the pipe organ, Japanese drums, and Native American flutes with his music when he performs at the Cathedral of St. John the Divine in New York. In Japan, koto ensembles play Bach and Mozart, and experimental musicians in Hong Kong use pentatonic, five-note melodies with African chants.

In the album *Bach to Africa* (Sony Classical) by the group Lambarena, the music of Bach and of traditional African musicians blend together brilliantly. Dedicated to Albert Schweitzer, the music is reminiscent of the great works that he brought from Germany to patients in his missionary hospital in equatorial Africa.

To do this exercise you have to buy the album. Put it on, close your eyes and then, on one side of the room, visualize a German Bach orchestra with an organ and keyboard player. On the other side, visualize Gabonese musicians with their drums and other traditional instruments. As you play the album, imagine a transcendent conversation taking place between these cultures, a conversation that would not be possible in their respective spoken languages. Now experience the joy and brilliance of this north/south collaboration as each begins to blend into the other.

At a recent concert in Boulder, I accompanied a Methodist minister from a white upper-class community to hear the remarkable group of singers Sweet Honey in the Rock. At the end of the concert, she said, "I've learned more, felt more, and sensed the political and social realities of women and justice more in the last hour than I have in my whole life." Ysaye Barnwell, a singer in Sweet Honey in the Rock, whose range spans bass, baritone, tenor, and alto, conducts international workshops in vocal expression. Whether in Findhorn, the inner city, or at Carnegie Hall, she is a singing minister to the mind.

In his autobiography, *Lift Every Voice,* Dr. Walter Turnbull, founder and director of the Boys Choir of Harlem, describes how music took him from the Mississippi cotton fields to the Radio City Music Hall, the White House, and the leading concert halls of Europe. When he founded the Boys Choir of Harlem twenty-six years ago, he did not set out to establish an internationally known performance group. "I simply wanted to share the joy of music with African-American children. It has the kind of power to lift people above any particular circumstance and inspire the heart. Music is very magical, able to transform children with no more than lint in their pockets and honey in their throats into grand performers on the world stage."

Noted for taking poor, untrained youngsters and teaching them to sing accompaniments to Bach, Mozart, Handel, and Leonard Bernstein, as well as jazz, gospel, and hip hop, Turnbull was once asked by Morley Safer of *60 Minutes,* "What makes your kids different from the other kids that we read about, the ones that go out and assault people and use drugs?" He replied, "My kids are no different. They come from the same projects. They come from the same kinds of families. The difference is that there is somebody here willing to do something for them, and they are willing to do something. There is an opportunity here."

At a local hospice in Louisville, music-care coordinator Dr. Joy Berger uses gospel music with patients and their families. Once she played it for a woman whose veins had collapsed, making it impossible for a nurse to take blood. "It was painful," she says. "I played 'Balm in Gilead,' and we focused on each other and the music, and she was able to get the blood. Afterward, [the woman] looked at me and said, 'This is gonna sound crazy, but I think that music helped my pain.'"

⟩ Drumming Therapy

Among all the instruments used in healing, the drum produces some of the most powerful effects and bridges the traditional and modern, the individual and the community. John K. Galm, a professor of ethnomusicology at the University of Colorado, demonstrates at schools around the country how the traditional *djembe* drum from West Africa is used to build a sense of community through entrainment of heartbeats and breathing.

The djembe is an ovoid drum that is held on the lap or between the knees. Galm strikes specific spots on the drum to stimulate sensations in selected areas of the listeners' bodies. Once, during a performance at Angevine Middle School in Lafayette, Colorado, his audience included a student with muscular spasms who was accompanied by a nurse. "As I played the djembe, I noticed that he seemed to relax and started to hum with the sound of the instrument," Galm told me. "Afterward I was informed that the boy had listened to a recording made of my performance and has been able to relax as he did during the live performance."

Remo is a light, hand-held synthetic drum used in healing and community events. It was invented by Remo Belli, president of Remo, Inc., in Los Angeles, and its sales grew exponentially once Belli realized that the percussion industry in the United States was moving away from rock & roll into "rhythm and restore" and marketed the drum accordingly.

With the invention of the synthetic drumhead, there is now a lightweight instrument that never goes out of tune from humidity and whose manufacture does not take the life of an animal. The drums—as small as a saucer or as big as a coffee table—are inexpensive, durable, and exceptionally beautiful sounding; depending on their size, they can be played by one person or five. It is not unusual now to find drums, drumsticks, and other musical instruments beside slings, crutches, and wheelchairs in the closets of hospital rehabilitation wards.

On one occasion, Galm led a small group of Alzheimer patients—mostly withdrawn elderly men and women—and their caretakers in a drumming circle with a handheld Remo. "I controlled the tempo and dynamic level by playing a bass drum," he observed. "After about forty-five minutes of steady playing, we stopped and were savoring the silence when one of the patients said, 'I haven't heard this silence since I was in Catholic boarding school before dinner.' This woman had not spoken all evening and was now able to communicate with her caretakers. The drumming had brought back her sense of the present, and this window of communication lasted from five to ten minutes. On other occasions it lasted as long as a few hours."

At the Senate Hearings on the Elderly, Mickey Hart reported on the successful use of drumming in organizations ranging from women's groups to twelve-step programs like Alcoholics Anonymous to Robert Bly–influenced mens clubs. He also addressed the question of percussive instruments for the elderly: "Our bodies," he said, "are multidimensional rhythm machines with everything pulsing in synchrony, from the digesting activity of our intestines to the firing of neurons in the brain. Within the body the main beat is laid down by the cardiovascular system, the heart and the lungs. . . . As we age, however, these rhythms can fall out of sync. And then, suddenly, there is no more important or crucial issue than regaining that lost rhythm." Drum therapy for the elderly was, he said, as good an idea today as it was thousands of years ago.

♵ Spontaneous Musical Healing

Today there are many mind/body therapists, New Age counselors, and sound healers who have incorporated music into their practice. In most cases, they do not have modern medical training. Their approach is largely spontaneous and intuitive. One of the most famous cases of spontaneous healing in history was portrayed in the film *Farinelli*. The title character, an Italian castrato, was summoned to sing for King Philip of Spain in the 1730s. Upon hearing Farinelli's incredible high-pitched singing, the King's chronic pain, depression, and mental illness miraculously disappeared.

Athough there are thousands of such tales, music therapy researchers frequently criticize the "soft data" of healing stories, which cannot be recreated under experimental conditions. We should realize, however, that the psychological disposition of the listener, the individual sound environment, and what one might term "the magic of the moment," tend to interact in ways that are impossible to duplicate in controlled studies. Modern medicine regards all human bodies as comparable machines that may be fixed with the aid of the most up-to-date repair manual. A better metaphor would be a group of highly sensitive musical instruments, each with its own unique artistic properties and preferred methods of "tuning." In new mind/body medicine, therapists typically insist on the importance of the intuitive, the spontaneous, and the spiritual, as well as the behavioral and clinical. Once again, healing is viewed as an art.

In his popular book, *Spontaneous Healing,* Dr. Andrew Weil relates that over the years he has received hundreds of testimonials extolling the specific virtues of herbs, special foods and diets, vitamins and supplements, yoga, prayer, music, chants, and other therapies. "Like my colleagues, I also question the simple cause-and-effect interpretations placed on these reports and hesitate to endorse products and practitioners," he explains. "But unlike most of them, I do not throw out the reports. Testimonials are important pieces of evidence. They are not necessarily testimony to the power or value of particular healers and products. Rather, they are testimony to the human capacity for healing. The evidence is incontrovertible that the body is capable of healing itself. By ignoring that, many doctors cut themselves off from a tremendous source of optimism about health and healing."

Although music is still considered an unconventional therapy— and physicians sensibly reject New Age albums that claim without documentation to heal certain organs, functions, or conditions— listeners intuitively sense its therapeutic effects. The phenomenal rise in popularity of this kind of music suggests that the public is more eager now than it has been in centuries to participate in its own wellness.

⟨ Physician, Heal Thyself

In 1993, the *New England Journal of Medicine* reported that one in three Americans uses unconventional medical treatments such as relaxation, chiropractic, therapeutic massage, special diets, music, and megavitamins. The most frequent users are college-educated and relatively well-to-do. Many have felt humiliated or ignored by physicians in the past, and at some point they decided that alternative medical approaches were more humane, less judgmental, and gave them more room for participation. Although alternative mind/body disciplines and creative arts therapies have been clinically demonstrated to offer patients significant control of stress, hypertension, digestive disorders, and other conditions with much less medication, many physicians still consider such approaches silly and useless at best and dangerous at worst.

I am concerned about this skepticism on the part of scientists, behaviorists, and clinicians, especially with regard to sound and music. Skepticism can easily evolve into fundamentalism. Just as we need no further proof that pollution is killing us to change our habits of energy consumption, we should not wait for the *definitive* answer to the question of why sound and vibration work before we turn to musical and other promising alternative therapies to treat our escalating personal and family ills. There are many effective mainstream treatments for which the mechanism of action is not fully understood, yet withholding such medicines or therapies would be, in the presence of suffering, inhuman.

What constitutes therapy, medicine, and healing is constantly being redefined. "Whatever happened to healers?" Dr. Larry Dossey recently asked in an editorial in the journal *Alternative Therapies*:

We were training to become surgeons, internists, and pathologists, not healers. . . . Whatever happened to healers? Have we simply run out of them? Surely not; all cultures seem to have produced them in abundance. They continue to abound—those passionate, idealistic young persons whose desire to be involved with healing is mysterious, powerful, and inexplicable. They simply "know" they must become healers, and they will do almost anything to fulfill their calling. Harkening to a deep and primal drive, they often migrate to medical schools, the healing path that currently enjoys the most emphatic social sanction. Yet, this can be a painful, suffocating experience for many of them, because most medical schools have a completely different view of the nature of healers and healing than that of the natural-born healers themselves. Thus we encounter a paradox: Our medical schools, which of all institutions should be most attuned to nourishing and developing the natural healing talents of gifted young people, seem adept at extinguishing them.

Fortunately, the climate is changing. As a result of the public's growing dissatisfaction with traditional medicine and managed health care, as well as the innovative and visionary work of Larry Dossey, Jeanne Achterberg, Andrew Weil, Linda Rodgers, Deepak Chopra, Joan Borysenko, and other mind/body pioneers, the National Institutes of Health (NIH) in 1992 set up the Office of Alternative Medicine (now the Office of Complementary and Alternative Medicine) to "facilitate the fair, scientific evaluation of alternative therapies that could improve many people's health and well-being." In addition to funding such promising holistic therapies as meditation, biofeedback, therapeutic touch, macrobiotics, and Native American medicine, the OCAM awarded one of its initial thirty grants to "investigate any beneficial effects of a specific music therapy intervention on empirical measures of self-perception, empathy, social perception, depression, and emotional expression in persons with brain injuries."

While minuscule compared to the funds spent on drugs, vaccines, artificial body parts, and other invasive treatments, alternative therapies are gaining credence and popularity. In a report to the National Institutes of Health, *Alternative Medicine: Expanding Med-*

ical Horizons, a distinguished group of mind/body researchers headed by Larry Dossey included music therapy, as well as other arts therapies, in the medicine of the future. It seems all but certain that, from a single tone, a mighty symphony (with a healing chorus) will one day grow.

⸬ From Eurythmy to Elvis

Movement and dance often enhance the healing power of music, and curative dramas have been developed based on mythological stories, specific patterns of movement, and indigenous sounds. Rudolf Steiner, an early twentieth century Austrian mystic, helped create a type of healing known as Eurythmy. Combining movement, music, and poetics, Eurythmy is an elegant form of ritual. Its slow, graceful movements are said to contribute to general health and well-being and have been used to treat asthma, stuttering, and respiratory ailments. Practitioners learn to move around a circle and make gestures that symbolize musical intervals and tonal colors while a trained facilitator plays the piano. Several modern forms of psychotherapy have also combined extended movement and dancing with music, singing, or toning, all with the goal of allowing the information held within the body to move into consciousness and play a role in the healing process.

Judging by the number of people who swear by pop music, it could be that contemporary sounds produce some of the healing and transformative effects of music therapists, indigenous practitioners, and mind/body healers. Certainly there are mythic overtones in much of rock. It may be that Bruce Springsteen is a contemporary working man's Orpheus, embodying the plight of modern youth in the act of slogging its way through the Underworld, in search of some lost beloved and making countless mistakes and wrong turns. The image of the deejay as urban shaman is a staple in modern mythology.

I am often asked about the place of rock music in healing and whether the music of Pearl Jam, Elvis, or Elton John creates the Mozart Effect. The answer is complex because rock is so varied.

Heavy metal is different from Phil Collins. To people in their fifties, some of today's bands make Little Richard and Jerry Lee Lewis sound positively Baroque.

In general, loud, pounding music is destructive to the ear, yet the body, to grow, needs to drum and move, sing and dance, release pressure, and find its own natural rhythm. Modern society doesn't always allow for this, however, and so a potent form of music has arisen to fill the void. My father, growing up on a farm in rural Arkansas, had no need to rock & roll. By one o'clock every afternoon, he was baling hay with that full pelvic motion that helps the body in its adolescent years to develop. When it hasn't got that kind of outlet—when people don't have the opportunity to throb and gyrate and throw themselves around—society comes up with, say, an Elvis the Pelvis.

On the one hand, rock music creates tension and frustration; on the other, it releases it. Rock music, one might say, is a two-sided coin that keeps flipping.

CHAPTER 6
Sound Images

ORCHESTRATING THE MIND AND BODY

Hold fast to the Great Image and all under heaven will come.
They will come but not be harmed, rest in safety and peace.
Music and food will make the passerby halt.
—LAO TZU, *TAO TE CHING*

Jerry was a twenty-six-year-old African-American man with autism. He had been born nearly brain-dead from oxygen deprivation after his mother was in a car accident, but with the help of modern medicine, he survived. Unable to speak, Jerry grew up attending schools for the mentally retarded and was finally institutionalized after virtually destroying the family apartment during repeated temper tantrums. He would express his frustration by hitting his ears and face or pounding his head against walls and floors. Jerry was six feet tall and powerfully built, and it took three trained staffers to control his violent behavior. According to specialists, his mental age was between two and eight years old.

Jerry began therapy with Ginger Clarkson, a music therapy instructor at Yale University. He beat patterns on drums, played accompaniments on a selection of melodic instruments, and danced to recorded music. After several years, a new technique called facilitated communication was introduced in the field of autism, and Jerry began to verbalize his feelings on a small, hand-held computer as he continued his musical healing. In his first message, he wrote: GINGER I LOVE MUSIC. WE DANCE VERY WELL TOGETHER CAN WE DANCE FOR LONGER PERIODS OF TIME.

"Stunned," Clarkson recalls, "I began my first conversation with this man whose intellect, empathy, and sense of humor I had greatly underestimated." Oliver Sacks, the neurologist and author, met Jerry and was impressed with his progress. In one memorable session, Jerry typed, I DREAMED I AM NORMAL.

Using a therapeutic method known as Guided Imagery and Music, in which he listened to different selections and drew a picture inside a circle, Jerry learned to express his emotions. (Practitioners of this method have found that providing the subject with a piece of paper on which a circle has already been drawn focuses him or her and elicits more revealing imagery.) He was even able, painstakingly, to print his name. The pictures Jerry drew depicted deer, snakes, and a person named Fred, who seemed to function as his alter ego. Through a combination of music and imagery, Jerry expressed long-standing feelings of resentment toward his father, who had abandoned the family when he was a little boy. Dianne, a graphic designer in the supervisory team, was so impressed with Jerry's progress and artistic talent that she enlisted his help in starting a greeting card company. Jerry came up with the name: "Flew the Coop." Today, Jerry helps design greeting cards and writes beautiful poems that Dianne prints and sells through an arts cooperative. With the help of music and imagery, his dream of living a more normal life came true.

As Jerry's story shows, it is often the combination of image and sound that creates the "healing shift." You may recall from my own story how Jeanne Achterberg, the mind/body researcher, warned me that the initial images I formed to heal the blood clot behind my right eye were not especially healing. She pressed me to go deeper inside myself, and, after five or six attempts, I came up with a vision of a small room next to a quiet ocean—a fortuitous discovery, and one that I'm convinced played a major role in my eventual recovery.

In this chapter, we will look at how imagery can enhance the Mozart Effect and take the healing process to an even higher level.

♩ Imagery: Not Just Visual

Most people think of "imagery" as exclusively visual, but, for me, the term embraces all the senses and the kinds of "sense memory"—the recollection of a sound or voice, the smell of a place, the anticipated taste of a special food. Images, many of them sensory, bubble up in our consciousness constantly, and they motivate much of what we do—from making an appointment for a new hairstyle to planning a new den for a house, to making reservations at a talked-about restaurant. Imagery may be stimulated from the outside, as when you watch a film or TV show or drive past a billboard, or it may arise spontaneously, as when you dream, daydream, or simply have a sudden "aha!" of inspiration.

Images elicit physiological and psychological responses: They set your blood racing, cool you off, evoke a cascade of memories, inspire visions. Some words are experienced as images—*fire, house, mother*. And some images transcend themselves. We call them *archetypes* when they're associated with such abstract concepts as goodness or evil, or when they resonate deep within us, seeming to point to the deepest mysteries of life. We call powerful images *icons* when they're fraught with religious or cultural associations—a bust of the Virgin Mary, a reproduction of the Mona Lisa, a picture of JFK, a lithograph of Marilyn Monroe.

Many forms of prayer and meditation employ imagery, including archetypes and icons, as a tool to focus and concentrate energy. Psychoanalysis, with its use of free association, harnesses the power of imagery to bring unconscious thoughts and feelings to awareness. Advertising is synonymous with manipulation through images. Detroit and Tokyo don't sell cars, they sell sex, nature, freedom. Now, mind/body therapies and traditional healing techniques use visualization and imagery to treat everything from back pain to blood pressure, from sluggish immune systems to energetic tumors. Clearly, imagery has enormous power to shape human life.

Music enhances the power of imagery, multiplying its physical, mental, and spiritual impact. It can create a current on which images flow; and it can, at the same time, catch an image in its net— fix it so that it may be analyzed and, in an instant, summoned back. After a decade of studying and using combined imagery and music for the purposes of healing, I have come to realize that explanations are elusive—that various approaches must be experienced to be fully understood. The simplest and safest way is to close your eyes, put on a piece of music, and see what happens. But I believe that there are even more interesting and effective ways of integrating thought and sound.

Take one of my college friends, a trombone major, who used to "rehearse" for history tests by listening to music. Before an exam, he would review the text, close his eyes, put on a march by John Philip Sousa, and visualize the information that he wanted to remember. He would then listen to part of the *Nutcracker Suite* by Tchaikovsky, a Chopin waltz, and finally a Bach fugue. Each work, he told me, gave him a different view of what he had to know, so when he read a question on the exam, he would recall the specific piece—almost singing it silently to himself—and the music would evoke the correct information. Although he was a straight-A student, I dismissed his way of studying as bizarre. It was not until many years later that I realized the practical value of his intuitive use of imagery and music as a mnemonic device.

Or consider the highly charged words that I spoke of above: *fire, home, mother*. Say them while you play open, free-form music like Jonathan Goldman's *Dolphin Dreams* or Brian Eno's *Music for Airports,* and then repeat them to the accompaniment of something more defined and robustly rhythmical, such as a Sousa march. The power of the words changes with the music: intoned to one piece, the words can make you feel fear or apprehension; to another, they can instill a sense of peace and contentment.

⸘ Releasing Images from the Body

Music has charms to soothe a savage breast,
To soften rocks, or bend a knotted oak.
—WILLIAM CONGREVE, seventeenth century British dramatist

Every part of the body has its own memories, whether of the mending of a broken bone or the pressure on the shoulders during passage through the birth canal. Research shows that the way our muscles tense and relax and the way we sleep, speak, think, and worry are all recorded within us—not just in our minds but our cells. Dr. Deepak Chopra explains that atoms, cells, and tissues are held together by "invisible threads" composed of faint vibrations—what Ayurveda, the traditional medicine of India, calls "primordial sound." The infinitesimally small vibrations that hold DNA together, he contends, are the strongest force in nature. However, there are times when a DNA sequence is altered—for example, following an illness or accident. "In that event," Chopra says, "Ayurveda tells us to apply a specifically chosen primoridal sound, like a mold or template slipped over the disturbed cells pushing them back into line, not physically, but by repairing the sequence of sound at the heart of every cell."

Practitioners of traditional Chinese medicine and philosophy agree, teaching that each cell in the body is the terminus of a tiny capillary and a meridian, bringing together blood, *ki* or life energy, and consciousness. According to this vibrational model, sound and images are received, archived, and transmitted not only through the brain, but also through other organic structures and functions. That means that, as a result of sickness, accident, or trauma, painful emotions and experiences can become locked in the body, and can remain there for weeks, months, and even years until released—in many cases by the right sounds and images.

Here's an illustration. Driving home one night with her twelve-year-old daughter, Lizzy, Alana crashed into a car that was making a dangerous U-turn in the road. Both cars were destroyed, but, fortunately, no one was seriously hurt. Lizzy sobbed uncontrollably but was unharmed and resumed her normal life. Her mother, however, suffered severe whiplash in her left shoulder and sought out sound and toning instructor Joy Gardner-Gordon for help in controlling the agony. Gardner-Gordon guided Alana to release her pain by visualizing the accident and screaming and making other sounds that expressed the terror for her life and the life of her child that she felt at the moment of impact.

"Her body had become frozen in a posture of tension since the powerful message she had sent to her muscles and tissues was to be in a state of ready alertness," Gardner-Gordon writes in her book *The Healing Voice*. "The scream was a message to her subconscious mind that the impact had, in fact, occurred, and now it was time to release." After two months of toning, Alana felt whole again.

The human voice is our most powerful tool for transmuting pain and sorrow into radiant well-being. In her book *Sound Medicine,* Laeh Maggie Garfield attributes the popularity of opera to its ability to purge strong emotions. "Opera buffs go to hear favorite singers not so much for their total performance but for the special notes they are known to hit during successfully written arias," she writes. "Most often the operatic devotee awaits the high pitch of the dramatic soprano, who unknowingly strikes a healing chord for the rapt listener. The fan is thereby revitalized by the evening's performance."

In the 1980s, I spent three years writing music based on listening to rhythms of the breath and observing cycles of relaxation, rest, and insight—music to help energy to circulate more freely and keep the inner organs, systems, and functions "in tune." During this period, I also composed for a fascinating, guided-imagery project by Dr. Victor Beasley, author of *Your Electro-Vibratory Body.* Instead of a progressive relaxation process, in which you visualize a movement through your body from head to toe or toe to head, Beasley had you regard different bodily systems in a holistic way. For example, he would ask you to think of your skin—the body's largest organ—and imagine every cell at once. Then he would ask you to imagine all the fluids in your body or the neurons pulsating through your nervous system. It fell to me to translate these strange mental pictures into sound and music. The result was the recording *Symphony for the Inner Self,* the ballet *Dances for a Sleepwalker,* and other pieces designed to summon forth images and, in some cases, alter physical function. Along these same lines, I also composed music to accompany Lamaze training for natural childbirth. The music suggests deep, long breaths, a constant reminder to the woman giving birth to breathe deeply, push down, and relax.

≀ Music and the Inner Landscape

As we saw in Chapter 3, music can alter our sense of space. This is one of the greatest contributions of the synthesizer. Until the 1960s, composers and performers were dependent on cathedrals, domes, watersheds, and echoing mountains to create a kind of architectural spaciousness in their music. Gregorian chants, amplified by long reverberations in monasteries, chapels, and cathedrals, along with the long-toned, repetitive Buddhist chants, are examples of sound that has been used to enhance states of awareness, prolong prayer, and improve concentration. Slow compositions of the Romantic, Classical, and Baroque periods have also offered balm for the psyche, allowing the mind to fairly float on sound. With the advent of synthesized music—often called New Age, ambient, or atmospheric music—composers now have the power to recreate the sound effects of certain spaces to release memories held in the body.

Although some trace its roots to Tony Scott and Paul Winter in the 1960s, this genre of music actually goes back over a century. While walking through the Bois de Boulogne in Paris one day in 1889, Claude Debussy heard the strangest music in the distance—it seemed to swirl around and through him. The young French composer realized that he was hearing not melodies, but space. The strangely tuned, pentatonic tones enveloped him, overwhelming his sense of chromaticism and counterpoint. What he heard was actually a gamelan orchestra from Indonesia, performing for the Grand Exposition to celebrate the hundredth anniversary of the French Revolution and the construction of the new Eiffel Tower. Following this encounter, Debussy realized that music had space, vapor, essences, and colors that had not yet been expressed, and, thereafter, his music took on a new sensibility. From his compositions, "Footprints in the Snow," "The Sunken Cathedral," "Moonlight" ("Claire de Lune"), and "Afternoon of a Fawn," Impressionism was born. The new age of atmospheric music had dawned.

Traditional Indonesian folk orchestras, known as the gamelan, continued to visit Paris through the 1960s. In my view, no sound has had such a profound influence on the shape of the new music in the West, and yet few Westerners are familiar with the gamelan.

On each of my nine visits to Bali, one of Indonesia's most beautiful islands, I have been constantly reminded of the power of the ancient Hindu myths that is reflected within the metallic and watery sounds of gongs and xylophones. Gamelan sounds, with their fiery cascades and placid ripples, evoke the heights and depths of our psyches. Like Debussy, I have come to realize that a world of sound exists far from my overstructured conservatory training; and I can easily see how he became obsessed with the coloration of the piano, the "essence" of sound, the space within the self. Much of his music functions as a sort of incense for the heart.

As we move into new electronic forms of deep listening—combining environmental music, brainwave synchronization, and minimalist structure—we are discovering, like Debussy, the importance of slowing down in order to stay in touch with ourselves. "As our world gets faster and more crowded," writes Joseph Lanza in *Elevator Music,* his entertaining history of Muzak and easy-listening sounds, "our music must get slower and more spacious in order to make peace with the biological clock." Ambient music is not created to entertain or to stimulate the intellect, but to act upon the body and emotions, helping us reclaim our inner landscapes, restore spaciousness to our lives, and reconnect with the rhythms of nature.

Despite these benefits, relaxing music has distinct limitations. Frequently, active, dynamic music that grounds us in the moment is more appropriate. In an emergency, jazz may even save your life—or at least keep it on hold—while New Age and ambient music can imperil it. That's the implication of a 1993 study designed to reduce the number of lost calls to a statewide abuse hot line.

In a ten-week experiment, the Florida Protective Services System Abuse Registry Hot Line played different types of music over the telephone until counselors were free to talk to callers. Each day the crisis center received nearly a thousand calls reporting the abuse, neglect, or exploitation of children, disabled adults, and the elderly. And each week, for five weeks, the answering system played a different type of music: classical, popular, relaxation and nature sounds, country, and contemporary jazz. Then the experiment was repeated. During both trials, the smallest number of disconnections came during jazz sessions, which featured selections from Miles Davis, Art Farmer, John McLaughlin, and Esther Phillips. Relaxation, nature music, and the *Pachelbel Canon* yielded the highest number of disconnections.

❧ Imagery and Relaxation

The most obvious therapeutic use of music is for relaxation and stress reduction, which helps the body to access and then discharge deeply locked-in material. And yet, approaching the unconscious demands special care. Too much relaxation can actually increase the pain for some physical conditions, causing symptoms to be released too rapidly—thus interfering with the body's natural healing process. And for deep-seated psychological difficulties, music-induced relaxation may give only superficial relief. Unless the listener has some training or guidance, evocative music can even serve as a catalyst for summoning up dire images of abuse that have been repressed for decades.

Fearful images can arise without music, of course. Consider an accident. The ambulance arrives; the victim is strapped into a cot; the loud, invasive siren conjures up a sense of panic along with constriction—the ride to the hospital alone can hinder recovery! It would be far more therapeutic (and compassionate) inside the ambulance to provide the patient with headphones and soothing music—preferably nonvocal music, patterned around sixty pulses or beats per minute. This would help relax the victim, stabilize his or her breathing, and lessen the shock of the emergency.

The same approach should be applied to the hospital itself. My friend Judy accompanied her husband to the emergency room when he had severe chest pains. After his admission, she went to the waiting room and found the TV turned full blast to *ER*, which was teeming with frenetic images of surgery and general pandemonium. On the next channel, a man was being blown away by a shotgun; on the next, a lion was stalking and eating a gazelle. By the time she switched off the televison she was half-mad with anxiety. And she wasn't even the patient! In a book on the psychology of medicine, Norman Cousins recounts a study which found that hospitalized cardiac care patients were more apt to die in the presence of their chief physician than at any other time. Apparently, their fear of the doctor contributed to fatal heart attacks!

The use of imagery as a presurgical tool is extremely effective as well. I recommend that a patient select an album of light classical music that is neither too slow nor too fast, and that is not associated with a text, which might generate uncomfortable images. It is better not to use vocal music loaded with emotion, but instrumental recordings of your favorite hymns can work well. For three days before surgery, listen to the music with your eyes closed, visualize a successful outcome to the operation, and practice this affirmation: "I am recovering well." This is a rehearsal for post-operative recovery and helps familiarize you with the rhythm and texture of the music. The nurse or nurse's aide can be instructed to let the music play in the recovery room after the operation on an auto-reverse tape deck. As you begin to awaken, the music immediately grounds you, letting you know that the operation is past and that you are recovering.

⸮ The Placebo Effect

Imagery has often been treated as a placebo, a thing that has no intrinsic medicinal properties but may, through the power of suggestion, produce a healing effect. It's difficult, of course, to measure clinically the differences among wishful thinking, faith healing, and imagery—and most allopathically trained clinicians have little incentive to research such distinctions. Yet, by acknowledging and (repeatedly) verifying the "placebo effect," modern medicine has been forced to admit, in its own skeptical way, that placebos work.

In my own professional life, I am constantly aware of the power of the mind. I remind my students, who are largely health-care professionals, teachers, and musicians, that for most reversible illnesses 20 percent of all people get well, regardless of the system, technique, or practitioner. Unfortunately, another 20 percent never get well, no matter how many systems, therapists, or, for that matter, Mozart violin concertos, they employ. My hope is to reach the

60 percent in the middle, who can benefit tremendously from music and creative arts therapies.

Yet the real miracle is not the rare recovery from an incurable illness, but the phenomenal possibility of using music and tone easily and inexpensively to improve the quality of our day-to-day lives. From Darwin's lowly earthworms, which perform so much of the invisible work of evolution, to Zen Master Dogen's teaching that "each drop of water makes the sea a little deeper," we are reminded that the greatest changes in life are the result of slow, gradual, cumulative effects.

The placebo effect has a unique musical history, which is important to understanding the Mozart Effect. In Latin, the word *placebo* means "I shall please," and it made it into English as early as A.D. 1200. *Placebo* is the first word of the first antiphon in Psalm 114 and was sung during vespers, a special Catholic service held on Sundays or holy days. Vespers is also the sixth of the daily canonical hours, a time of prayer in the late afternoon or evening. At this time, the psalms were traditionally sung to praise God, heal the living, and pray for the dead.

It's not hard to trace how the concept of "placebo" became secularized. In the medieval world, placebo signified the power of listening to sacred music, which healed the mind, body, and spirit. In modern times, when the power of the Church declined sharply and sacred music, especially Gregorian chant, all but vanished, the word jumped into the medical lexicon. *Hooper's Medical Dictionary* in 1811 defined placebo as "any medicine given more to please than benefit the patient." Sir Walter Scott used it in a romance, *St. Rouan's*: "There is nothing serious intended—a mere *placebo*—just a divertissement to cheer the spirits, and assist the effect of the waters." Many of Mozart's compositions, as well as those of the Baroque and Classical music of that era, were commissioned as background music—a divertissement, a placebo—for nobility.

Today, placebo has come to mean not only something administered to soothe, but also an inactive substance used as a "control" in a scientific experiment. Medical studies have shown consistently that about one-third of all test patients given a sugar pill, a saline solution, or some other nostrum, note improvements in their symptoms. Physicians routinely treat with placebos such complaints as coughs, colds, headaches, seasickness, anxiety, and pain of various kinds.

So if imagery has a placebo effect, how does it work? A clue is provided by experiments going back to the 1930s, when Edmund Jacobsen developed his progressive muscular relaxation techniques. In research on muscle physiology at the University of Chicago, Cornell, and Harvard, Jacobsen determined that when he placed electrodes on a subject's muscles and asked the person to think about taking a walk, the EMG (electromyography) indicated electrical signals solely in the walking muscles. The same was true if he asked subjects to imagine resting, chewing, or jumping. We may understand this better if we recall the stimulation that occurs in our bodies and muscles during dreams. Dream images create the sensation without the phenomenon.

Further research has begun to shed light on the physiological mechanism behind the placebo effect. At the University of California at San Francisco, twenty-three patients who had teeth pulled were injected with a placebo several hours after dental surgery. Over a third reported that the placebo eased their pain. The power of suggestion stimulated the release of endorphins, the body's natural opiates, which can elevate mood and provide quick, safe relief from pain and discomfort. However, when the subjects were subsequently given another medication that blocked the action of endorphins, their pain returned in every case. The power of suggestion, or mental imagery, was neutralized. The experiment elegantly demonstrated that the mind/body connection allows the body to supply its own, very real, painkiller in response to belief in a dummy medication.

In research on the effects of guided imagery, taped music, and progressive relaxation on shift workers, Jeanne Achterberg and Frank Lawlis reported positive effects on daily rhythms, finger temperature, and hormonal levels. In another study, Achterberg, Lawlis, and associates found that imagery and music produced higher levels of the chief marker in an enhanced immune system (IgA).

News of these experiments, along with the emergence of psychoneuroimmunology, a new field, has done much to sway doubters about the power of music and imagery. Norman Shealy, M.D., who works with pain and health rehabilitation in his clinic in Springfield, Missouri, reports that relaxation, music, and visualization techniques are the single most important therapy he offers his chronically ill patients. Dr. Neal Olshan, another chronic pain specialist, reports that almost 60 percent of his patients have learned to control their pain through imagery and have resumed an active lifestyle.

⟨ Swimming in the Unconscious

It is as if everyday awareness were but an insignificant island, surrounded by a vast ocean of unsuspected and uncharted consciousness.
—KEN WILBUR

How can imagery and music be used to tap into the unconscious? For twenty-five years, one of the most prominent researchers to pose the question has been Jean Houston, whose experiments employ music and creative visualization in an attempt to evoke mythic images. In sessions that last three to five days, Houston and her staff of actors, musicians, and dancers reinvent a mythic story, such as *The Odyssey, Parsifal, The Wonderful Wizard of Oz,* or the tale of Isis and Osiris, and use it to illustrate the ways in which the participant's life follows patterns and rhythms that are strikingly similar.

How many modern-day Orpheuses dwell among us who need only discover their talent for playing the lyre, for charming everything from trees to rivers to wild beasts? Who among us has not, like Odysseus and his men, been enchanted by the chorus of Sirens determined to lull us into the abyss? Houston finds that using the whole body to reenact archetypal dramas generates more complex images than visualization alone.

Music and imagery can lead us into inner worlds. I often compare it to travel. For one thing, people experience similar phobias—the ones about leaving home and being stranded in a place with strange signs and symbols, a foreign language, and an unfamiliar climate. Sometimes it's good to explore on our own, with nothing but our intuition. At other times, it makes sense to read guidebooks, study maps, and make all our hotel reservations in advance. We might also opt for a structured trip with firm itineraries and tour guides. Despite his or her fears, the curious traveler will find ways to explore the unknown, balancing adventure and safety.

In my training seminars, I serve as a guide for participants. Sometimes, I let them journey through the music alone, because it's important for them to discover things for themselves and learn to survive in new locales. At other times, I am more active, working with the music to ease them deeper into their unconscious.

To journey through inner worlds is to leave our logic and our emotional bearings behind. We swim differently in the bathtub than along the beach, and it is an altogether different experience to find ourselves alone in the middle of the Pacific Ocean. There are different ways to feel at home in the depths. To some, the ocean is a beautiful place full of wondrous fish. To others, it's a dark, cold abyss, teeming with unseen sharks and barracudas ready to devour us. The unconscious contains all these things, from the loveliest to the most ghastly, and the right music can enable us to explore these depths like trained divers, ready for the glory, the terror, the intensity of the inner world.

INTERLUDE

Conducting Your Life

Imagine tapping into the power of the great conductors: Toscanini, Bernstein, Osawa, or even John Williams. The non-musician, the wounded musician, and the inhibited musician can all gain from a simple exercise that begins and ends in the imagination.

Select a recording—say, Paganini's "Violin Concerto No. 2 in b minor," Wagner's "*Flying Dutchman* Overture," a Beethoven symphony or piano concerto, or the soundtrack to *Star Wars*.

Close your eyes and stand for a minute or two, relaxing

the body, exhaling, releasing tension from the feet, the knees, the hips, the torso, hands, arms, elbows, shoulders, and head. As the music begins, imagine yourself as a great conductor in front of a world-renowned orchestra. From your hands spring the rhythms, the emotions, the eloquence of the music; yet, at the same time, the music is conducting *you*, flowing into your body, animating your hands and arms.

Conduct at times with your knees; at other times, your hips; at others, your head. Try not to dance. Just let your hands and body mold and shape and caress the music. Think of yourself as a sculptor of sound.

Experiment with the same piece of music for five days in a row. As you become more familiar with it, let its spirit surround and infuse you. Then, memorize how an orchestra would be seated in front of you: the violins on the left; the violas, woodwinds, and brass in the middle; the percussion in the back; and the cellos and double basses on the right. Let each, in turn, fill you.

A ten to twenty minute conducting session each day balances the brain waves, serves as an aerobic workout, and unlocks the creative spirit within.

Unlike drugs, which some people use to generate altered states, music does not foster diabolic patterns and dependencies. When we travel with music, we have a far easier time remaining lucid and in control. We are free to turn the music down or off, and if something unnatural or threatening swims up from the depths, we can stay very still and let it swim away. Exploring imagery and music with the assistance of a trained therapist or guide ensures that we will remain alert as we traverse these new waters.

Our choice of music, the amount of time we need to test the waters, the temperature, and the undercurrents—these are unique in each case. Some music is so safe and comforting that the water seems rich and nurturing, and we feel as if we're seeing all the way to the bottom. With other music we gaze into the void—we have a vision of our own death. Since we sometimes glimpse this void in life, music and imagery afford us the chance to survive and even thrive in the presence of our worst fears. We can learn to tread water, or to swim *around* the source of trouble. At the same time, music can help us learn to love the unseen, and give us the confidence to search out the eternal.

On a trip to Switzerland in 1956, Margaret Tilly, a concert pianist and music therapist from San Francisco, visited Carl Jung at his home in Kusnacht. In the course of their conversation, she asked the great psychoanalyst about his approach to music. "My mother was a fine singer, so was her sister, and my daughter is a fine pianist," Jung replied. "I know the whole literature. I have heard everything and all the great performers, but I never listen to music any more. It exhausts and irritates me." Surprised at his response, Tilly asked why. Jung said, "Because music is dealing with such deep archetypal material, and those who play don't realize this."

During the visit, Jung asked Tilly to demonstrate how she used music with her clients. Visibly impressed with her work, he exclaimed, "This opens up whole new avenues of research I'd never even dreamed of. Because of what you've shown me this afternoon—not just what you've said, but what I have actually felt and experienced—I feel that from now on music should be an essential part of every analysis. This reaches the deep, archetypal material that we can only sometimes reach in our analytical work with patients. This is most remarkable."

Although he did not systematically integrate music into the work of his final years, Jung came to regard music as a gateway to the collective unconscious. He was particularly interested in the cyclical form of many compositions and saw the sonata, with its four movements, as a symbol of unconscious processes. "We know that the creative power of the unconscious seizes an artist or musician with the autonomous force of an instinctual drive," observes Patricia Warming, a Jungian analyst in Seattle who uses music. "It often takes possession of the person without the least consideration for his or her life, health or happiness. Such an individual is an instrument of the transpersonal. Great musicians such as Mozart and Beethoven knew that the spirit blows where it will."

In the late 1980s, Warming took a workshop with me, and I asked her to do a vocal scan. As her sounds become more animated, I coached her to turn them into a song. Eyes closed, she allowed me to lead her around the room to a piano, at which I sat down and accompanied her. It was as though she were "singing in tongues." Patricia said afterward that she never would have guessed that a song would swim up from her depths. But that wasn't the end of her experience. That night, she dreamed she was at the ocean, staying in a cabin where she had to supply her own cookware. A small earthquake occurred, and she could not recover her utensils. She interpreted the dream to mean that something had shifted in her psyche and that she could no longer cook—nurture herself— in the same way. By using her voice, Warming had discovered a new way both to nurture herself and to help her patients dredge up deep archetypal material.

≀ Guided Imagery and Music

The leading therapeutic use of music and imagery today is known as Guided Imagery and Music (GIM). This approach—the method that helped Jerry recover from severe autism in the story at the beginning of this chapter—originated in the 1960s at the Maryland Psychiatric Research Center at Johns Hopkins University in Baltimore. At first, the project revolved around LSD and its ef- fects on art, drawing, and other forms of creativity. Out of those early experiments, art therapy (including the spontaneous drawing of circles, mandalas, and other images), breathing techniques, and music-evoked imagery emerged as clinical tools.

Originated by music therapist Helen Bonny, Ph.D., GIM has been refined into a model of one-on-one therapy in private psychological practice. In her early work with LSD research in Maryland, Bonny found that music helped subjects to relinquish control and enter fully into the experience, heightening emotions and sustaining con- sciousness for longer periods—which proved an aid to natural heal- ing. Bonny found that peak experiences—moments of great insight, surrender, wisdom, or the awareness of being fully loved—could be invoked by music. Anchoring an experience in time, music could nonetheless create a feeling of timelessness. In short, Bonny and her associates found that music cut a path to the deepest regions of the psyche, a road through emotional pain, physical disability, loss, and even death. Music permitted the conscious mind to explore the unknown in a safe, directed fashion, rather than through the chaotic, sensory overload that often accompanies an LSD experience.

Although generally misunderstood and confusingly named (there is no guided imagery in the process), GIM is a technique in which music itself becomes the guide that allows images to emerge. "GIM involves listening in a relaxed state to selected music, a programmed tape, or live music in order to elicit mental imagery, symbols, and deep feelings arising from the deeper conscious self," Bonny explains. During GIM sessions, the therapist helps the client (actually referred to as "the traveler") explore images as they arise, rather than interpreting the symbols and offering a diagnosis. The therapist's most important tasks are to keep the flow of images coming and to encourage the traveler to express or release emotions.

INTERLUDE
Music for Massage

Music enhances massages.

In this exercise, you play three selections for the friend, family member, or client receiving the massage.

First, to relax the person, play very slow, ambient music that creates a safe environment, facilitates deep breathing, and encourages the release of thoughts and feelings. Examples include quiet harp music, Erik Satie's *Gymnopedies for Piano*, and New Age music with flute (such as the works of Carlos Nakai and John Ranier).

During the middle part of a massage, the deepest body work usually takes place, and the brain may enter into a relaxed, sleep-like state. For this, play music that has a very slow pulse or one that encourages tension to be released from the body. Selections include Pauline Oliveros's *Deep Listening,*

Brian Eno's *Thursday Afternoon,* or Stuart Pempster's *Music from the Abbey of St. Clement.*

In the third and final stage, put on music that is pleasant, melodic, and has a slightly faster beat, between 50 and 60 beats per minute. This kind of music—the slow movements from Mozart piano or harp concertos, for example—builds a bridge between the deep, revitalizing experience of a massage and the world to which we must return.

Relaxing the jaw and humming while body work is taking place can increase the benefits of the massage. As a variation, suggest that the person receiving the massage gently hum an *ah* sound during the first 5 to 10 minutes. This constitutes a self-generated internal massage that acts as a marvelous complement to an external one.

When listened to in a deeply relaxed state, music becomes a catalytic agent, giving rise to a kind of waking dream. During a GIM session, which usually lasts from thirty to forty-five minutes, the unconscious and conscious selves begin to communicate through music, speech, symbol, and emotion. GIM creates what Bonny calls "a meeting ground for subpersonalities or parts of the self." Through the medium of symbols, Bonny observes, music serves as "a field of safe combat, as well as a comfortable container where disparities and inequalities of the personality coexist."

GIM practitioners have fashioned tapes of classical music using the entrainment principle (matching the physical and emotional pace) and iso principle (gradually changing speed), and medical studies have documented the physical and psychological results. At Jefferson Hospital in Port Townsend, Washington, doctors and nurses recorded lowered heart rates and blood pressure in patients who listened to Bonny's *Music Rx* tapes, and significant positive changes occurred on the Emotional Rating Scale, a widely used measure of patient anxiety and well-being. In tests with surgical patients, pain and anxiety decreased, and half the usual amount of anesthesia was required.

Through years of rigorous training, GIM professionals have learned to analyze every image that emerges during sessions. Practitioners are certified by the Association for Music and Imagery (AMI). Some graduate schools offer GIM training, but most students receive their training at regional institutes. The upshot is that this approach has benefited thousands of people, from those with multiple personality disorder to those struggling with substance abuse.

GIM has influenced my own teaching. Johannes, a graduate student studying poetry and writing, participated in one of my classes on imagery and creativity. His writings were dreamy and vague, and his teachers had called him a romantic without structure. Like many young people suffering from an overdose of the New Age, he needed to find ways to bring his sensitive nature into concrete reality. During the third session, Johannes had a great insight. The "epiphany" began when he closed his eyes, relaxed, and breathed deeply for ten minutes, while I spoke to him about feeling comfortable with all styles of creativity. Then I played the first movement of Sibelius's *Second Symphony* and continued with Vaughan-Williams's *The Lark Ascending,* Fauré's *Sanctus,* Bach's *Prelude in b minor* for keyboard, and, last, Mozart's *Alleluia.*

During the first piece, Johannes experienced images surrounding the trauma of a car accident he was in at age eight. He spoke of the nightmares and fears he suffered all through elementary school about someone unexpectedly hitting him from the side. Listening to *The Lark Ascending,* he saw himself flying as a bird and living in the clouds, knowing he'd never have to worry about being hit. He felt safe in this vague, wispy, dreamlike milieu. During the Fauré piece, he spoke emotionally of swimming, floating, never needing to put his feet on the ground.

During the Bach, the transformation began. He saw himself standing now, back on terra firma, moving and feeling strong. He was in his graduate-school classroom with the clouds and air above, a small pond outside, and a comfortable, old-fashioned wooden desk in front of him. He envisioned himself sitting down and writing poetry with both hands, drawing thoughts and words from the air and water, but feeling the strength of his body and the power of connecting to the solid wood of the desk. During the Mozart, Johannes felt himself integrating the disparate elements of his life. His fear vanished. He felt he could go forward.

After these sessions, Johannes's writing changed immediately. He began an epic poem with an imposing order and structure.

Today, he works as a journalist in the Midwest, producing tightly written articles and meeting strict deadlines.

As Jerry, Patricia Warming, and Johannes's stories demonstrate, the power of music holds enormous promise for dimensions of our lives beyond basic health and well-being. In the next chapter, we will look at additional ways in which sound affects how we learn, how we earn, and how we can unlock our creative potential.

CHAPTER 7

Sound Intellect

ENHANCING LEARNING AND
CREATIVITY WITH MUSIC

*I believe that a nation that allows music to be expendable
is in danger of becoming expendable itself.*
—RICHARD DREYFUSS, star of MR. HOLLAND'S OPUS,
at the 1996 Grammy Awards

Bobby was a hyperactive boy in my classroom. He could
not be quiet. He shouted nearly all the time, intimidating the other
children. When he wrote a paper, you could sense the tension and
anger inside him—the coiled force of his personality impressed itself into the words on the page. At home, Bobby was just as unruly,
and his parents had given up trying to control him.

After a few months of plying him with imagery of food or of
activities he enjoyed, I was at last able to get Bobby to close his
eyes and hum: "Ummmm, Ummmm." He did this for several minutes, and there was an amazing turnaround: the tension left his
shoulders and his voice dropped. The other teachers found, too, that
when Bobby hummed, or when he began his day with a few minutes
of humming, his nervous tension lightened appreciably. When he
became involved in musical activities over the next year, the whole
atmosphere in the school changed.

"The music teacher in our school has had more success with

'one potato, two potato, three potato, four' than all the psychologists, child psychiatrists, and counselors have had with drug-induced stability," the former principal of an elementary school in Washington, D.C., told me after a career of overseeing teachers who deal with children like Bobby.

And the impact is not just on emotional growth. A Texas study has found that students who participate in orchestra have SAT scores that are higher than average.

Alas, because of a lack of understanding on the public's part of the importance of music for neurological development, funding for music and art educators is vanishing. The story told in *Mr. Holland's Opus,* a heartwarming American film with a bizarre, near-tragic ending, rings too true. The movie chronicles the journey of a composer and performer (Richard Dreyfuss) who needs money and decides to spend a year teaching in a public school until a better gig comes along. Thirty years later, after a thousand musical epiphanies, the beloved mentor is fired on the eve of full victory, as his former and current students and colleagues hail him with a performance of his grand opus.

Mr. Holland represents teachers in the arts who have lost their jobs because they have not had the knowledge of science or psychology to defend their field. Yet sound and music, as we have seen throughout this book, are integral to maintaining good health and to developing communications skills. In this chapter, we will explore how the Mozart Effect can strengthen memory, improve learning, and enhance creativity. We will also look at how music is being used successfully in education, business, and in society as a whole.

‹ More Harmonious Learning

In *The Symposium,* Plato describes a banquet at which the great ideas are discussed. Against a backdrop of music and charming conversation, a drunkard, Alcibiades, enters and upsets the atmosphere, creating havoc with his loud, raucous sounds. Plato describes how Socrates tries to bring Alcibiades into the harmonious rhythm of the group. He has little success on this front, yet the banquet isn't fatally disrupted; Socrates is aware enough of his own and other people's rhythms to keep the proceedings from spiraling into chaos. If we can emulate Socrates' awareness, we can successfully orchestrate the rhythms of our days and thereby create an optimal learning environment.

We can, for a start, use rhythm as a tool to develop memory and intellect. Although short-term memories can be stored as images, they are often stored as sounds—especially when we're remembering words. Short-term memory has the capacity to hold about seven bits of information (the length of this clause, for example). But related groups of information are remembered as a single bit, and thus the volume of material that can be stored increases exponentially. Information spoken in a rhythmic pattern will easily hold together as a unit.

In addition to noting how rhythm aids memory, researchers have found that memory has its own circadian rhythm. Short-term memory processes are at their peak in the morning, while long-term storage is best attempted in the afternoon.

As noted above, playing an instrument or participating in a music program in school (or incorporating music into classroom activities in such areas as history and science) has been shown to have broadly positive effects on learning, motivation, and behavior. Here are some highlights of the new research.

- The College Entrance Examination Board reported in 1996 that students with experience in musical performance scored fifty-one points higher on the verbal part of the SAT and thirty-nine points higher on the math section than the national average. "Study in music and the other arts generally seems to have a cumulative effect and is undeniably correlated with improvement over time in students' standardized test scores," concluded Edward J. Kvet, director of the School of Music at Central Michigan University in Mount Pleasant.
- In a study of approximately 7,500 students at a medium-size university between 1983 and 1988, music and music education majors had the highest reading scores of any students on campus, including those in English, biology, chemistry, and mathematics.
- Walt Disney film scores and New Age music had the most

positive impact on the mood of 255 first and second graders, with classical music coming in third. How was this determined? The children were asked to make freestyle drawings while listening to the music and to rate their feelings before and after listening by drawing happy or sad faces.

The study revealed something more surprising to researchers. The drawings revealed a much higher degree of unhappiness than the children had reported before listening to the music. One researcher, who had a background in working with at-risk youngsters, said she was amazed at the levels of anger, depression, and violence manifested in the artwork—about 40 percent of the drawings. The researchers concluded that the combination of music and art enabled the children to release feelings and emotions that they had hesitated to express verbally.

- Other studies showed that playing music lessened children's inappropriate behavior on a school bus, and that scheduling arts activities, including music, on Mondays and Fridays reduced student absences on those days.

- Researchers reported that light pop music, primarily songs by the Beatles, reduced the rate of inappropriate or disruptive behavior in young children in a special preschool class.

₹ Musical Intelligence

In the early 1980s, Howard Gardner of Harvard wrote *Frames of Mind,* one of the most influential books on education for this generation. In it, he introduces the notion that we have multiple intelligences. In addition to linguistic, logical-mathematical, spatial, and bodily-kinesthetic intelligences, he believes that we have interpersonal, intrapersonal, and musical intelligences. He cites research showing that infants as young as two months are able to match the pitch, loudness, and melodic contour of their mother's songs, and at four months they can match rhythmic structure as well. Science has found that infants are predisposed to these aspects of music—far more than they are to the core properties of speech—

and that they engage in sound play that clearly exhibits creative properties.

In examining traditional music education in Africa, Gardner looks at the Anang of Nigeria. In this society, infants scarcely a week old are introduced to music and dancing by their mothers, while fathers fashion small drums for their children. When they reach the age of two, children join groups where they learn many basic cultural skills, including singing, dancing, and instrument playing. By the age of five, the young Anang can sing hundreds of songs, play several percussion instruments, and perform dozens of intricate dance movements. In some cultures, broad individual differences are recognized. Among the Ewe of Ghana, for example, less talented persons are made to lie on the ground, while a master musician kneels over them and beats rhythms into their body (and, it is thought, soul).

Since *Frames of Mind* helped bring musical intelligence into the educational mainstream, hundreds of books have elaborated on this theme. In my book, *Introduction to the Musical Brain*, I wholeheartedly endorse the belief that the more stimulation a child receives through music, movement, and the arts, the more intelligent she or he will turn out. Of course, stimulation must be followed by quiet and reflection; otherwise, the benefits may be lost. As most parents of teenagers know, a steady diet of music alone doesn't necessarily make kids brighter.

Music brings a positive and relaxing atmosphere to many classrooms, as well as allowing the sensory integration necessary for long-term memory. It also serves as a background in some classrooms to mask industrial or traffic sounds, and it can be used successfully to instill excitement, release stress before testing, and reinforce subject matter. In a comprehensive review of hundreds of empirically based studies between 1972 and 1992, three educators associated with the Future of Music Project found that music instruction aids reading, language (including foreign language), mathematics, and overall academic achievement. The investigators also found that music enhances creativity, improves student self-esteem, develops social skills, and increases perceptual motor skill development and psychomotor development.

In 1997, during the debate on the future of arts education in public schools, Gardner expanded his earlier views and said that

musical intelligence influenced emotional, spiritual, and cultural development more than the other intelligences. He said that music
helps structure people's thinking and working by assisting them in
learning math, language, and spatial skills. Legislators and school
boards that "lop off" music in elementary education, he stated, are
"arrogant" and unaware of how the human mind and brain have
evolved. Like Gardner, I believe that children deserve to be exposed
to the rich diversity of human art and culture.

♩ Language Skills and Music

From Jiminy Cricket's "E-N-C-Y-C-L-O-P-E-D-I-A" song
to more sophisticated rhythmic tools found in elementary schools
across America, sound and music are used to teach language, spelling, and even basic social skills. This is not music education per se;
it is educating with rhythmic and auditory components.

During my five years with the Guggenheim Education Project
in Chicago's inner city, I realized that many of the students could
not spell well because both the auditory stimulation provided by
the teacher and their ability to track the information were faulty.
I discovered, however, that rhythmic tools, combined with movement, almost instantly boosted their memory.

This was brought home one morning when a particularly sympathetic teacher in the lower elementary classes called roll and came
out with some of the finest triphthongs I'd ever heard: A girl named
Alora Smith became "Y-a-lor-a Sa-me-ia-tha," while Myra Sue Robbins was now "Ma-y-ss-u Rau-bn." Although these children were
being loved and mothered, they had never heard consonants! We
began by forming Ls with our elbows, spelling As with our fingers
in the air, and making Us by pointing our toes to the ground. We
strung together the first names of everyone in the class by spelling
them in the air with our noses and chins. With imaginary paper
in the sky and on the floor we shaped the letters on the left side
of the body, then the right, then with the head, and finally with
the heels. Within two days, the spelling list was being spoken in
rap, and each child was using his or her whole body in the play-

ground outside to spell words with the grandest gestures possible. What had seemed initially a gimmick became a powerful tool for learning and development. Needless to say, the childrens' ability to spell improved.

Research has confirmed the crucial role of music in the inner city. A 1993 study found that African-American high school students identified music teachers as their principal role models (36 percent), followed by English teachers (28 percent), history and social studies teachers (14 percent), and sports coaches and physical education instructors (7 percent). Other studies have found that elementary students who received daily music instruction had fewer absences than other students, and courses in music, as well as in art and drama, positively influenced the decisions of high school students not to drop out of school.

INTERLUDE

Reading 101-a and a-two-a

At Brainworks, an innovative school in Carrollton, Texas, it is common to hear a child with reading difficulties reading aloud while a metronome beside his or her desk ticks at 60 beats per minute. After a few minutes, the voice of a child becomes smoother and more rhythmic.

As an exercise, read out loud to the slow second movement of a baroque concerto (by Bach or Handel, for example). At first, the sound might create a distraction, but soon the soft, regular music will improve your concentration.

Needless to say, if you have a young person in the house who is just learning to read or who would like to read better, this can be a fun and instructive way to pass an hour.

At an experimental school in Tokyo, I witnessed an innovative use of music, akin to the one in Chicago. Teachers played classical, Japanese, and folk music, and even "My Darling Clementine" in the background during language classes to anchor the instruction and enable the children to develop linguistic skills in a clear tonal, rhythmic manner. Meanwhile, children were learning *kana,* the Japanese phonetic script, with 3- or 4-inch-wide brushes dipped in light watercolors. To music, they painted on the wall characters almost as big as themselves—large ovals and striped shapes, not quite calligraphy. They learned to make strokes with the full gesture of the arm and the sound of the phoneme, performing a graceful dance that made this "graffiti" seem both eloquent and primal. After a few weeks, the large brushes, which made what I called "Tom Sawyer" strokes, were exchanged for smaller markers. With these implements and medium-size strokes, students practiced making characters on paper on the wall. The third step was to write with soft-colored pastels on drawing paper—at a desk.

In the month during which I was privileged to observe this training, I noticed the sounds the children made with their voices evolved from aggressive and rhythmic to—by the time they had reached pastels and appreciated the artistry of making these symbols—relaxed. Finally, each pupil was given a soft lead pencil for the first time. After only a few weeks' instruction, the children had begun to write with ease and beauty. The pressure of learning the fine motor skills that are required to write had been relieved by this gradual transmuting of dynamic rhythms and voice into focused penmanship.

₹ Accelerative Learning

The most in-depth use of music to accelerate learning was developed by the Bulgarian psychologist, Georgi Lozanov, whose comprehensive study of suggestion, imagery, and relaxation has become one of the foremost methodologies in mind/body education. Developed initially for adults studying foreign languages, his technique—known as Suggestopedia—has brought creative modifications to curricula throughout Europe and the United States, and has popularized the concept that slow baroque music improves learning.

The international best-seller *Superlearning,* by Sheila Ostrander and Lynn Schroeder, introduced Suggestopedia to the general pub-lic. It describes how Lozanov began to look into music while work-ing on his doctorate at the University of Kharkov in the Ukraine. Researching the powers of suggestion for learning during sleep, Lozanov found that hospitals and sanitariums in Russia, the Ukraine, and Bulgaria used music amplified through loudspeakers to speed up recovery in patient wards. The music appeared to help regulate heartbeat and blood pressure.

At the Bulgarian Academy of Sciences and Sofia Medical Insti-tutes, Lozanov continued his investigations, discovering that slow Baroque music could bring students into a state of alert relaxation and was more effective than sleep-induced learning for optimal re-sults. With educator Dr. Aleko Novakov, he developed a method of breaking up information into four-second "data chunks." These brief sound bites, sandwiched between four-second pauses, con-sisted of seven or eight words that could be repeated in different combinations, patterns, and intonations. Against a backdrop of in-strumental string music, reciting the data chunks improved overall memory and accelerated learning. Lozanov found that the best music for learning was that of the violin and other string instru-ments rich in harmonic overtones and pulsing at sixty-four beats per minute. Subjects learned in a fraction of the usual time it took to complete complex tasks such as designing dresses or machine tools. With the addition of music, a semester's training could be reduced to a few hours.

Lozanov's accelerated program spread throughout the Commu-nist bloc and included a government-funded institute in Sofia, the capital of Bulgaria. In a single day, students reportedly learned half the working vocabulary, or up to a thousand words or phrases, in a foreign language, with an average of 97 percent retention. "Human memory is virtually limitless," Lozanov asserted, after demonstra-ting that yogiclike retention skills could be developed by practi-cally anyone.

Like Tomatis, Lozanov determined that the time of day and the posture of the learner influenced the effects of music. He also dis-covered that brainwaves receive concrete information in both highly stimulated (beta) states and extremely relaxed, near-dream-like states. Lozanov concluded that when information is coded in both the conscious and unconscious minds access to memory is far greater.

Lozanov's emphasis on auditory and visual tracking created what schools of accelerated learning now refer to as *active* and *passive concerts*. A passive concert involves the reading of stories or vocabulary by the teacher in the late afternoon while the lights are subdued and the students sit in chairs reclining to 40 or 50 degrees. This is akin to a low-budget passive listening room I observed at the inner-city Guggenheim School in Chicago. As there were no funds for recliners, the children had to make do with aluminum loungers from a sale at K-Mart. It was quite a sight: a small classroom filled with multicolored deck chairs and dozens of kids jumping over each other to show their teachers how well they could close their eyes, relax, and listen.

In the passive concert phase of accelerated learning, which lasts about forty-five minutes, new materials, vocabulary, and sounds are recited at a leisurely pace, with slow Baroque music in the background. Concertos by Telemann, Vivaldi, Scarlatti, Corelli, Handel, and Bach fill the air, their rhythm between fifty-two and sixty-eight beats per minute. The teacher's voice entrains with the music; he or she takes time to accent or repeat new words, giving each its own tonality, richness, and inflection.

A parent came to me once with concern about my "hypnotizing" her child in a language class. She had seen her daughter's improvement in verbal dexterity, stress reduction, and greater self-esteem, but her religious beliefs led her to question the propriety of teaching deep relaxation in school. I invited her to attend the class and observe for herself. "This is amazing!" she said. "What you did for my daughter is what the doctors recently taught her father for his blood pressure so he wouldn't have another stroke. Even if my daughter doesn't learn language, she won't be prone to high blood pressure. Keep up the good work."

On the second morning of an accelerated learning session, an "active concert" by the teacher reinforces what has been presented passively. In an active concert, the teacher typically recites the same text, phrase, poem, or story incorporating the new vocabulary, only this time to highly dramatic, nineteenth-century music—for example, a moderately loud Paganini violin concerto. The teacher's voice rises and falls to the music's contours, repeating key phrases and accenting its emotional texture. Compositions used include the full-length concertos of Mozart, Beethoven, and Brahms. After the active concert, students echo key words and phrases back to the teacher. Only when the ear and voice have been engaged are reading and writing skills introduced, as students for the first time examine the text and words directly.

♩ Music Education and Orff Schulwerk

As you may have begun to suspect, learning *about* music can be just as important to a child's intellectual and emotional development as learning to the accompaniment of music. Happily, modern music education has come a long way. In the United States, it goes back to New York educator Horace Mann, who proposed "the introduction of music, drawing, and the study of natural objects" to the curriculum in 1844. Thanks to Mann and Lowell Mason, who was influenced by the teachings of the Swiss reformer Johann Heinrich Pestalozzi, music entered the public school system by the early twentieth century. Yet, in the decades that followed, music education was often overly structured, the teachers dryly academic. By the mid-twenties, the focus had shifted away from performance to "appreciation."

Oberlin College offered the first four-year training course in undergraduate music education. By the early 1940s, a variety of skills, including listening, composing, and performing (known as *musical process*), began to emerge in schools and conservatories. Today, most programs have evolved from European and Japanese teaching methods that synthesize movement, improvisation, and *solfège* (sight-singing and theory)—methods that originated in Germany through Carl Orff, in Hungary through Zoltan Kodaly, in Switzerland through Jacques Dalcroze, and in Japan through Shinichi Suzuki. In addition, computers, synthesizers, and MIDI electronic systems offer young learners a multitude of innovative training routines. Sometimes a clear, focused method works best for students and teachers; at other times, a mix of styles and strategies encourages growth and self-expression.

During the 1930s, Carl Orff, the elemental yet progressive composer of *Carmina Burana,* developed a system to integrate the natural into "the moving, expressive auditory world." His approach, which came to be known as the Orff Schulwerk training, combined rhythmic, raplike speech; gesture; movement; and improvisation with the singing and playing of simple percussion instruments. Thus, in a typical Orff classroom, children recite nursery rhymes, poems, or stories as they move, clap, and play drums and xylophones. The idea is to use simple melodies and chants borrowed from natural folk traditions in order to understand music without having to read "paper" music—to approach music through movement, song, dance, and playing instruments rather than in a left-brained, analytical way.

"Just as humus in nature makes growth possible, so elemental music gives to the child powers that cannot otherwise come to fruition," Orff explained, in a typical analogy drawn from the natural world. "It is at the primary school age that the imagination must be stimulated; and opportunities for emotional development, which contain experience of the ability to feel, and the power to control the expression of that feeling, must also be provided. Everything a child experiences at this age, everything that has been awakened and nurtured, is a determining factor for the whole of life."

Through the Orff method, the child woke up to a world where musical vocabulary was woven into movement, speech, rhyme, and instrumental and vocal work. At present, over three thousand schools in the United States use Orff Schulwerk in their elementary programs. International activities are coordinated by the Orff Institute, located in the Mozarteum, a venerated school of music, in Salzburg, Austria.

The story of Liz Gilpatrick illustrates the attraction of the Orff method. Growing up in Wisconsin, Gilpatrick filled her days with the unself-conscious joys of singing, trumpet-blowing, and fiddling with an old harmonium she found in the basement of the family home. She taught herself to play guitar on a finger-torturing $13 Stella—but she was so happy that she never felt the pain. The songs she wrote were the innocent expression of a child whose best reason to get out of bed was to make more music.

Even when these blithe interludes diminished and the loneliness of early adolescence arrived, music was the one friend to accompany

Liz on her long treks along the shores of Lake Michigan or in her quiet moments watching a slow winter sunset from her bedroom window. Sometimes it was Mendelssohn's incidental music to *A Midsummer Night's Dream* or Mozart's *Requiem*; at others it was vintage Harry Belafonte or her own improvised melodies. "But it was always present, either out loud or in my head, and it made all days meaningful," Gilpatrick says. "I had no need for conventional religious exercises because music filled my spiritual needs. Any ecstasy my spirit needed was just a toot, song, or spin of the old monaural record player away."

In high school, Gilpatrick discovered the French horn and began to sing madrigals. At the University of Wisconsin, she majored in the horn and went on to teach, but soon suspected that the field of music education was "more swamp than field." For the first four years, she was convinced she had made a dreadful mistake. Her only fulfillment came when she taught kids the music she enjoyed herself, or wrote simple arrangements for a grade-school brass choir— "which could barely blow its collective nose, but whose efforts called forth angels when we played music the teacher loved."

As an antidote to the stifling atmosphere of music education, Gilpatrick registered for the Orff Schulwerk program. The first class, she recalls, "was like that exquisite, visceral pain we experience when we fall in love. My God, someone was encouraging *me*, adult musician, to make up my own music and dance. There was no printed music to get in the way—just me and my ears and the rest of the ensemble." When tapping out a simple repetitive pattern on a metallophone, Liz would close her eyes and experience pure sound. "Bodies no longer existed, just us angels," she quips. During her Orff program, Gilpatrick recognized a powerful force for creativity that tugged her back to childhood days when she was "the music, not just the player."

Gilpatrick went on to become an Orff Schulwerk instructor. She loves being in the midst of an ensemble of children playing a pentatonic accompaniment as much as she loves making sophisticated music with adults, writing a song, or playing Bach on the recorder. "The sound of a seven-year-old singing her heart out is as beautiful as a Brahms choral work," she exults. "It took a personal epiphany not unlike Mr. Holland's to recognize the legitimacy of my passion as a vehicle for bringing music to children, and Orff Schulwerk brought it about."

⟩ The Suzuki Method

Mozart's variations on "Ah, vous dirais-je, Maman," better known as "Twinkle, Twinkle, Little Star," make it possible for children to learn their ABCs in, well, a twinkle. Hundreds of little people with undersized violins begin with this theme, thanks to Dr. Shinichi Suzuki, who founded the School for Talent Education in Matsumoto, Japan, over fifty years ago. Every child, he has said, has unlimited potential. Just as young children speak their mother tongues effortlessly, music is basic to the brain and the body. Through imitation, Suzuki teaches children, some as young as two and three, that skills for sound expression can be allowed to mature and ripen throughout childhood. Recordings of good music are played daily in the home, and parents are asked to attend all of their child's lessons to help create "a noble mind, a high sense of values, and splendid abilities."

Vicki Vorreiter, a violinist and Suzuki method clinician, introduces people worldwide to the effects of early childhood education on the brain and learning. She tells the story of Sophie, a three-and-a-half-year-old who attended a Suzuki workshop held in an old monastery in La Sosailles, France, with her mother and baby brother. Sophie's slight figure, spiritless body language, whispery voice, and shallow violin sound indicated a fragile and apprehensive personality. In her first lesson, she was shown a stance that rooted her feet solidly on the earth. Then, along with her mother and teacher, she sang "Twinkle, Twinkle Little Star" to energize her voice. Finally, she was asked to play her violin so that the strings vibrated as widely as possible with a "diamond tone," as Dr. Suzuki calls this register. (When the violin is fully vibrated, a small interior piece of wood called *l'âme*, or the soul, conveys resonance throughout the instrument.) "By the end of the week-long workshop," Vorreiter reports, "Sophia's body was more open and solid, her tone full. She had begun to move inside herself and her violin to create tone with soul."

INTERLUDE

Theme and Variations

Contrary to myth, Mozart did not write "Twinkle, Twinkle, Little Star" as a small boy. It was a children's song of his time called "Ah, vous dirai-je, Maman." But Mozart did compose a set of twelve variations (K. 265), probably in 1781 when he was sixteen years old.

What at first seems artless and childlike can actually inspire enormous creativity, insight, and trust. Try the following exercise while listening to Mozart's variations on "Twinkle, Twinkle, Little Star." (You can find these variations on my compilation *Music For The Mozart Effect, Vol. III— Unlock the Creative Spirit: Music for Creativity and Imagination.*)

1. Sit comfortably with your eyes closed. Release six or eight breaths and let go of any tension or thought.

2. Consider a task that you perform daily that is getting boring or that makes you extremely tense. See yourself performing that task as the music begins.

3. Then, with your eyes still closed, imagine twelve variations of that task being executed. Jot down notes if you wish, but be careful not to break the flow of images.

Does this sound like kindergarten? Perhaps, but it has been used with brilliant results in brainstorming sessions at both small and large corporations.

If this exercise works especially well for you, then consider using Mozart's ten variations on another folk song, "Unser dummer Pöbel meint" (K. 455).

David, another French youngster, was experiencing emotional problems following his parents' divorce. His lifestyle was chaotic, moving between the homes of unhappy adults, and he practiced ineffectively, if at all. Music lessons, attended by his mother, were frustrating, and he masked his discomfort by acting out. After several weeks, the Suzuki teacher tried a new approach. She asked the mother to hold David in her arms while she performed a concert of classical pieces on her violin for the entire hour. Listening to the music and holding each other, mother and son became more receptive. The next week, David returned in a quiet, happy state of mind and played his best lesson ever.

The Suzuki method grew out of a musical heritage going back centuries. Last spring I attended a *shakuhachi* flute lesson in Japan given by Fujita Daigoro. He is considered a living national treasure in the ancient style of flute playing that emerged in Noh drama, which dates back to the fourteenth century and is known worldwide for its masks, subtle but dynamic costumes, and powerfully emotive characters. Now over eighty years old, Sensei (teacher) Fujita passes on this ancient tradition.

Jeff Clark, an American teacher and translator who has lived in Japan for twenty-five years, began studying with "Fujita-san" twelve years ago and invited me to sit in an anteroom during his lesson. I had forgotten, since my own Japanese musical studies in the early 1970s, how music was taught there. Sensei Fujita sat alone in a traditional Japanese room of *tatami* floors and *shoji* sliding screens with a small wooden block in front of him. Attired in a kimono, the master sat on his knees and held two small mahogany-colored sticks that looked like scalpels with extended paddles on the ends.

All students come on Tuesdays between 1:00 and 7:00 P.M; no one is scheduled. Fujita-san takes them in the order of their arrival for fifteen minutes at a time and charges an inexpensive tuition by the season. At times, the students listen to those ahead of them in line as they work on their own five-minute excerpts from a medieval Noh play. If a wait is necessary, Mrs. Fujita appears from nowhere with a cup of green tea and then seems to disappear before your eyes.

What I found remarkable, even overwhelming, was that the teacher never played the instrument during the lesson. Sensei Fujita merely reproduced the rhythms of three drums used in Noh music—the *kotsuzumi,* the *otsuzumi,* and the well-known *taiko*—by beating a little wooden block. As he recited the text, the student, perceiving the absent part, filled it in with the haunting beauty of the shakuhachi flute. After thirty years of study (that is not a misprint), the student is finally invited to perform. This is the opposite of accelerated learning; it's prolonged, eternal, *and internal* learning.

} The Brain-Music Connection

How does music boost the intellect and enhance learning? Does it stimulate an area of the brain associated with creativity? Are children's musical preferences wired into the brain or culturally determined? Do musicians' brains differ from those of other people? These are some of the subjects that scientists, medical researchers, psychologists, and educators consider as they ask the question, Why does the Mozart Effect work?

Tracing neurological development through childhood provides clues to this quest. When children first come to school, they have a facility for rote memory, and many simple facts have been imprinted in their minds through songs and musical games. *Comprehension* of what they are able to repeat eludes them until at least the age of six (with many boys, eight). Phonics are learned through a kind of nonsense process that involves matching sounds to different objects, movements, and activities. While not linear and seemingly meaningless, this process is actually essential in developing thinking skills that will last a lifetime.

Until a major leap takes place in brain growth in the elementary school years, learning occurs through movement and quick emotional associations; by age two, the brain has begun to fuse with the body via marching, dancing, and developing a sense of physical rhythm. Take rap, which makes sense to children even though they may not know what it means. (Second graders in parts of Chicago and New York can easily rap for fifteen or twenty minutes, but it's hard to hold their attention in a conversation for more than a minute or two.) A great spurt of neural integration occurs between ages seven and nine. The more music children are exposed to before they enter school, the more deeply this stage of neural coding will assist them throughout their lives.

Between second and third grades, the child commonly develops more complex skills—listening, processing visual information, coordinating movement in the brain and mind. It could be that after the fourth grade the basic patterns of sensory awareness are set, and any further learning is remedial. But there is, of course, more work to do. Phonics, music notation, and math link auditory centers to the left and right brains. Then the real conversation in consciousness begins, between symbols in the outer world and meaning in the inner world. The Swiss child psychologist Jean Piaget calls this "concrete reasoning."

From ages nine to eleven, auditory pathways undergo a further spurt, enhancing speech and listening. Choral reading, poetry, and varieties of pronunciation and dialect become important, as the brain and auditory system begin to process the voices and the wisdom of the world at large. Children who have never heard dialects or foreign languages tend to regard such unfamiliar speech as weird for the rest of their lives. Hearing a variety of dialects on TV or at the movies helps slightly, but learning to sing simple folk songs in Japanese, Swahili, German, or even regional accents like those of Texas enable the brain to encode new sounds—and thereby understand the world more fully.

During this stage, the *corpus callosum,* the bridge between the left and right sides of the brain, completes its development, allowing both hemispheres to respond to an event simultaneously. Recent studies have found that the corpus callosum of musicians is thicker and more fully developed than in other people, reinforcing the idea that music enlarges existing neural pathways and stimulates learning and creativity. The *planum temporale,* located in the temporal lobe of the cortex, is also more pronounced in musicians. This area of the brain appears to be associated with language processing and might also "categorize" sounds, suggesting a perceptual link between language and music. Studies like this, notes science writer Richard A. Knox, are "part of a growing body of evidence indicating that human brains are designed to process, appreciate, and eventually create music—an activity whose importance for the species scientists are only beginning to appreciate in biological terms."

In 1996, educators reported that by about age eleven, the circuits of the neurons that govern perceptual and sensory discrimination undergo a change. Children who have not had music in their education may no longer be able to develop the ability to identify pitch and rhythm after this age.

From the ages of eleven to thirteen, as Piaget and other child educators have observed, a self-consciousness begins to develop as the right hemisphere of the brain becomes harder to access. From thirteen to fifteen, the voice in boys drops and they often lose the more intuitive, emotional characteristics that were readily available before. At these ages, music, art, and creative physical education, all of which stimulate right-brain function, are important to full mind/body integration.

Consciousness continues to develop throughout the teen years. Thinking becomes more abstract, and musical skills more mathematical. Performance becomes more self-conscious. By the end of high school or the late teen years, music, art, and other rhythmic activities have done much of their work. The brain will continue to grow into early adulthood, but the potential for the greatest neurological development has passed.

The nervous system is like a symphony orchestra with different rhythms, melodies, and instrumentations. There are many rhythmic and melodic systems that keep the brain synchronized. When any part of the brain is damaged, the natural rhythms of brain and body are disturbed, and the neurons may fire at the wrong time, or not at all. Often external music, movement, or images help bring the "neurological music" back in tune. Music mysteriously reaches the depths of our brain and body that call many unconscious systems into expression.

From Chaos to Creativity:
♭ Jazz, Samba, and Improvisational Music

Dee Coulter, Ed.D., Director of Cognitive Studies at Naropa Institute in Boulder, and author of *The Brain's Timetable for Developing Musical Skills*, specializes in the relationship between musical patterning and neurological development. She explains that the Mozart music used in the IQ and spatial intelligence experiments at the University of California at Irvine stimulates high-quality beta waves, or ordinary consciousness. But for optimal creativity, and for grappling with issues that do not lend themselves to simple, linear solutions, she recommends jazz. Jazz moves into chaos, and from chaos creates order. Coulter finds that the music of Miles Davis, John Coltrane, and avant-garde composer John Cage can lift the listener into theta consciousness—the highly creative brainwave state associated with artistic and spiritual insight.

In contrast, she finds that rock, rap, and other music centered on the beat constitutes an intense statement about *time*—particularly well-suited to refining the abilities of children who labor under an oppressive sense of it. "Some of our inner-city environments are war zones," she says. "In order to survive, inner-city kids do not dare dull their awareness. This music can keep them focused. Within a chaotic, unpredictable environment, it sharpens their ability to organize." New Age and ambient music is organized around *space*. For people living a highly mental, structured life, such music helps them to unwind and float freely.

Although it shares the same roots as rock and rap, jazz is not a survival tool; it is neither driven nor relaxing, according to Coulter. "Jazz is an ideal state in some ways," she says. "It involves paying attention, while in a community, and being able to respond without being sure what's coming next. Our lives are like that these days. If we learn to live them well, we're going to be attracted to jazz." The music, she says, is unbelievably subtle and has a soulful quality that promotes meaningful conversation. "You have to hold the beat to meander off it. Jazz's level of cognitive complexity stuns me. Its sense of timing, jokes, repartee, attentiveness, respect, and listening is fascinating."

When I listen to contemporary jazz artists such as Wynton Marsalis, the virtuoso trumpet player and artistic director of jazz at Lincoln Center in New York, I tend to agree. In a recent interview, Marsalis explained, "Playing jazz means learning how to reconcile differences, even when they're opposites. That's why it's such a great thing for kids to learn. Jazz teaches you how to have a dialogue, with integrity." Perhaps our inner order must be Mozartean, but to go out and know the world at large—to go through an airport, watch television, shop at a mall, surf the Internet—to function socially in the world—we need the sophistication of jazz. Jazz helps us to go out of that world and come back into it, in an orchestrated phasing that prevents us from getting too neurotic.

While I am an admirer of jazz and often improvise on the piano, I find samba and Brazilian music to be the healthiest and most accessible contemporary genre. Brazilian music, which fuses elements of Latino, Indian, African, and indigenous South American traditions, has the improvisational quality of jazz, but just enough pathos, sweetness, and drive to keep the listener attentive. It also allows the mind/body as a whole to feel safe, soothed, and energized.

After visiting the province of Bahia on a trip to Latin America, Lee Cobin, a Los Angeles educator and musician, started offering after-school classes in samba and other Latin music at Cheremoya Avenue Elementary School, inviting children to meet native Brazilian drummers living in the L.A. area. The response of the children, parents, and school administrators was so enthusiastic that it led to the development of the Cheremoya Escola de Samba (School of Samba) program, in which students learn to play and dance to samba, bossa nova, bloco, timbalada, and other styles.

In addition to enhancing a sense of personal achievement and self-esteem, the program has brought together youngsters of different cultural backgrounds and helped to break down racial stereotyping and isolation. "I like Cheremoya because I know what it did for me," says Victor Garcia, who participated in the program for eleven years before going on to major in engineering at Cal State University. "It kept me away from gangs even though I had a lot of peer pressure to join. Playing drums relieves all of the tension you have—after you finish you feel rejuvenated." Says Angelique Bermudez, a sixth grader who has been making music for four years,

"With Brazilian dance, you can shake everything. I like *bolero*. It's faster, you make all the movements strong, lots of samba rhythm." She adds, "The group is like my family. The older members in the drum section help me with other school problems."

Music adds color to the palette of consciousness. Coulter concludes, "If we are to give children a full repertoire of ways of being with their body, mind, and heart, there is no better template—and no less judgmental one—than music."

♪ The Sound of Positive Thinking

Sound and music can enhance the workplace as well as the classroom. Forty-seven-year-old Bill, a successful businessman with a happy marriage and strong family life, was nonetheless plagued by chronic worry and depression. Over the years, he had read every book on positive thinking and had tried countless positive affirmations and motivational strategies. Nothing worked. Diagnosed with adult ADD (attention deficit disorder), he could not tolerate Ritalin, the standard treatment, and remained negative and hyperactive, rarely staying focused or completing tasks. The larger his business grew, the more overwhelmed he felt.

One day, while driving home from work, he heard me giving an interview on National Public Radio. I was explaining that sound was being used successfully for the treatment of learning disabilities and depression and that people could be trained to use their own voices to function better in the home and office. He obtained one of my books and tapes but didn't have the patience to tone or hum.

About six months later, still searching for relief, Bill came across an audiotape in the library on overcoming depression by Dr. Art Ulene, a television commentator. The key to overcoming depression, Ulene stressed, was movement: Act first, feel better later. According to Ulene, physical exercise is crucial to well-being because it increases the brain chemicals called endorphins that cause euphoria and control pain. Ulene suggested marching in place for 20 minutes to pieces by John Philip Sousa—all the while pumping the arms and getting the creative juices flowing.

Bill dutifully followed Ulene's suggestions. He pulled out a Nor-dicTrack that had been parked in a corner for a year and exercised to "Stars and Stripes Forever." But he still felt terrible, because the cadence was fast and he was in poor shape. Then, on the third day, he experienced a minor miracle. Switching to a New Age music tape that slowed his cadence and felt more soothing, Bill inadvertently began to hum softly. After five minutes, he realized that his whole body had begun to relax.

INTERLUDE:

Hum a Happy Tune

For much of my early musical life, I dismissed the notion of "whistling a happy tune" as a naive and trite way to elevate mood or reduce stress. Then, a few years ago, I was on the New York subway, and the sounds were so loud and obnoxious that I felt my eardrums buckle. To arrest the damage, I experimented with humming and toning, and quickly realized that other subway riders, even those standing next to me, could not hear me. I found I could sound nearly the entire time I was on the train. My ears would not ring, and I didn't feel any tension as I left the subway, even during rush hour.

While living in Tokyo and traveling by train for over two hours a day, I found I could hum such upbeat songs as "Climb Every Mountain," "Gonna Build a Mountain," "On a Clear Day," or "Whistle a Happy Tune" and mask all outside sounds and pressure. I could read a book or the morning paper and still keep these songs repeating over and over in my mind with a gentle hum. Reaching my destination, I'd find myself refreshed and relaxed.

This method also works well on planes, buses, and cars. Fellow passengers rarely notice when you hum quietly to yourself, and if they do, just explain to them what you're doing and chances are they'll join in.

Bill remembered my book *The Roar of Silence* and continued humming another five minutes. The humming and the exercise felt good together, and the sound distracted him from the strain of the workout. "I had slipped into a runner's high without the normally required extreme exertion," Bill observed. "I felt great at the end of the workout. And remarkably, I felt great three hours later."

After two days, he repeated the routine but this time listened to ten minutes of "Stars and Stripes Forever," followed by ten minutes of relaxed humming to lullabylike music. The result was the same. Three days later, he did it again. He'd had a terrible day and was ruminating on the same old morbid thought that his business couldn't grow, that it would go into decline, that he'd be a miserable failure. By the end of the workout, Bill couldn't remember why he had been worried. The only difference in his technique that day was to switch from a gentle "Mmm" to the resonant vowel sound "Ahhh." He allowed the sound to get very loud as he let anger and frustration flow out of his body. Bill realized that he could change his brain chemistry at will, discharging bottled-up frustration without having to intellectualize it. Each time he exercised and hummed, obsessive fear gave way to a full day's worth of optimism.

Since he started humming and toning four years ago, Bill has been free of chronic fear and depression. He now works out two or three times a week for twenty minutes. Of course, he still has his bad days. But now he knows how to break the cycle. "The glass remains half full, regardless of how my business is performing," he says. "I was at last becoming a positive thinker without trying. My self-confidence bloomed. I felt great."

Three years ago, Bill enrolled in my Transformational Sound School, and he now periodically teaches toning to others, instructing co-workers and employees on how to dissipate anger and stress and to make themselves feel better. The training is nonintrusive, quick, and long-lasting, and it has likely saved the jobs of several people in crisis and on the verge of quitting or being fired. "The productivity gains in my business were priceless," Bill concludes. "We got results that Dale Carnegie would envy. I now consider knowledge of this training to be a competitive edge. I have become a more understanding parent, a more effective employer, and a much happier person."

⟩ The Muzak of the Spheres

Nowhere is it more apparent how sound and music have entered the workplace, changing the ways in which we do business, than in the transformation of Muzak. The bland background music that we first heard in a dentist's office or elevator has come a long way. Along with several other competitors, the Muzak Corporation now provides a variety of styles of environmental music (including jazz, New Age, and rock) to corporate offices, factories, shopping malls, hospitals and clinics, airliners, and even the Vatican, all of which are striving to create a more balanced soundscape.

The evidence is in: Music in the workplace has been shown to raise performance levels and productivity by reducing stress and tension, masking irritating sounds, and contributing to a sense of privacy. (A side benefit of the sense of well-being it can foster is reduced health-care costs.)

Forty-three of the world's fifty largest industrial companies provide music to employees. Dupont introduced a listening program in one department that cut its training time in half, reduced its training staff by a third, and doubled the number of people trained. A large Southern utility company tested music in the finance department and found that clerical errors decreased by 37 percent. Productivity in the mailing room of Prentice-Hall rose 6 percent after background music was piped in. In Cincinnati, 64 percent of employees at nine branches of Fifth Third Bank reported that by masking surrounding sounds and creating a strong sense of privacy, programmed music encouraged a feeling of trust between them and their clients. Even the Pentagon vouched for music's potential to increase alertness and efficiency. At the height of the Cold War, operators listening to Muzak in missile silos had a .27-second faster reaction time than those exposed to ordinary background noise. Thankfully, this musical "achievement" was never put to the acid test.

Designer music can also be a valuable tool to promote consumerism. In one department store survey, sales to shoppers under twenty-five years old jumped a whopping 51 percent when music was present, while purchases among those aged twenty-six to fifty rose 11 percent, and among those over fifty 26 percent. Overall, 17 percent more shoppers purchased items when listening to the music. Supermarkets, discount stores, and other retail outlets report comparable results, especially when slower, lighter music is played. One supermarket found that grocery sales increased 28 percent when people walked in rhythm with the slower pace of moderate-tempo music. Another study found that slower instrumental music was the most effective in a dining setting. While it did not increase the amount of money spent on the meal, it encouraged customers to drink an average of three more beverages per table. A liquor store reported that when classical music was introduced in the background, sales of wine—and overall profits—shot up dramatically.

Voice mail offers another opportunity to introduce sound business procedures. To streamline her division, Melissa, a midlevel manager of a new information technology company in the Sun Belt, had a state-of-the-art answering system installed. Yet instead of increasing efficiency, sales began to lag. Melissa attributed the decline to overmechanization. Convinced that people want to connect with a human voice, not a machine, she modified the phone system and had a receptionist answer all incoming calls before directing them to different offices.

Sales picked up, but not to previous levels. There was still something wrong. Melissa decided to find out what it was by testing the system. Placing a few calls to herself, she was cordially put on hold by the receptionist, whereupon the answering system switched to hard rock music. After several idle minutes, Melissa began to feel angry. She resented being forced to listen to this throbbing music for more than a few seconds. She just wasn't in the mood—nor, evidently, were many of her customers.

Melissa switched the recording to a Mozart string quartet. Not only did the intimate chamber music soothe her waiting customers, but sales increased. One client on hold even rebuked Melissa when she finally took his call, saying she had interrupted an enchanting selection.

Melissa's clients are not alone in feeling this way. We all want to be held, not just put on hold.

⟮ Sound Breaks

In my training seminars, I tell businesspeople that the body is a corporation. *Corpus* means body. And this corporation has a need for procurement, advertising, sales, development—all the departments of a large office. The body has to answer the phone, take out the garbage, and attend to daily maintenance. But the mind and heart are also part of the larger corporation. Sound breaks are a way to enable all of these corporate divisions of our existence to work together.

George, a Los Angeles office worker, found himself unable to work after lunch. He did fine in the mornings, but by 2:00 P.M. he was always groggy, his thinking slow. Although his job was not particularly stressful, he couldn't wait to get home. Management was alarmed and viewed him as a half-time employee drawing full-time pay. George agreed. Together, he and his manager searched for a way to raise his productivity and restore his creativity. First, he used music to take five-minute sound breaks twice an hour in the afternoon to repattern his mind and body. George enjoyed Mozart, Mannheim Steamroller, and other activating, popular music. He changed his diet and took short walks after lunch. And almost immediately, his performance climbed. Soon he was more than making up for his past losses, and, by the end of the month, many of his colleagues, impressed with George's turnaround, were taking sound breaks, too.

INTERLUDE
The Paper Plate Dance

A few years ago I was invited to give a talk on music, stress reduction, and creativity to the board of a major computer company. The group of fashionably attired and serious professionals greeted me with proper reserve. The meeting had a long, grueling financial agenda, and the executive who introduced me told the trustees that my presentation might offer a creative solution to their company's dilemmas.

I began with a short exercise, playing music from Bach's Brandenburg Concertos. I asked the trustees to jot down the most vital points for their financial discussion. After six or seven minutes, I asked them to turn the page and set aside momentarily what they had written.

I passed out two cheap, flexible paper plates to each person and asked everyone to move their chairs back a few inches from the boardroom table.

Then I played an Irish folk dance with a simple, spirited, and predictable melody, and asked them to follow along and imitate me. I brought the paper plates together as if I were playing the cymbals, then bounced them off my knees, chest, and head. After a few grumpy looks in my direction, all fifteen men managed to participate. Within three minutes, they were smiling and, after the six minutes of this paper plate dance, their entire bodies had loosened up. They were laughing and relaxed. I put on the Brandenburg Concertos once again and asked them to write solutions to the problems that they had mentioned earlier. They wrote vigorously and pensively. After ten minutes, I excused myself and let them have their meeting.

The next day, I was called and told the board meeting was the most fruitful, creative session they had ever had. The board found itself able to concentrate more clearly after my visit.

Whether in a classroom, a boardroom, or in a retirement center, using the hands to clap and tap rhythms (especially along the midline in front of us) can synchronize the hemispheres of the brain. Music can activate the creative right brain and the more logical left brain, which enables us to find more creative solutions to our problems and tasks.

Because of the dangers of habituation, it is important not to overuse music and risk losing its effectiveness. Whether at the of-

fice, school, or home, a good rule of thumb is to play it in the background no more than twenty-two minutes per hour. A continuous twenty-two-minute selection is stimulating, but shorter blocks of time distributed throughout the hour work well also. Three five- to seven-minute selections at the beginning, middle, and end of an hour, or just twice a day, once in midmorning and again in midafternoon, can be very effective. Active sound breaks, in the form of short musical activities that increase alertness and energize the individual or the group need take only two to three minutes. Brisk, upbeat music like the kind George used is good to energize and activate. To let go of tension and relax, slow, stable music such as *Essence* and *Relax with the Classics* is effective.

Commuting to work affords an optimal time to tune up. The music you listen to can set the tone for your entire day. If you are tired, then up-tempo, progressive music can give you a boost of sonic caffeine to get you going. If you need to slow down, more leisurely music can help you unwind. While commuting, I've found that playing a classical tape or tuning into a classical FM station provides an excellent environment in which to rehearse a speech or presentation. Speaking aloud for ten minutes with Bach, Vivaldi, or Mozart in the background can help pace your delivery and allow your voice to find its rhythm.

In the morning, I especially like to spend five to ten minutes humming. What I recommend is a fairly deep utterance in the lowest part of your voice, not a high, whimsical humming. Put a hand on your chest and feel the sound "*Hmmmm*." Now move your hand to your cheek and continue to hum. You can feel the vibration coming into your hand, and sense the way in which humming massages the body from the inside out.

Every time I'm on a plane, or a train, or a bus, I hum, and hardly anyone has ever noticed. It may take you three or four days of practice to feel comfortable humming in your car or on your train ride. But once you get the hang of it, you will have a reliable way to modify and equalize your brain waves, generating relief, relaxation, and clarity of mind. You can hum almost anywhere, any time, whether working at the computer or walking. (Jogging is one of the few times I refrain from humming.) The long exhalation is the first step to deep relaxation.

As you experience the benefits of "*Hmmm*," you may wish to

experiment with different vowel sounds. *"Ahhh"* releases energy and conveys a sense of space. *"Aaaa"* and *"Eeeee"* are, as I have noted, more charging sounds. Following a training program at the Sound Listening & Learning Center in Phoenix, an attorney from one of the nation's largest corporations commented that he could feel his body resonating at a different frequency. He said he felt subtle but positive shifts in his posture, was more relaxed, and noticed improvements in his reading habits. A real estate developer said that he was able to project his voice better, and an electronics specialist marveled that his balance and handwriting had improved.

Using music in the workplace goes beyond providing background music to employees and customers, taking sound breaks, and installing listener-friendly telephone answering machines. A friend convinced Randall, a city manager in his early fifties, to take a seminar in shamanic drumming. "In the beginning, I was thinking, 'Why the hell am I here?'" he confessed. "Then I began to feel secure and happy. There was no thinking about day-to-day issues. I was just more or less experiencing the experience." In the course of the weekend, Randall was transported into many different sonic environments, including that of an African tribal society and a Native American tribe. During his "journey," he related, "I felt the movement UP, like being in a channel. I had no clue how I got in it. All of a sudden, I was there. It was dark, but I had a real sense of freedom. It was great."

He reported feeling very different when he went back to work after fifteen minutes of this brainstorming exercise. The world looked new. And he was not so uptight or rigid, especially when it came to doing business in a modern, multicultural community. He began to relate to people better and to come up with fresh, original approaches.

Creativity is often seen in terms of an artistic product: a painting or sculpture, a musical composition, a dance, or a literary work. But there is creativity in a tantalizing casserole, a satisfying relationship, a new marketing idea, or any other product of living. These are also the results of the creative process, and you don't have to be a sorcerer's apprentice to make them come to life for you.

INTERLUDE
Raindance

Over the years, I have served as a consultant for IBM, Canadian Bell Telephone, the Michigan Department of Health, and other corporations and agencies that wanted to use music to stimulate creativity in the workplace. In Dallas, I give seminars teaching Fortune 500 trainers how to use sound and music to enhance memory and focus, improve communication, and increase efficiency. One of the greatest challenges in the business world is developing new product ideas, marketing approaches, and advertising copy. In staff and sales meetings, I recommend the following exercise for my business clients to keep the creative juices flowing.

1. Create a target. Take a long piece of paper (for example, a 6-foot length of fan-folded computer paper), draw a red dot in the middle of three or four thick, black concentric circles, and lay the paper on the floor or on a small table in the middle of the room.

2. Find a piece of popular music that everyone likes, one that invites movement and some degree of participation. Begin the music and have everyone walk clockwise around the target. The person who is presiding should start by saying clearly as he or she walks, "Our goal is to create ten new ways to market this product"—or whatever the actual goal is.

3. One by one, each person walks around the target, focusing on the dot, saying, "We want to come up with the ten best sales ideas." Don't get too close to the center or you'll get dizzy. Say it over and over and move to the music. This part of the exercise is an invocation—literally an invoicing—in which the left brain, right brain, midbrain, and hindbrain are charged simultaneously. (While seated, we lose much of our thinking and creative potential.)

4. Next, let the ideas be spoken aloud as everyone continues to walk around the target. Have one person be a scribe and jot down their spontaneous suggestions. Participants may also write them on a chalkboard as they go by. No matter how silly they are, talk them out. (If you are embarrassed or overwhelmed by giggles, you don't need to make eye contact.)

5. After fifteen minutes of this rainmaking (or brainstorming) dance, the participants can resume their normal way of discussing things, paying particular attention to the ideas that have just emerged, and come up with a plan.

This exercise may seem like child's play, but it really works. It charges the breath, activates all areas of the brain, and revs up one's whole system. In the Far East, it's called attaining beginner's mind—seeing the world fresh and new, as a young child would. And it's astonishing how many top executives, athletes, writers, cooks, and other creative individuals have routines like this to prime their pumps. In Greek myth, Orpheus played the lyre to inspire Jason and the Argonauts in their quest for the Golden Fleece, a symbol of both personal and corporate achievement. Music moves energy, and energy, as Blake observed, is eternal delight. With the help of music, work can become more like play, our lives a joyous adventure.

♩ Music for the Millennium

As the year 2000 approaches, composer Homer Hooks has proposed a Millennial Symphony as a way to celebrate the last thousand years of sound and to prepare for the epoch to come. The first movement would draw from Gregorian chant and the Hebrew psalms, as well as other early religious utterances. The second movement, starting with the Middle Ages and ending with Stravinsky, Wagner, Leonard Bernstein, Ella Fitzgerald, and the Grateful Dead, would also invoke the dances of Polynesia, Africa, Ireland, and Brazil. *The New York Times* called it "a bonanza of musical frequent flier miles." The last movement would set off into deep space, with "futuristic and visionary themes . . . scientific wonders yet unseen, and the mystery of the unknown."

For the past century, we have looked at how to move music and the arts into the sciences, but it may be more useful to see the sciences as a subset of music and the arts. "Music for the millennium" does not imply that we will have ten times more albums to buy, while being stimulated by market-research-driven music beamed into our local department store by satellite. Rather, it suggests that music holds the map to integrating multiple systems of intelligence, with broad applications in health, education, and business.

Music might be a polyglot, but its many languages are understood intuitively by nearly everyone. Through its judicious use in our schools, workplaces, and daily lives, we can stimulate our intellects and unlock our creative potentials. In its broadest sense, the Mozart Effect reveals a path to a higher, more comprehensive IQ than any we have previously envisioned.

CHAPTER 8

Sound Spirit

THE BRIDGE BETWEEN LIFE AND DEATH

What is this holy emptiness,
this loss of full presence,
this mystery?
—THERESE SCHROEDER-SHEKER

From the primordial explosion, the cosmic Om, the first
utterance of the Logos, sound has been both fact and metaphor.
Sound and vibration pulse and throb, transmuting energy into matter and creating time in the vast, endless reaches of space. The earth
is inherently musical, and all life responds to and makes rhythmic
motions and sounds. Thus far we have explored music and sound
in this book throughout the human life cycle—from the nurturing
of the fetus to the birth of the child to experiences in school and
the workplace. We now bring the symphony of human life to a
close with songs of death and transfiguration.

{ Steal Away Home

Is a soul greater than the hum of its parts?
—DOUGLAS HOFSTADTER, THE MIND'S EYE

Work with the terminally ill constitutes a major part of nursing care. Karen Quincy, a registered nurse at the Community Hospice in Fort Worth, Texas, tells the story of Grace, eighty-seven, a retired high school teacher, whose Alzheimer's disease had worsened following her husband's death fourteen months earlier and who now had pneumonia. Grace's only daughter was understandably distraught. Karen often visited Grace, listening sympathetically, and the two women talked, touched, and cried.

One day, responding to a beeper call, Karen found Grace agitated and fearful, her breathing rapid and labored. Grace's daughter left the room to make a phone call, and Karen remained to hold Grace's hand and head, comforting her as she had in the past. The dying woman remained agitated. Karen noticed the cassette player on the dresser. She knew Grace enjoyed classical music, and Karen had *Steal Away Home*, a cassette by soprano Lynda Poston-Smith, in her car. She got the cassette and played the music, which was composed as an aid to the chronically ill and dying, for Grace. She put on "Sanctus," and Grace's daughter, who had returned, immediately relaxed when the music began. When "Swing Low, Sweet Chariot" started, Grace's breathing relaxed. As Lynda's angelic voice sang "Ave Maria," Grace took her last peaceful breath and her heart gently stopped. She was not on morphine or any other drug. Karen was convinced that the music was the primary factor in easing both this woman's transition into death and her daughter's pain.

There are many hospice stories like Grace's. Gladys, ninety-four, had lived in a nursing home for three years, suffered from severe dementia, and was nearing death. As Ruth Hinricks, a music therapist from Arvada, Colorado, who works with older adults, arrived in the dayroom, she became aware of a commotion. The frail, petite Gladys, seated in a geriatric chair much bigger than she, was flailing her arms and body with immense energy so as to move the chair across the floor for no apparent reason. Two nurses were standing by, hoping to prevent Gladys from injuring herself or the other residents. This scene had been going on for three hours. The nurses needed to be relieved, so Ruth offered to take over. Gladys was surrounded by pillows and a restraint and left in Ruth's care. Ruth sat in front of her with her keyboard on her lap. Gladys lunged for the keyboard and would have thrown it, but Ruth quickly set it on the floor and took Gladys's hands in a gentle but firm way to restrain them and protect herself from injury.

Ruth began to sing "Let Me Call You Sweetheart." Gladys immediately looked directly into her eyes. Ruth said, "Sing with me, Gladys," and she began to sing. The two women then sang "Springtime in the Rockies," followed by "Children of the heavenly father safely in his bosom gather, / Nestling bird no star in heaven such a refuge e'er was given." Gladys stopped singing, and Ruth continued again. Her violent movements had ceased. Ruth sang "Savior, Like a Shepherd Lead Us," and Gladys remained calm. Ruth began to hum the hymns, and Gladys's eyes began to close. Ruth moved her hands to rest gently on top of Gladys's and hummed improvised melodies. Gladys's eyes closed in what appeared to be peaceful sleep. She slept much of the afternoon and remained calm the rest of the day. "She joined her heavenly father early the next morning, a Sunday," Ruth adds.

In my own work, I have occasionally comforted seriously ill or dying patients. I will never forget an older man whom I nicknamed Archie because he reminded me of Archie Bunker, the ill-tempered television sit-com character. We were working in a therapeutic setting in a hospital in Texas. Archie had suffered a heart attack and was angry about being in the hospital. He was angry at having to lie in bed and eat poor food, all the while confined in a room painted the same green as a latrine. His blood pressure was high. Emotionally and physically inhibited, he said he preferred dying to submitting to any kind of treatment. After seeing me for a few days, he finally trusted me enough to say, "Look, I'll try anything. I like the nice music you're playing in the background, but I really want out of here."

We began by talking about his anger. As trust built up between us, Archie was soon able to express his frustration, anger, and pain through his voice. He did not use words directly. I would ask him how it felt to be confined; was there a sound that expressed the way he felt? During the therapy, I was afraid the nurse would come in and scold me for raising his blood pressure. No doubt I did raise it for a few minutes, but after thirty or forty seconds of *Oou-urrgghh*—the sound of Archie releasing his anger through his voice—the long sigh of relief, *Aahh*, signaled that the emotional and physical tension was beginning to leave his body. I gave him a few vocal exercises, and within a few days his blood pressure went down. Archie felt better, and through his voice, he released a great deal of tension he had carried with him through the years. Without the toning, Archie's will to live had been so low he might not have survived.

The Chalice of Repose

Therese Schroeder-Sheker has devoted much of her life to resurrecting the music of Cluny, the medieval abbey in the south of France, where chant and hymns were used for centuries to heal the sick and assist the dying. Therese tells the story of her first patient, a tough old man in his eighties, who was living in a geriatric care facility for elderly Russian emigrants. He was "a mean old buzzard," she says, prone to mischief and viciousness, disliked by the staff and residents. He had been fighting a losing battle with emphysema and was in his last days when Therese met him. She found him in agony, thrashing about, frightened, unable to breathe. There were no more surgeries or drugs available. A sense of desperation and misery filled the room.

Therese climbed into the man's bed and propped herself behind him in the midwifery position. She recounts how she sat with her head and heart lined up behind his, supporting his enervated body. Not quite sure what to do, she held him in silent prayer, then leaned down into his left ear to sing Gregorian chant in an almost inaudible voice.

"He rested in my arms and began to breathe much more regularly, and, as a team, we breathed together," she related. "It was as if the way in which sound anointed him now made up for the ways in which he had never been touched or returned touch while living the life of a man." The chants seemed to calm his fear. "How could they do anything less?" she asks. "These chants are the language of love. They carry the flaming power of hundreds of years and thousands of chanters who have sung these prayers before. It seemed that the two of us were not alone in that room."

The man soon died, peacefully, a holy silence filling the room as his struggle ended. "What is this holy emptiness?" Therese asks. For her, this silent space evokes not fear or sorrow, but awareness, a sense of presence with dying people as their spirit shines through the final process of decay.

That was more than twenty years ago. Therese subsequently founded the Chalice of Repose Project, a palliative hospice program combining music and medicine, now based in Missoula, Montana, at Saint Patrick Hospital. Music-thanatology (as Therese calls her work, from the word signifying the science of death and dying) is now a standard component of end-of-life care in institutional settings in Missoula. Local hospitals, hospices, geriatric homes, and many private homes are filled with music. Therese's dream has come true. "In what other hospital in the world," she muses, "can you find between twenty and thirty harps and a fine *scola cantorum* (school of singing)?"

During the course of their two-year curriculum, Chalice students serve at the deaths of more patients than most physicians in a decade of practice. Chalice members work in teams of two, playing harps, singing, and chanting, "weaving tonal substance over, around, and above the physical body of the patient, from head to foot." In addition to soothing the dying, their music serves to mask the unpleasant sounds they are commonly exposed to. For the comatose or dying patient, Therese sees the constant clicks, beeps, and buzzes of heart and respiratory monitors and life-support systems in the hospital as a source of noise pollution that can disorient and interfere with the last moments of life. The music her program provides eases this strain.

The Chalice workers perform a sort of musical midwifery for a variety of conditions, including cancer, heart disease, respiratory illness, and AIDS-related syndromes. The combination of harp and voice helps to restore the dignity, intimacy, and immediacy of dying, often for the family as well as the patient.

In the late 1980s, there was no support system to assist people who were dying alone. Therese recalls receiving an anonymous phone call from a young gay man dying of AIDS. Driving to the address he left on her answering machine, she grew increasingly apprehensive. The neighborhood was frightening, and Therese realized the risk in answering this call. "It was a moment of truth. Everything from Boethius to El Salvador to Dachau crossed my mind, because in essence, I am part nun, part boring middle-class working-girl idealist, and part chicken," she says, looking back. Tim, the caller, turned out to be a young, inner-city college student whose medical coverage had run out. He lived in a wretched apartment, without windows or ventilation. Completely alone, without friends or family, he had somehow stumbled across her number.

Instead of the usual chants and hymns, Therese decided to sing lullabies to Tim, who was bereft of all human contact, including motherly love. Ten days later she heard he had been moved to another place. She was with him as the end came mercifully on the night of the full moon. Therese played her harp and sang Irish and Romanian lullabies for Tim on the loading dock of the private-home facility where he died homeless, surrounded by the clanging of forklifts, the roaring of engines, and the jibes of truckers, who cursed her for sitting with "a queer."

"I don't know where or when or if he was buried," she recalls. "I am only certain that his much-longed-for release involved expansion into the blessed quiet of a silvery night."

Those days of dying alone and unattended are largely gone. Chalice of Repose members have now kept over twelve hundred vigils with patients suffering from all kinds of afflictions. In the last three years, fifty students have graduated and received certification. As her team fans out throughout the United States, there is a greater chance that people like Tim will die within the chalice of love.

⟩ The Final Refrain

His voice goes into his mind; his mind into his breath; his breath into heat; the heat into the highest divinity. That which is the finest essence—the whole world has that as its soul.

—CHANDOGYA UPANISHAD, describing the moment of death

For many people, music is the bridge between life and death. Death and near-death experiences have frequently been accompanied by stories of a mysterious tunnel of light and sound, where a type of celestial illumination or sacred magnetism guides the spirit on its journey.

Tibetan Buddhists speak of being awake at death so as to break the endless cycle of reincarnation. They regard life as eternal, requiring constant preparation, remembrance, and release. From the *Tibetan Book of the Dead*, monks and nuns memorize and rehearse chants during life so that, at the moment of death, they will not fall into the illusion of nonexistence. Prayers and chants around the deceased function as an air control tower for the spirit's release from the body; the monks and nuns serve as a distant voice directing the airborne soul in its flight toward the eternal return.

From an early age, Catholics are taught to utter, "Hail Mary, Mother of God, pray for us sinners now and at the hour of our death. Amen." Thus they prepare to invoke the sound of Mary's voice as they embark on the final journey through judgment, purgatory, and paradise. Southern Protestants commonly sing the traditional hymnal refrain, "Will the circle be unbroken, by and by, Lord, by and by?" Through traditional musical invocations such as these, we are able to embark on our last passage, while our ancestors' voices continue to sing and pray for us.

Gregorian chant seems to allow practitioners to prepare for this journey and live in two worlds at once. The Benedictines' basic law, or *trellis,* has supported monastic life for nearly a millennium and a half. The trellis reminds them that, whenever they sing, they are in the presence of angelic choirs. As they praise the angels and saints, the heavenly host blesses them in a never-ending cycle of sonic inspiration.

At the end of every day, Benedictine monks conclude with Compline, the last of the canonical hours, which means "completion." Though the day's chanting is completed during the sixth hour of vespers, Compline serves as the final prayer, recited not in the chapel, but in the cloisters or private quarters. The concluding refrain, "A peaceful night and perfect end grant us," says Brother David Steindl-Rast in his heart-inspiring book, *The Music of Silence,* "connects the end of the day with the end of life itself. It reinforces the theme that the rhythm of our days parallels the rhythms of our life. And the way we live each hour each day determines the character of our life. The paced hours teach us how to pace our life."

Spiritual practices related to music are not unique to Tibetans, Buddhists, Catholics, or Hindus. American psychic Edgar Cayce spoke of the importance of singing and called it "the pouring out of soul." In her book, *Music as the Bridge,* Shirley Rabb Winston quotes the sleeping prophet: "Hum, sing to the self, not to be heard by others, but to be heard by the self."

INTERLUDE
Grieving Through Music

Music helps in the ritual of release, allowing us to let go of our emotions, and to grieve. While the sickness and death of friends and loved ones causes deep sorrow, we often try to keep a "stiff upper lip" and choose not to allow our hearts to experience the natural healing that can come from grief. We also try to insulate our children from pain.

This exercise is not designed to conjure up all the agonies of the world—a strategy that goes to the opposite extreme, and is equally unwise—but to help us keep in touch with our feelings in an often anesthetized world. Although this exercise may seem to consist merely of talking to yourself, think of it as a new way to listen to yourself.

Play "Lacrimosa" from Mozart's *Requiem* (K. 626) or other music that has a special meaning for you.

1. Repeat this affirmation: "I release my grief and pain and allow it to be replaced with peace, richness, and appreciation."

2. With your eyes closed, exhale twelve times and allow your thoughts to arise and pass away without holding on to them.

3. Imagine your body as both a storehouse for all memories and a library of vast potential. Visualize a temple of light, shadow, and sound tones, representing thousands of new ways to experience feelings.

4. With every exhalation, let go of the fear of experimentation. With every inhalation, take in a breath of fresh air that will free your mind and spirit to explore new dimensions.

If you perform this exercise with someone who begins to cry in the course of it, gently comfort the person as he or she lets go of old thoughts and emotions. You might, at some point, need to switch to more calming music or to turn off the music altogether. If appropriate, meditate or pray together, visualizing lasting peace and harmony.

To bring *The Mozart Effect* to completion, it is fitting to describe Mozart's own death at age thirty-five and the commanding role that music played in his final moments. In the last year of his life, Mozart simultaneously composed *The Requiem* and his opera based on Freemasonry, *The Magic Flute*. For several months of this time, Mozart was seriously ill and suffered depression, delusions, and delirium while he strove to complete these twin masterpieces.

As his symptoms worsened, he took to bed for the last time on November 20, 1791. His fever heightened, his pain intensified, and he experienced attacks of vomiting and diarrhea. On the final evening, December 4, family and friends gathered around him in Vienna to sing selections from the unfinished *Requiem*. Only seven stanzas of the "Lacrimosa" were completed, and Mozart began to sing the alto part, imitating the trumpets by puffing out his cheeks. "Here is my death song," he said, invigorated by the music. "I must not leave it incomplete."

Shortly after midnight, Mozart died. On his deathbed, the child prodigy who had been bathed in music while still in the womb and the composer who could channel heaven-sent concertos and symphonies asked to be surrounded by music and singing. "A creative force" radiated from Mozart's music, Goethe observed, commenting on the tragedy of his early death, "which will continue from generation to generation and will be neither readily consumed nor expended."

The songs, prayers, and chants that surround the body after death create a powerful vehicle for the soul to travel beyond the physical senses. The rosary and the sutras, repeated around the deceased body, continuously remind the released spirit that it is dead and not dreaming. If one has spent one's life helping others through the portal and transition, one will more easily understand that one has left this world. For centuries, the dead have been provided with the sonic tools for the spiritual journey to the next life through prayer and song. Music and sound weave a magic carpet for the soul's journey home.

The Eternal Song

The Weaver God weaves, and by that weaving is deaf-
ened, that hears no mortal voice, and by that humming,
we too, who look on the loom are deafened. And only
when we escape it will we hear the thousand voices
that will speak through it.
—HERMAN MELVILLE, *MOBY DICK*

Thank God for the serious musicians who must compose and play it right, who feel duty bound to interpret the gods in the right measure on the perfect instrument in the perfect hall. Thank God for those who sing the blues to ease the pains of addiction and abuse. Thank God for those who sing all night, who know no better bliss than surrender to the eternal voice that sings us.

Praise to the living loudness, the raging seas and subways whose chaos and cacophony conceal a mathematical fugue as splendid as Bach's. Let roar the angry warsongs, nuclear guitars, and rhythmic ring of fire that purge the furies of modern life. Sing out the forgotten chants and hymns whose radiant sounds and rhythms sustained generations. Praise to the music teachers, the drummers, organists, and cantors who give spirit to our souls and bodies.

In *A Path with Heart*, Jack Kornfeld tells the story "Song of the Spirit" about a tribe in Africa in which music is the thread of life. In this community, the child's birth is reckoned not from the day of its birth, or even its conception, but from the first time the mother thinks about it in her mind. After deciding to have a child with a particular man, the woman will go off to sit by herself under a tree. She sits there and listens until she can hear her child's song. When she has heard it, she returns to her home and teaches it to the father, with whom she then sings it as they make love and invite the child to join their family. While the baby is growing in her womb, she continues to sing to it and teaches the song to the midwives and old women, so that when the baby is born it is welcomed into the world with its song. As the child grows up, the villagers all learn the song and sing it to the child whenever he or she is injured. They sing the child's song during rituals, triumphs, and losses. The song is sung at the wedding ceremony, festivals of harvest and thanksgiving, and around the deathbed when friends and family gather for the last time.

Whether on the edge of the African savannah, at the heart of the Austrian empire, or on the cusp of a new millennium, this is the ultimate Mozart Effect—discovering our unique song or voice and becoming one with it as we blend with other songs, rhythms, and instruments in the eternal symphony of life.

Miracle Stories of Treatment and Cure

Each illness has a musical solution.
The shorter and more complete the solution,
the greater the musical talent of the physician.
—NOVALIS, THE ENCYCLOPEDIA

The use of music for healing goes back to Pythagoras, David, and the abbess Hildegard of Bingen. But in the wake of the Renaissance and the Enlightenment, a new analytical approach to medicine emerged, and few physicians or musicians would admit to using sound to enhance health or to treat a specific condition. One of the last classical musicians to devise a harmonic balm was Johann Sebastian Bach. In 1742, a certain Count Kaiserling sent his emissary, Johann Gottlieb Goldberg, to the composer to obtain some keyboard works with a sufficient "soft and lively character" and a "constant sameness of the fundamental harmony" to enable him to sleep. And so were born the Goldberg Variations, a series of thirty harpsichord pieces. Needless to say, they have been soothing troubled minds and bodies ever since.

After several centuries in eclipse, the medicinal use of music has made a comeback in the West. In this chapter, I have summarized material related to treating many physical, mental, and spiritual conditions drawn from current scientific and medical research, as well as personal accounts.

You may have picked up this book and fast-forwarded to this section wondering what to do for a cold or sore throat. Is there some music you can play to make a migraine go away? Will a few minutes on the synthesizer or bongos clear up congested nasal passages? Alas, it doesn't work that way. The cure is not a dose of B flat or C sharp. And if you look up "Depression," you're not going to find a prescription to listen twice a day to ten minutes of a Mozart concerto, followed by five minutes of Elvis's "Jail House Rock," topped off by three minutes of Kitaro's "Silk Road."

What you will find are stories, all of them illustrative and most of them inspiring. Janis Page's experience illustrates some of the intangibles of musical healing. Page spent time with her seventy-five-year-old father during the last months before his death from cancer. She found that when she prayed and played her *didgeridu,* an Australian Aborigine flute, close to his spine, where the cancer had settled, his pain would lessen, and his spirit would soar for hours.

What's the prescription here? Principally time, patience, and love. Often we become so desperate to aid our loved ones that we call in physicians or healers who have neither a rapport with the patient nor the patient's permission to invade his or her body. Real harmony depends on listening and acting with compassion. The bond of trust between Janis and her father created an atmosphere in which healing could take place.

A main theme of *The Mozart Effect* is that music heals but is not prescriptive. Its power varies according to the composition, the performer, the listener, the posture assumed in listening, and other factors. Rather than focus on symptoms and conditions, I have tried to emphasize the treatment of the whole person. The material here is palliative, not remedial, and few causal conclusions should be drawn from the limited sampling. In fact, some of the following material deals with treating the anxiety, pain, or isolation surrounding the illness rather than the illness itself.

That doesn't mean there aren't some practical uses for music, which is commonly employed to help diagnose disease (by encouraging verbalization about an illness), increase motor function, motivate the patient, enhance communication with the therapist or family members, and facilitate conventional treatment. Musical healing can also be part of a holistic approach combining sound therapy (listening, singing, toning, or chanting) with dietary changes, exer-cise, and meditation.

Although some of the personal accounts here are dramatic, the work of music therapists is still evolving. As far as I know, no one has yet been able to duplicate at will the feat of the sons of Auto-lykos who sang incantations over the wound of Odysseus and "stayed the black blood . . . healing him well." However, as a cross-section of empirically based studies, therapeutic reports, holistic approaches, and miracle stories, the following sample is representa-tive: Music can be a powerful catalyst in the healing process. As Andrew Weil reminds us, regardless of what patients think cured them or scientists treat skeptically, this is prima facie evidence of spontaneous healing.

As the new century begins, further research will provide a firmer foundation for the use of music and voice as a therapeutic tool. New biomedical models will be constructed, modifying and possibly replacing those that have governed health care until now. This knowledge may also influence musical performance, composi-tion, and listening tastes, contributing to the development of indi-viduals and fostering a world community more attuned to the healthful and peaceful rhythms of life. Let this be an invitation for you to participate in this joyous revolution.

≀ Abrasions

Many childhood ailments consist of bruises, scrapes, and cuts. Although minor mishaps can be treated simply, they are painful and disorienting. I recall Flo, a nurse at a Dallas public elementary school, telling me that her job became easier when she started playing music tapes when children came to her office. She kept a library of ten cassettes that she had developed for the kids, cassettes of gentle, playful music that had lullabylike effects. She used *Toy Symphony, The Nutcracker Suite,* and themes from Disney movies.

When an injured or sick child arrived at the infirmary, Flo knew immediately which tape to put on to help mask the pain or soothe his or her fears. She was also a master healer. Once she told me, "I pass my free time trying to find images that will give the children power over their injuries. Instead of telling them, this antiseptic will sting for a few minutes, I tell them that it's going to put a tingling healer right into their scrape or scratch. I tell them that if they hum when I do it, the healing will go deeper, and they will feel better more quickly. Humming is one of the best ways to change tears of pain and fear into wellness. Music and the humming enable me to help them get better."

⟩ Abuse

Melanie, age ten, came to see Alice H. Cash, Ph.D., a social worker and musician at the University of Louisville, with severe emotional and behavioral problems. She had been sexually abused as a small child and had been hospitalized many times for violent, aggressive behavior. She was brought to Cash because she loved music and had an exceptionally good voice for a young child. Cash showed her how to play the Omnichord, an electric autoharp that makes many musical chords, and Melanie spontaneously made up songs that dealt with the pain of her current life. Over an eight-month period, Melanie began to sing about the pain and fear connected with her early abuse. She sang about her suffering, but absolutely refused to talk about it. "Music was the only pathway into her psyche!" Cash says. Today Melanie is less violent and aggressive and, as trust was reestablished, has slowly begun to talk about her feelings.

Mary, a young woman suffering from ritual abuse for the first fourteen years of her life, had been terrified to go out in public. She had been listening at home to *Serenade at the Doorway,* an album by Ann Mortifee, a composer and singer from West Vancouver, British Columbia, who works therapeutically with the voice. Mary played the album over and over every day, and the music calmed her. Mary's therapist finally called Mortifee and asked if she would be willing to have Mary come to a workshop. Mortifee agreed. But an hour or so into their first session, Mary panicked.

"I went to her and began to sing into her ear," Mortifee recalls. "Gradually she relaxed and then she began to sing with me. She changed the song into another song with the words, 'I won't stay silent any longer.' From a tentative, fearful place, Mary moved into a place of choice and personal power." Mary's life changed radically. After completing her sessions with Mortifee, she went back out into the world and to school, and she is now successfully employed.

When working with battered women, music therapists evaluate and treat such physical problems as muscle tension, anxiety, and numbness. With children, who have less capacity for self-expression, therapists strive to improve their ability to hear and process verbal information, and to raise their threshold response to sounds and visual stimulation. In other words, they try to coax them out into a world that in the past has been a source of pain. Often, therapists use imagery along with music to gauge a child's concept of family and self.

A survey of eighty music therapists who worked with victims of domestic violence found that music could be used with some success to restore the sense of self that's often stripped away by abuse. (Seventy-five percent of the women and fifty percent of the adolescents had drug problems.) The battered women and children were led in songs, chants, and instrumental improvisations, and were especially encouraged to play woodwinds, which can improve one's breath support and overall feeling of well-being.

≀ Acute Pain

One week after extensive knee reconstruction, Wendy, age forty-two, sought help from Ruth Hinricks, a therapist with Eldermusic Associates in Arvada, Colorado. Wendy had leg spasms—pain that she rated, on a scale of one to ten, a "twelve." Hinricks asked her to visualize her pain in the form of concrete objects and colors. To the accompaniment of musical patterns in my own composition "Rune Dance" (from the album *Essence*) and in Dr. Emmett Millet's *Healing Journey*, Hinricks talked Wendy into pushing the "object" of pain off her body. Then, changing to Mozart's "Adagio" from the *Clarinet Concerto* (K. 622) adapted for the flute by James Galway, Hinricks guided her patient toward increased sensory awareness. Wendy later described a vision of herself on the beach by a warm ocean with waves that lapped over and pulled the pain away with them.

By the end of the session, that "twelve" pain rating had dropped to "three." The next time Hinricks saw her, four days later, Wendy reported that she had been able to sleep well for the first time since the surgery. Her leg spasms ceased thereafter, and she went on to heal normally.

♩ Aggressive and Antisocial Behavior

From ancient times, it has been known that music can soothe the savage breast. Well, nowadays, there are a lot of savage breasts. In a world rent by family disunity, racial and ethnic antago-nism, crime, violence, and warfare, sound and music can heal con-flict, or can at least dissipate tension and anxiety. Perhaps its most astonishing benefits come not from listening, but from performing.

Consider Tommy, the only African-American in a class of His-panic and Anglo children in Corpus Christi, Texas. His father was serving a life term in prison. Much of his mother's time and atten-tion were spent on her new boyfriend. Tommy, the only child in the family, was handsome, always immaculately groomed, and well dressed. But he arrived at school each morning ready to punch out the lights of any child who got in his way. In music class, Tommy always sang louder than anyone else. He would not allow his voice to blend in because of a need to maintain his identity. When he played an instrument, his part stood out like a sore thumb.

Judy Cole, his music teacher, worked with Tommy to help him achieve a sense of individuality while blending and balancing with the other players. She used instruments from the method developed by educator Carl Orff. First, it was the lower sustaining tones of the bass metallophone (a percussion instrument consisting of tuned metal bars), which allowed him to hear his part as unique, yet con-nected with the entire ensemble. Next, the glockenspiel and soprano xylophone parts allowed him to make a successful contribution to the whole. Because he was so skillful, Tommy was able to play rhythmically intricate patterns that could be easily distinguished within the orchestra.

Music teachers often experience progress like this, but there is no way to follow the long-term effects. Cole resigned from her position at the end of Tommy's fourth grade, but returned to the school to work on a project with a selected group of children about nine months later. "Word spread like wildfire that I was in the building," Judy told me. "Tommy bounded from his classroom to seek me out. When he found me, he fell to the floor and grabbed me around the ankles with both arms as if to hold me there." Music helped Tommy overcome his deep feelings of rejection and isolation and express his appreciation.

⅔ AIDS

Although a cure for AIDS remains to be discovered, a promising new generation of protease-inhibiting drugs, nutritional therapy, and the adoption of safer sexual practices are beginning to slow this deadly epidemic. In the meantime, sound and music can have a palliative effect. For example, at Horizon House, an assisted living facility for people with HIV/AIDS in Jacksonville, Florida, sound therapy is an important part of daily activities, and the staff employs a vibrotactile technology called Therasound, involving a special mattress with built in speakers. "They swear by its effectiveness," reports Anne Bozzuto, R.N., executive director of the Mind/ Body Institute of Florida, "especially in the treatment of pain, anxiety, depression, sleeplessness, and hypertension."

Within the HIV community, the music of Constance Demby, a New Age composer who weaves electronic sounds into sonic architecture through which the mind can wander, is especially popular. Her album *Novus Magnificat,* combining Baroque influences with crystalline, harplike effects, moves like a symphony in vapor, spontaneously exploring multiple themes, textures, and rhythms.

Demby has received hundreds of testimonials about her recordings. "As my AIDS patient lay dying," one physician wrote her, "*Novus Magnificat* filled the halls of the hospital. He was hooked up to machines that showed us his life signs and with the last note of the music, he flatlined and passed over. The halls were filled with doctors, nurses, and patients either weeping or wondering what was happening." Of the dynamics in her music, Demby observed, "In the climax of 'Part I' of *Novus Magnificat,* a tremendous amount of boiling energy is brought to a fever pitch, and the darker elements are redeemed by a triumphant chorus crashing through. Composers can heal when using the darker tones, and they have to realize how powerful music really is in terms of eliciting emotions."

Music, combined with imagery, has been particularly helpful in coaxing deeply felt but unexpressed emotions to the surface. When Matt first sought help, he was twenty-six and had been recently diagnosed as HIV positive. Tall, gaunt, and with dark circles under his eyes, Matt chain-smoked and look scared. He was taking AZT and Xanax for his symptoms, which included dizziness, tremors, nausea, and fever. He explained to Kenneth Bruscia, professor of music therapy at Temple University in Philadelphia and his therapist, that although he was gay, he had contracted the AIDS virus through his work as a hemodialysis technician in a hospital. To compound his troubles, neither his employer nor his insurance company would cover any of his medical bills.

Matt told Bruscia that he saw terrible images. He could see himself dead and felt as if he were falling backward into a deep black hole. He lived in constant anxiety, dreading the images' return. Gradually, Bruscia guided Matt through the visions that emerged while they listened to tapes of classical music. In one session, Matt impulsively decided to let sunlight flood a dark cave and illuminate its contents. What he found were long-buried memories of early childhood sexual abuse. Finally, the images shifted to those of healing, including one in which he stood over his own grave and felt the presence of a strong, fatherly, Christlike man telling him to go back into his body and live. Matt revealed to Bruscia his history of alcohol and substance abuse, and confessed that, for years, he had felt more dead than alive. If he were to live, he realized, he had better do something about it before it was too late.

Matt underwent detoxification for several months and then joined a support group of alcoholics affected with HIV. He later told Bruscia, "You really helped me to take a look at myself, and to begin embracing the life I still have to live."

♩ Allergies

It was a Sunday afternoon in mid-July. Stephanie Greene, a Santa Fe music teacher, had been suffering from an allergic reaction for over a month. The flesh under her left eye was puffy and wrinkled, the eyelid was irritated and itchy, and the eye itself was constantly filling with tears. By evening she could only read with her right eye. Three weeks earlier, a physician had prescribed a homeopathic remedy, cautioning her that it might take time to experience any relief. Greene knew that sometimes things get worse before they get better, but this particular Sunday she was alarmed that her right eye was starting to be affected as well as her left. She feared that soon she wouldn't be able to read at all.

Wracking her mind for a solution, Greene remembered attending a meeting of the Noetic Society (a research group well known in the transpersonal and scientific communities), where a lovely young woman had played several ancient clay flutes that produced haunting, animal-like sounds. She recalled that the woman had prayed over each instrument and, as she played, seemed to go into a trance-like state. Greene had felt transformed. After the performance, she had bought the tape but hadn't yet played it.

Now Greene decided to listen to the tape for the first time, hoping it would at least lift her depression. With the stereo on, she lay down on her bed, closed her eyes, and put a crystal over her left eye. While listening to the music, she imagined pink and golden light traveling in a circle through her eyes. She prayed. As the melodies and the strange, haunting sounds of the twelve-hundred-year-old clay flutes enveloped her, she grew calmer and more accepting of her suffering, and she surrendered to the healing power of the sound.

Two hours later, Greene looked into the mirror and realized her eyes were completely clear. The itching and the burning had gone. For the next two months, she listened to the tape once a week and then tapered off. Her eyes have remained clear. While it is possible that her improvement was caused by the delayed effects of her medication, Greene thinks the music made the difference.

ꕢ Alzheimer's Disease

A large proportion of music therapists devote themselves to treating the elderly, whose suffering tends to be more intense and longer lasting than the rest of the population. Many work with Alzheimer's disease, which currently afflicts about 6 percent of the elderly (including nearly half of those in nursing homes) and is showing up at progressively earlier ages. Rhythmic interaction or listening to music has resulted in decreased agitation, increased focus and concentration, enhanced ability to respond verbally and behaviorally, elimination of demented speech, improved ability to respond to questions, and better social interaction.

In a study of ten elderly men and women with dementia and probable Alzheimer's disease who resided in a state hospital, researchers at the University of Alabama and the University of Oregon found that the patients could recall the words to songs dramatically better than spoken words or information. All the patients were from the Bible Belt in the rural South, and the selections that were used in the study included "What a Friend We Have in Jesus," "Amazing Grace," Psalm 23, "Happy Birthday," and the Walt Disney song "It's a Small World." Sessions averaged twenty minutes, and, overall, patients recalled 62 percent of the sung material compared to 37 percent of the spoken material. When they were asked to sing, hum, or keep time while the therapist sang, memory retention rose to 75 percent. Although memory recall was short-lived and concentration was lost soon after singing, the researchers concluded that singing, especially long-familiar songs, was an effective way for family members or caregivers to momentarily engage Alzheimer's patients in vocal communication.

Sometimes the effects are longer lasting. Arriving for a sing-along at a Ridgewood, New Jersey, nursing home, music therapist Grant J. Scott noticed a striking woman sitting at the back of the room in her wheelchair, silent and withdrawn. He was told that the woman, Ruth, did not speak or interact with other patients. But partway into his program, while he was singing the standard "You Made Me Love You," Ruth suddenly straightened her back, and, after two years of silence, broke into song, with a well-defined contralto voice that once must have been thrilling—as it was again that magnificent night. Scott hasn't seen Ruth since then, but he understands that Ruth continues to sing and that she talks once again to her loved ones and to other members of her community.

At a nearby veterans home, Scott led a program of songs for a group of old soldiers and their spouses. Gradually, those who could got up to dance, and that attracted others. The sleepers awoke and began to tap their wheelchairs with their hands and fingers. Eventually, the dancing became more vigorous. Couples formed and embraced, reaching a climax with "Sweet Georgia Brown." As Scott began the song, he looked over to see Fred, an Alzheimer's patient who had been watching and chewing gum for more than 45 minutes, struggle to his feet, leaning heavily on his silver walker. A volunteer asked if he would like to dance, and Fred replied that he couldn't walk without his walker.

But then he grew steadier on his feet, made motions like a trombone player, and smiled broadly at the volunteer. He was having a wonderful time. "From silence and quiet," Scott observes, "he had come alive to the beat of this old-time, down-home Southern song. When I looked back at him, I was overwhelmed by what I saw. Fred was dancing with his walker. He swung it from side to side and dipped as the beat carried him to the end of the song. Fred continued with our farewell song and then, in complete satisfaction, put the walker down and shook his finger at it with what I called his inner joy of 'wasn't that the cat's meow?' "

﹛ Anxiety

One of the most widespread therapeutic uses of music is to alleviate the anxiety or pain surrounding surgery and other medical procedures. Many studies extol the benefits of music in the operating room. Researchers at the Bethesda Naval Medical Center in Maryland reported that men who listened to music during sigmoidoscopies—a procedure that requires a tube to be passed through the anus into the colon and is performed to diagnose colon cancer and other colorectal conditions—felt more relaxed than "control" subjects.

Ralph Spintge, M.D., executive director of the German-based International Society for Music in Medicine, studied the effects of music on nearly 97,000 patients before, during, and after surgery. He found that 97 percent reported music helped them relax during their recovery. Many said that, with it, they felt less of a need for anesthesia. Soft, tonal music was particularly effective. Listening to slow Baroque or classical music several days prior to surgery and hearing it again in the recovery room reduced their postoperative disorientation.

At the University of Massachusetts Medical Center in Worcester, patients are encouraged to listen to soothing music and to perform relaxation exercises and meditation derived from Buddhist practices. The innovative program, developed by Jon Kabat-Zinn, director of the stress reduction and relaxation program, and harpist Georgia Kelley, offers a safe, natural alternative to tranquilizers and other mood-altering drugs.

One of my associates, Jeanne Achterberg, Ph.D., a pioneer in transpersonal psychology, shamanic healing, and imagery who assisted me in my own healing, used music during an operation on her jaw. "The musical pieces that I asked for were grounding, to carry me through the surgical process," she explained to me after the operation. "You and I had a talk, and I used your selections 'Memories of the Alhambra' and the Mozart piece 'Laudate Dominum' from *Cosmic Classics*. I didn't want any airy-fairy music. I wanted to feel alive and not come out of surgery thinking I was dead. I used pieces before surgery and in the recovery room to remind me that I was okay and coming back. These pieces were very helpful for that kind of grounding."

⟩ Arthritis

For years, Jack, a forty-four year old actor and director, had suffered from ankylosing spondylitis, a crippling arthritic disease that involves the progressive degeneration of connective tissue. It is considered incurable. (One of the few reported recoveries was that of Norman Cousins, who said he overcame it with laughter and megadoses of vitamin C.) Jack sought therapy for severe depression and began sessions with psychotherapist-musician Stephanie Merritt, director of the Southern California Center for Music and Imagery in San Diego.

Listening to classical music, Jack came to a deeper awareness of his condition—and its origin. "My spine had been literally a bony prison for my most vital core," he said, after treatment had helped him to get in touch with the emotional sources of his pain. "My back pain was the jailer that has kept my anger and my vitality imprisoned. I made my rib cage an inflexible place for my heart, so that my chest was unable to expand when I breathed."

The rhythm and vibration of the music, and the images it invoked, released memories and emotions locked in Jack's body that were felt as pain. The kinesthetic energy of the illness was shifted, allowing a kind of spiritual integration that hadn't been possible previously. And there was nothing abstract about the outcome: Jack overcame not only his depression, but also found his pain reduced by about 90 percent.

Rheumatoid arthritis. An immunological disease that strikes older people in particular, rheumatoid arthritis lends itself well to treatment with music therapy. In a study on the efficacy of Guided Imagery and Music (GIM), a therapeutic technique that uses classical music to stimulate inner experiences and help sufferers to express their emotions, researchers at Lutheran General Hospital in Chicago found significant physical and psychological improvement in twenty-seven rheumatoid arthritis patients. Over an eighteen-week period, researchers found both pain and psychological distress declined, and walking improved. The study concluded, "Patients often experienced themselves beyond the limitations of their disease as they moved easily, joyously, and without pain."

♩ Attention Deficit Disorder

Attention Deficit Disorder (ADD) and Attention Deficit Hyperactivity Disorder (ADHD) affect an estimated 10 to 15 percent of young males in the United States and are characterized by restlessness, inability to concentrate, mood swings, and difficulty relating to peers. In a study of nineteen children aged seven to seventeen with ADD or ADHD, researchers played recordings of Mozart during thrice-weekly neurofeedback sessions for some of the subjects and nothing for the others.

The music used was a CD entitled *100 Masterpieces, Vol. 3: Wolfgang Amadeus Mozart,* which included selections from "Eine Kleine Nachtmusic," *Piano Concerto No. 21 in C, The Marriage of Figaro, Flute Concerto No. 2 in D, Don Giovanni,* and other concertos and sonatas. The researchers reported that those who listened to Mozart reduced their theta brain waves in exact rhythm to the underlying beat of the music, and displayed better focus and mood control, diminished impulsivity, and improved social skills. Among subjects who improved, 70 percent maintained that improvement six months after the end of the study without any further training.

Music therapy has been helpful in treating individual cases of ADD. Jacob suffered from idiosyncratic speech, verbal outbursts, fixation on particular objects or ideas, impulsive touching (especially of anything to do with plumbing and electricity), and lack of perseverance. Two neuropsychologists independently diagnosed the thirteen-year-old with ADHD, developmental receptive language disorder, and developmental perceptual disorder. In addition, his optometrist gave him a visual and perceptual evaluation and reported an eye tracking problem and perceptual integration difficulties. The Cleveland clinic conducted tests for allergies and found that he was allergic to yellow dye #5, which is present in most processed foods. He was also allergic to salicylates, which are present in most fruits and vegetables. To help control these allergic reactions, he was given a variety of antihistamines, as well as Ritalin for his hyperactivity.

Jacob also had sound treatment with music therapist Mary A. Scovel. After evaluation, he was given a set of musical cassette tapes designed to increase his theta brain wave levels. He listened for one week and then went back to his optometist, who found that his eyes were now tracking. A neuropsychologist who administered an EEG found no dysfunction. Jacob's teachers reported that his concentration and reading showed significant improvement. Jacob has continued to listen to the cassettes after school and during periods of stress. He is now on homeopathic remedies and has no need for psychotropic drugs.

Across the country, nine-year-old Cindy had been diagnosed as having ADD. Her reading comprehension was low, and she retained little of what she read. Unable to concentrate, she moved about continuously, often performing handstands and other inappropriate behavior. Her frustrated parents brought their daughter to the Sound and Listening Center in Phoenix to begin the Tomatis listening program. Following the training, Cindy calmed down. She joined in conversations and showed improved concentration and motor coordination. Cindy had experienced vision problems, seeing everything slightly tilted to the right, a condition her opthamologist said could be corrected by surgery. However, after the first week of listening training, the vision corrected itself and has remained stable. Cindy's mother told Center director Billie M. Thompson that the world had suddenly made sense to her daughter. It was like having a new person in the house. Cindy could read, follow directions, put together puzzles. "She has not had to *learn* anything," she said. "It was all there—her large vocabulary, sense of humor, reasoning. It all was covered up and just had to be uncovered."

} Autism

Annabel Stehli's life was a nightmare. Her elder daughter had died a lingering death from leukemia and her younger daughter, Georgie, was autistic. After being declared "hopeless," by her doctors, Georgie was put in an institution at the age of four. On a trip to Europe with her husband, Stehli heard about a therapy developed by Guy Bérard, a French doctor. Over objections from Georgie's physicians, she took her daughter to his clinic in Annecy, France, where Bérard found that her hearing was so hypersensitive that even the slightest tremor brought on pain, and loud noises could throw her into fits of hysteria and agony.

As a result of her auditory reeducation, Georgie recovered, went on to develop normally, and, after graduating from college became a successful artist. Stehli told her daughter's poignant story in the book *The Sound of a Miracle* and founded the Georgiana Foundation to use music and sound therapy to help other children with autism.

Brain-damaged, blind, and autistic at birth, Tony de Blois developed a remarkable memory for thousands of songs and is admired for his jazz improvisations. He can play practically any tune on the piano just by hearing it once. However, in other areas, he is deficient and has been classified by doctors as an "idiot savant." His musical interest began at age two when his mother, alarmed that he had still not learned to sit, gave him a small electronic keyboard. She thought he might at least reach for it and learn to sit up.

"For the first six weeks it was hell," she recalls. "Tony played every possible combination of notes randomly over and over again. But one day when I was in the kitchen, I heard the first three notes of 'Twinkle Twinkle'—I went in and showed him the rest of it." Now, his gift is such that he can switch effortlessly among Bach, Andrew Lloyd-Webber, and complex jazz scats.

At six weeks old, Wendy Young's son, Sam, developed a case of colic—an acute abdominal pain caused by various abnormal conditions in the bowels—that stretched her and her husband to their limits. The child could find no way to settle himself; he would begin to cry around ten or eleven in the morning and continue until ten or eleven at night. The parents tried everything—rocking, singing, walking, car rides, herbs, old family remedies.

A professional musician, Young always had music playing in her house, but nothing seemed to calm her son. One night, she intuitively began to tone, though she didn't know it was called toning at the time. The two pitches she sang resembled a foghorn, and to her amazement, her son stopped crying. In fact, he fell asleep in her arms. After several months the colic disappeared, and Young's family (and her patient neighbors) found peace again.

The story does not end there. At age two and a half, Sam was diagnosed with autism. Looking back, Young recognizes that his inability to process and prioritize sensory input began at a very young age. He is now seven and, along with many other autistic behaviors, has a low pain tolerance to sound. Sam has been known to curl up in a ball at the sounds of street traffic or walk around the house with his hands over his ears, mumbling. He also has tantrums, which became so severe that he was put on medication.

For nearly a year, Young has been attending my workshops and discussing ways to help her son with sound and music. But when she tried singing to him, Sam told her to "stop singing." When she toned, he told her to "go away." Drumming was met with "no drum." Then one day, while reading an anecdote about colic and music, Young had the inspiration to make the foghorn sound. The instant she began, her son came over and leaned against her, his back to her chest, where the sound resonated most. Sam reached around and pulled her head close to his and gave his mother a big, knowing smile. Young was astounded. She stopped and watched for his reaction. "More humming," Sam said.

Skeptical, Young put the foghorn sound to the test. In typical autistic fashion, her son was unable to stop watching a movie until he saw every last credit. He was singing along to *My Fair Lady* when she said they needed to turn the television off. As Sam began to get upset, Young said, "Sam, it's okay . . . (foghorn) . . . we have to go now . . . (foghorn) . . . we can watch it later . . . (foghorn) . . ."

Sam calmed down. He still wouldn't let Young turn off the TV, but suddenly he began to tone with her. Then he said, "Hold me," sat on her lap, wrapped his arms around her, and whispered, "Hum with me." Finally, Young was able to fast-forward through the movie (previously unheard of), so they could watch the credits and turn off the set.

In another case study, medical researchers in Wales reported that a noncommunicative three-year-old girl with autism improved significantly after completing two years of musically oriented Medical Interaction Therapy. In twice-weekly, twenty-minute sessions at home, the mother would engage the child in games involving swinging, patting, tickling, and stroking, as well as action rhymes, vocalizing, and singing. The girl was treated as though she were communicative, and mother and daughter took turns imitating each other as they played lap games and sang spontaneous songs. A musician participated, providing harp accompaniment like a pianist at an old silent film theater. The harp music was performed to correspond with the mood, timing, and perceived meaning of the parent-child interaction. The music softened when the child avoided her mother, for example, and increased in intensity when she approached her, gradually reaching a crescendo during dramatic interactions.

Results were profound. Before therapy, the child would acknowledge her mother's presence on average once every six minutes. After therapy, acknowledgment occurred within a minute. In the follow-up phase of treatment, the number dropped to nine seconds. Eye contact went from once every three minutes at the start of the program to twice a minute and then, during follow-up, six times a minute. Before therapy, the child initiated contact with her mother 20 percent of the time, afterward 75 percent. By the end of the training, the child spontaneously teased her mother and during a familiar hand-clapping song made eye contact and smiled while spontaneously lifting her jumper and clapping her stomach. She also "fed" biscuits to a stuffed animal and "washed" her dolls' clothes—pretend play in which she had not previously engaged. A two-year follow-up showed that these positive changes were sustained.

Nonverbal communication between an autistic child playing the drums and a therapist on piano can serve to bring a child out of isolation, the *Journal of the American Medical Association* reported. "When you have a child who is unable to relate to life successfully, cannot endure human relationships, or has communication difficulties, this improvisation [can] be very effective," explained Clive E. Robbins, Ph.D., director of the Nordoff-Robbins Music Therapy Center at New York University. "It's a way of reaching into the child's mind." Robbins compared the musical interaction to a conversation. "As we speak, we improvise," he said. "You ask a question, I respond. So it is with music. It can be used as flexibly as we use speech to reach children with language problems. It bypasses those difficulties. Neurologic research is discovering that the brain comes into synthetic activity in response to music. Some say the brain is fundamentally programmed so that the organic connections are symphonic rather than mechanistic."

⦃ Back Pain

The harp has always been linked to the soothing of pain. In the Bible, David played the instrument to rid Saul of his "evil spirit." In ancient Ireland, Celtic bards plucked it while telling stories, both to heal and to pass down centuries of unwritten lore. In France in the Middle Ages, monks at the abbey of Cluny used it in conjunction with vocals to assist the dying. "The poets did well to conjoin Music and Medicine in Apollo," Francis Bacon asserted in *The Advancement of Learning,* "because the office of medicine is but to tune the curious harp of man's body and to reduce it to harmony."

A pioneer in harp therapy is Sarajane Williams, a nurse, former director of a cardiac catheterization laboratory, and a biofeedback therapist specializing in chronic pain. Now running the Shepard Hills Counseling Center in Allentown, Pennsylvania, Williams treats patients suffering from chronic back pain, headaches, stress, anxiety, and depression. Her harp therapy makes use of a portable massage table that amplifies the sound and is usually performed in conjunction with biofeedback training or counseling. Before and after each session, patients rate their discomfort on a scale of one to nine so that any changes can be evaluated. In reviewing sixteen recent case reports, Williams found that pain and tension levels in all areas of the body were reduced on average by one-third, or three points. The greatest reduction occurred in the legs, back, and shoulders. She finds harp especially effective because its broad frequency range—low C 32.7 hertz to high G 3136 hertz—vibrates the entire body. It also offers "a varied palette of tone colors," many of which are soothing, and creates an ethereal effect through the unique glissando plucking technique (sliding from one pitch to another and playing all the pitches in between).

In counseling sessions, Williams customarily plays individual C's and "walks" her way up to the second octave C and back down two times. The client indicates where she feels the tones in her body. Then Williams moves on to D and repeats the process up and down the scale. If a particular part of the body is in pain, Williams looks for specific notes that resonate in that spot. Once she determines which tones are eliciting a favorable response, she plays or improvises a piece of music highlighting those tones. Reducing that tension, she finds, allows greater flow of energy through the body so that healing can take place. When the person is deeply relaxed, beta-endorphins are released, alleviating pain and elevating mood.

As an ancient healing instrument, the harp, Williams finds, opens doors to the collective unconscious, evoking images, past memories, and other symbolic material that can be addressed in counseling sessions and that sometimes lead to an awareness of deeper sources of the pain.

⟩ Breathing Difficulties (Asthma)

George's asthma had gotten progressively worse over the course of a decade. His lungs felt tight, damp, cold, and wheezy, and nothing seemed to improve his condition. Eventually, he came for instruction in toning with Joy Gardner-Gordon, a vibrational healer. Gardner-Gordon asked him to express vocally each sensation he felt in his lungs. Feeling self-conscious and awkward, George made several short, tight sounds to demonstrate the tightness in his chest, shivering sounds to convey the cold, and wheezy sounds to describe his wheeziness. It wasn't an especially evocative performance, and it certainly didn't make him feel that he was releasing anything.

George was clearly uncomfortable with his own voice, so Gardner-Gordon guided him in making an appropriate sound that would resonate with each symptom. He repeated each for about five minutes until he found the symptoms abating. George discovered he had a surprisingly strong and vibrant voice and could hold a tone longer than he imagined. By the end of the session, he was breathing freely. Back home, to his amazement, he found he didn't need his chest inhaler to get through the night. More important, since he started toning, his lungs have appreciably cleared.

♩ Burns

Excruciating pain usually accompanies severe burns and can last for weeks and months. Because of extensive bandaging and isolation in a sterile environment, burn patients have little outside contact. This is particularly hard on children. According to a study conducted by Elizabeth Bolton Christenberry, a music therapy intern in Tuscaloosa, Alabama, live music in a burn ward provides both auditory and, in the case of such things as hand-clapping and guitar-strumming, visual stimulation. Tight bandaging and pain, she found, could inhibit movement, but nearly all patients could sing or hum, thus providing sensory stimulation and giving patients an outlet for self-expression.

In Christenberry's experience working with burned children at the Children's Hospital in Birmingham, songs such as "The Eensy Weensy Spider" were helpful in improving finger or hand movement, walking, and other gross and fine motor movement. The song "If You're Happy and You Know It" was particularly good because it allowed patients to, in the lyrics of the song, "wiggle your fingers" or "make a fist." (Adults responded to "She'll Be Comin' Round the Mountain"; "Do, Lord," in which they were encouraged to clap their hands, tap their toes, and stamp their feet; and "Swing Low, Sweet Chariot," during which they were asked to lift a leg whenever the phrase "Comin' for to carry me home" was played.)

Music therapy is important for psychological reasons, especially for children. Unlike doctors, nurses, and other physical therapists, the music therapist's procedures do not produce pain, and they are frequently able to earn more trust and have better communication than other caregivers.

In visits to Dallas hospitals and clinics in the mid-eighties, I found that ambient and New Age music didn't work for teenagers with serious burns. Michael Jackson, Diana Ross, and the latest rock hits masked their pain better and made them feel more connected to their bodies than more tranquil sounds. Relaxing music was too painful to listen to. The most soothing image for these teenagers was a long-haired guitar player, not an angel with a harp.

♭ Cancer

Until now, music has been used in cancer treatment primarily as a palliative. *Oncology Nursing Forum* and *Cancer Nursing* reported in the mid-1980s that music therapy and guided imagery could reduce the nausea and vomiting caused by chemotherapy. Music therapy has also been helpful in patient rehabilitation after surgery—from enhancing fine and gross motor skills to increasing self-esteem.

Music therapist Deforia Lane, who received the first grant to study the therapeutic effect of music on cancer patients and is now a spokesperson for the American Cancer Society, has witnessed many amazing turnarounds. One was Duane Sullivan, a former pharmaceutical salesman who was hospitalized for colon cancer. A music lover, he had built his own dulcimer and spent many happy hours in the hospital playing his instrument. Eventually, however, Duane's condition worsened, and he dropped into a coma from which doctors said he would never emerge. Despite his condition, Carol, Duane's partner, refused to have the life-support disconnected. Instead, she came to see him every day and played dulcimer music beside his bed. Weeks went by, when, to everyone's amazement, Duane suddenly awoke and lived vibrantly for another year. "I heard these beautiful notes, strains of music, and I had to find them," he told Lane later. "The sounds forced my mind to function as a mind should and not just sleep. They made me realize that out there was something worth looking for, something I *should* look for."

Breast cancer. Since the era of Galen, the ancient Roman physician, it has been known that breast cancer—a disease that, according to the National Cancer Institute, will affect one out of every eight women in America—is strongly connected to the emotions. Beyond creating a harmonious environment, tone and sound may produce powerful effects on cells and tissues and even influence malignant growth. The cutting edge research of Fabien Maman, a French musician and teacher, offers intriguing evidence that sound and music may actually be capable of eliminating cancer cells and dissolving tumors.

The story begins about twenty years ago, when Maman was a

professional guitarist and jazz musician. During a 1974 concert tour with his group in Tokyo, he noticed that between pieces the audience didn't clap. They would clap at the end, but not after each selection. In the West he was used to applause and was initially shocked by the lack of response. But as he got used to this reaction, he noticed that he began to have more energy than ever before. After three months of touring in Japan, Maman realized that clapping in between pieces, however well intentioned, actually destroyed some of the benefits of the music. In the absence of clapping, he would enter fresh and exhilarating mental states as a performer. Japanese audiences—because of something in their emotional makeup—stayed with the experience. (At the end of the concert, they would clap and applaud for fifteen minutes.) Maman began to ruminate on the question of what music does to the cells of the listener. What kinds of effects does sound produce in our bodies?

A few years later, he met Hélène Grimal, a senior researcher at the National Center of Biological Research in Paris and also a nun. She was interested in music; she liked to spend her evenings playing the drums. Through their friendship, Maman and Grimal were able to devote a year and a half to an unofficial biological study of the effects of sound on cancer cells. They went to the University of Jussieu in Paris five nights a week for a year and a half, carrying out their experiments in the biological research laboratories from 12:30 A.M. to 5:00 A.M. when all the metros in Paris had stopped. Beginning with drums, flutes, guitar, bass, and xylophone, they investigated the effects of sound on both normal and malignant cells.

Grimal had access to many forms of cancer cells. They began with the *hela*, which is a cancer cell from the uterus named after *Helen Lane*, an American who died of the disease. Grimal attached a special camera to her microscope, and, in the course of the investigation, took thousands of pictures.

First, they played a xylophone at about 30 to 40 decibels (not very loud) about a foot away from the cells. Then they studied how one note affected the cancer over time. They struck an A every four or five seconds, and continued this for twenty-one minutes. Maman was intrigued by this particular time interval. "We have 7- to 7$\frac{1}{2}$-minute cycles in our body," he says, and goes on to suggest that tripling a cycle is the most efficient way to control the body's response. Eventually, Maman and Grimal found that when repeatedly exposed to this sound the nuclear and the cytoplasmic membrane of the cancer cell would break down, its structure thrown into complete disorganization after twenty-one minutes. The healthy cells, however, remained intact. Maman and Grimal next tried alternations of two notes, then added voice to the xylophone, then moved on to scales. They found that a combination of major, chromatic, and half-tone scales produced a much faster disintegrating effect.

These were *in vitro* or test tube experiments. In experimental sessions on actual cancer patients, *in vivo* or live testing, the music produced equally astonishing results. Two female volunteers with breast cancer were taught to tone with the whole scale—using a violin to keep a base note—for twenty-one minutes at a time. They spent 3½ hours a day at this, and did it regularly for a month. That's a lot of toning. One woman's tumor disappeared completely. The other had agreed beforehand with her husband to have surgery, whether she had the musical therapy or not. In the hospital, surgeons found her tumor reduced and completely dry. There were no metastases. The malignant part was removed and the cancer never came back.

Maman's preliminary results open up new vistas that need to be attended to in a clinical context. His new book, *A Sound Structure for the 21st Century*, includes dozens of photographs of sound-treated cells and chemicals.

Cancer in children. At the Ireland Cancer Center at the University Hospital of Cleveland, music therapist Deforia Lane reported in 1996 that children given a single half hour music therapy session had improved immune function. In nineteen subjects, she found a significant increase in salivary immunoglobulin A (IgA) after the music session, while in seventeen controls there was a small but not significant *decrease*. IgA, an antibody in saliva that protects against harmful bacteria and toxins, is a principal marker in enhanced resistance to disease.

In her book, *Music as Medicine*, Lane describes many young cancer patients whose lives have been enhanced by music therapy. Ginny, seventeen, was bandaged head to foot. Side effects of leukemia treatment had left her with practically no skin. Her suffering was excruciating, and for weeks she had been severely depressed and uncommunicative. Learning that Ginny liked music and played in the orchestra in high school, Lane brought an Omnichord (a hand-held instrument that makes up to twenty-seven chords) into her room and offered either to let her play it then or to bring it back another time. To Lane's surprise, Ginny extended three fingers on the hand that was not bandaged and said that she would play the instrument. For the next forty-five minutes, she rapturously sang and played, as her mother and aunt looked on with tears of joy. On her way out, Lane was told by Ginny's mother that this was the first time since her daughter had been hospitalized that she had been happy. A few days later, Ginny died, and her mother asked Lane to sing "That's What Friends Are For," a song they had sung together, at her memorial service.

⟨ Cerebral Palsy

Several recent studies have shown that music therapy is helpful for cerebral palsy, a degenerative nervous condition that affects about three million children and adults. In a study of twenty developmentally disabled children, including sixteen diagnosed with cerebral palsy, music designed to enhance learning improved speech and eating habits. At the start of the program, eighteen of the children (whose average age was two) could neither walk nor talk because of lack of motor coordination or delayed development. In addition to Baroque compositions by Vivaldi, Bach, and other composers, the children were exposed to contemporary and popular music that had a regular tempo of sixty beats per minute, similar to that of the heartbeat, as well as to the rhythms of sucking and walking. The music was further enhanced with Hemi-Sync signals, binaural beat patterns delivered through headphones that transmitted sounds alternatively between right and left ears. Overall, 75 percent of the children responded positively to the program, with benefits that included improved attention span, reduced hypersensitivity, less withdrawal, improved coordination during feeding, regularized breathing, and sustained posture.

In a study conducted at United Cerebral Palsy of Miami in 1982, six young adults who received three weekly twenty-minute training sessions over a five-week period showed a 65 percent average decrease of muscle tension when sedative music was added to biofeedback. When only biofeedback training was administered, muscle tension decreased only 32.5 percent. The music included "The Gift" and "Grandfather's Story" from *The Red Pony* by Aaron Copland, "Gymnopedies" by Erik Satie, "Aspen" from *Captured Angel* by Dan Fogelberg, and "Lullaby" from *Children in Sanchez* by Chuck Mangione.

₹ Cervical Exams

Women's reproductive disorders and their attendant operations are often accompanied by terrible anxiety and distress. In a study of twenty-two patients undergoing cervical examinations, a researcher at Florida State University reported that women exposed to music (a selection of tapes from such artists as James Taylor, Amerika, Van Morrison, Judy Collins, the Oak Ridge Boys, Enya, Steven Halpern, and Elton John) had significantly lower respiratory rates and pain than control subjects. During a painful biopsy, three of the controls experienced excessive bleeding, while none of the women listening to music bled. The researcher, Cynthia Allison Davis, M.M. R.M.T., now a music therapist at Gaston Memorial Hospital in Gastonia, North Carolina, concluded that further research was warranted to study the effects of music on blood pressure, stress hormone levels, and blood clotting.

Jim Oliver, an Emmy-award-winning musician, has developed (with G. P. McRostie, a doctor of natural medicine) Synphonics, an approach to healing using specific sound frequencies and wave forms to affect energy fields that may fundamentally influence mental, physical, and spiritual health. In his studio in Santa Fe, New Mexico, Oliver uses synthesizers, music samplers, and other equipment to create a library of more than 25,000 sounds. He also takes the "sonic fingerprint" of his clients (the unique vibrations that come from their voices and bodies) and blends their own voices with the music. One, a cytologist, came to see him in 1985 after a pap smear of four, indicating dysplasia and a possible precancerous condition. (Five is the highest level, zero the lowest.) The procedure had been performed on a Tuesday, and the woman had a sound therapy session with Oliver on Thursday.

The following Tuesday, her pap test was zero. (It wasn't a laboratory error, she said—she had hand-carried each test through the lab and had verified the results herself.) Weeks later, another test showed the condition had corrected itself. She has had normal pap smears ever since.

♫ Chronic Fatigue Syndrome

Floyd suffered from chronic fatigue syndrome, a debilitating disease that, along with Epstein-Barr virus, fibromyalgia, and other immune disorders, has immobilized or crippled hundreds of thousands of young adults. "I used to run, but now there are hand-carved hazel and cocobolo canes in my closet where running gear used to be," the longtime Portland resident wrote in an article "Thorn into Feathers: Coping with Chronic Illness" in a small literary magazine. "I can no longer work, so a wardrobe of baggy sweats and wildly patterned, floppy pants has replaced the trim three-piece suits and snug-collared shirts of days past." For years, it had been a challenge for Floyd to tie his shoelaces.

Before his illness, Floyd loved rock & roll, especially Elvis Presley, the Everly Brothers, Buddy Holly, Fats Domino, Chuck Berry, and Jerry Lee Lewis, as well as Broadway musicals such as *Guys and Dolls, Camelot,* and *South Pacific.* Music was for entertainment or to listen to on headphones as he jogged through Portland on early mornings. Then a friend introduced him to Mozart, and Floyd's whole world changed. "I thought classical music was, by definition, complicated and heavy and only to be discussed in hushed tones and pompous accents," he confessed. "It was written by people without first names, most of whom were cranky and tubercular and had wild hair."

For the next two years, Floyd listened to music by Schumann, Beethoven, and Chopin, as well as Mozart, for four hours a day while lying down. "Sometimes the music took me to the dark center of what I was experiencing, to my conflicting emotions about all that had changed in my life," he said. "But sometimes it took me outside myself altogether, into a realm of pure sound where there could be peace.

"It's not that I wouldn't have survived without music. But without what music taught me, I might not have been able to grasp that the score my body had followed for so long had been totally rewritten. I wouldn't have understood that my body's symphony now included a long movement of pure chaos: somber and discordant in itself, but leading somewhere worth going if I learned to listen."

In addition to music, Floyd made other positive changes in his life. He improved his diet and sleeping habits, devoted more time to developing a loving relationship, and moved to the country. "I found that eros is a remarkably restorative force . . ." he explained. Although he has not completely relieved his condition, these changes have brought Floyd new hope and a measure of inner peace. "Music has taught me that I may still contain harmony, if only I can hear the whole thing through."

⟩ Colds

"Is there something I can do for my cold?" This is one of the most common questions I am asked. Although there is no simple remedy (no surefire medical remedy at all, in fact), toning may prove helpful in controlling some of the symptoms.

For sinus problems, humming and making *Ah* sounds sometimes helps clear congested nasal passages. It's important to remain comfortable and not to force the sound. If your nose is completely stuffed up, you can't hum. In this case, making an *nggg* sound in the back of the throat (I call this Don's Tibetan Cold Remedy) may help move energy and provide some relief. Other than that, I advise staying in bed, listening to a lot of Mozart, and resting with the powers of Brahms or Kenny G.!

♫ Depression

Orpheus played the lute to heal melancholy. Johnny Cash ministered with the gospel. For all of recorded history, music has been used to ward off despondency. Even cases of clinical depression—one of the most intractable mood disorders—are yielding to the magic of music.

Jane, fifty-two, suffered from severe depression, which her psychiatrist believed was related to menopause. She had a history of dysthymia (a mild form of depression), but it had swelled to the point where she was unable to work or even to get out of bed. Jane thought her situation hopeless. Once she had dreamed of starting her own business, but now she was sure she would fail—as she had failed at most of her ventures into the business or professional world.

During two series of music and imagery sessions with therapist Stephanie Merritt, Jane began to explore her fears. "The two outstanding images that accompanied her in her musical travels," Merritt reports, "were the Phantom of the Opera and Pegasus, which allowed Jane to look at two completely opposite sides of herself: the part that lived underground, heavy with shame and isolated from all others, and the part that she had long disowned—the light and fun-filled Pegasus, who always told her to lighten up."

As the two aspects of her self began to reintegrate, Jane's pent-up energy found release. She eased up, and her self-esteem increased. Her psychiatrist, the director of a large hospital in San Diego, had been treating her with antidepressants for more than five years and found no improvement. Suddenly, toward the end of her second series, he asked Merritt, "What did you do with Jane? I can't believe she's no longer depressed!" Merritt shared the Guided Imagery in Music process with him and left him curious and interested to find out more. Out of her depression, Jane started her own health food franchise and, like Pegasus, the winged horse of mythology, is soaring to new levels of self-realization.

Since age five, Brigitte had been obsessed with death. When her mother brought her to French auditory specialist Guy Bérard, M.D., at age sixteen, she answered all of his questions with, "I want to die." Bérard learned from the mother that the girl had expected to die at an early age, suffered depression after a youthful romance, and had twice attempted suicide. She had visited several medical specialists, but the strongest drugs produced no beneficial results.

Bérard took an audiogram, an electronic hearing profile. As he expected, it showed a characteristic 2–8 curve—or hypersensitivity to sounds at 2,000 and at 8,000 hertz—in the left ear. Over the years, Bérard found that many disorders have auditory patterns that can be represented by lines, waves, or curves. Like a cardiologist reading the peaks and valleys of an EEG, a listening specialist can make accurate diagnoses by observing the patient's audiogram. A suicidal patient, he found, typically displayed hypersensitive listening at 2,000 hertz, a steady drop between 3,000, 4,000, and 6,000 hertz, and then a sharp rise at 8,000 hertz. Further study showed Bérard that the deeper the 2–8 curve, the more serious the tendency toward self-destructiveness, while the less pronounced the curve, the more latent the suicidal urge. The absence of strength in the high frequency range between 3,000 and 7,000 hertz may be an indication of depression.

By the end of ten listening sessions, the audiogram indicated improvement, although Brigitte's attitude remained negative. After the fourteenth treatment, she experienced a transformation. She began to take pride in her appearance and became suddenly communicative. "Her mother still cried, but with joy," Bérard wrote in his book *Hearing Equals Behavior*. The final audiogram revealed that optimal listening had been restored. Two and a half years later, an audiogram confirmed that her listening—and state of mind—had returned to normal.

In his book, Bérard reports having treated 233 depressed patients with suicidal tendencies. Two hundred seventeen (93 percent) were cured, he says, after the first course of treatment, eleven healed after two or three treatments (4.7 percent), and five failed the treatment.

} Developmental Delays

Ear infection (otitis media) is the most common childhood disorder, especially prevalent in children aged three or younger before their eustachian tubes descend and there's adequate drainage of the middle ear. A survey performed by the Developmental Delay Registry found a high correlation between recurrent childhood ear infections, treatment with antibiotics, and developmental delays. As a result, the D.D.R. encourages parents to reduce medication and consider alternative methods, among them music therapy, which enhances the immune system.

Occupational therapist Valerie DeJean, O.T.R., directs the Spectrum Center in Silver Spring, Maryland, where children with learning disabilities and special needs are treated. She reports that children with chronic ear infections often have intermittent hearing loss and may miss a critical period of language and speech development. Normal hearing levels my be restored, she explains, but irregularities in how the children listen to and analyze sound may continue. Through the Tomatis method emphasizing listening training, DeJean has found that certain frequencies in hearing that have been missed as a result of illness may be recovered. As listening improves, speaking improves. The voice is able to articulate restored hearing frequencies, and problems in reading and spelling can be corrected.

Michael lagged far behind the rest of his classmates. He struggled with every word on the page and almost gave up interest in learning to read and write. Because of his poor performance, he would often have emotional outbursts and cry in frustration. Michael had three older sisters who were all bright, which only added to his feelings of inadequacy and isolation. Michael's teacher was sympathetic and suggested to his mother that he might be dyslexic, a disorder that affects ten million American children and several million in England, where Michael and his family lived. Dyslexics have normal intelligence and motivation, but great difficulty reading single words. (They commonly transpose letters.) They also tend to have trouble hearing and generating speech. Many dyslexic children drop out of school and end up with drug or alcohol problems, or else have trouble finding and keeping jobs that require even basic verbal and written skills.

Michael was tested by a child psychologist, who concluded he was not dyslexic, but experiencing anxiety and educational delays resulting from his parents' separation. While Michael's mother worked to support her family and couldn't give him all the attention he needed, she felt her son's condition was misdiagnosed and moved to another school district. The new staff was supportive, but, despite special instruction, Michael failed to catch up.

One day, Michael's mother read a review of a new book, *When Listening Comes Alive,* by Paul Madaule, the director of the Tomatis Center in Toronto. The book was about the author's own nightmare growing up in a "dyslexified" world and how he had overcome his learning disabilities with the Tomatis method. Michael's mother immediately contacted the Lewes Tomatis Centre in East Sussex, England, for an assessment of her son.

From the first session, Michael responded to the listening training as supervised by David Manners. His mother described him as the opposite of how he was before—strong, happy, even overexcited. His teacher also noticed the difference. Michael was suddenly willing to compete in class for the first time. During the second session, his confidence soared even further, and his reading and writing began to improve. After the third and final session, Michael's progress continued unobstructed. In school, he received an 80 on a spelling test.

"He used to be *so* clumsy, always breaking things," his mother recalled. "Now, he is the opposite! He helps around the house, even taking control of activities. . . . He is such a different boy—more sure of himself, interested in lots of things, and optimistic. Today, Michael shines—he wasn't shining before. And now he has a great big smile!"

≀ Diabetes

Diabetes, the third leading cause of death from chronic disease (after cardiovascular disease and cancer), may respond to music or sound therapy. Bonnie, an insulin-dependent diabetic, recently came for a session with Santa Fe musician and sound healer Jim Oliver. She had taken no insulin that day, and at the start of her session had a fasting glucose blood level measuring 192. After the session, her glucose had declined to 120, well within the normal zone of 60 to 160. Without insulin, Bonnie told Jim, her glucose level would usually have risen to 300 or more. "The bottom line of this is its simplicity," Oliver reports. "We're presenting pure harmonious sound for the body to align itself with and to adapt to and reestablish its own resonance."

In another case, a scientist came to see Valerie V. Hunt at her office in Malibu, California, bringing with him a fifty-year-old diabetic friend. For many decades, Hunt, an author and retired UCLA scientist, had been investigating the high-frequency vibrations of the aura, the energy field that surrounds the human body. In the course of a conversation on the healing effects of sound and music, Hunt played for her guests the Music of Light—sounds she had produced by amplifying the light frequency data of the energy field. (She had correlated different sounds and colors and used electronic spectra analysis to confirm her results.)

After listening for fifteen minutes to the full spectrum of sounds, the diabetic friend jumped up and exclaimed, "I can feel my feet!" Like many long-term diabetics, he suffered from parasthesia, the absence of sensation in the feet. "He said he lost feeling twenty years ago and this was the first time he had experienced sensation again," Hunt wrote in her book, *Infinite Mind: The Science of Human Vibrations.* Several months later, the man called to tell Hunt that he rarely used insulin now, and that the sensations in his feet were those of a normal person.

♪ Down's Syndrome

At sunset on August 6, 1991, Clare Candela took her nineteen-year-old daughter Christine, who had Down's Syndrome and had been speechless for fifteen years, out in the yard to pray. The next day, she showed her daughter pictures in an angel prayer book; gave her a large, colorful, beaded rosary; and sang one of the songs, "Beloved Jophiel and Christine." "When the line, 'O blaze illumination from the Central Sun' was sung," Candela recalls, "an intense light from the sun lit up her face and hands." The girl sang the very next line—"Now let the joy of angels fill each day"—and then sang the rest of the song along with her mother.

Candela was ecstatic: Christine never spoke, much less sang an entire song. Keeping their composure, mother and daughter continued to sing together in perfect rhythm. "She didn't want me to slow down for her," Candela says, "so I kept an even pace and allowed her to stumble. Each time through, she memorized more of the words and rhythm. We were a symphony of two." By this time, Candela had cast her containment to the wind: "We hugged and kissed and rocked. I said, 'We are being healed,' and Christine whispered, 'Yes.'"

The family's teenage son came into the yard. "She's talking!" he exclaimed in total disbelief. "This is great!" Candela suggested to Christine that she chant her brother's name and tell him "I love you." Christine did. Her son's happiness, she said, "was as big as his smile."

The following morning, Christine was shy about using her new vocal skill in front of her father. He could only half believe what his wife had told him. After more prayers and songs with her daughter, Candela told her husband to come downstairs discreetly and listen to his daughter. "When he came down and heard her, I was able to witness him and he was beaming," she says. "We ended our session with 'God Bless America,' and it was rousing. But her dad had left and didn't get to hear it, so up the stairs we went to serenade Dad. The song took away all doubt that she could be on her own."

⟩ Epilepsy

Over the years, Margo Anand, author of *The Art of Sexual Ecstasy*, has used music in her seminars on human relationships. She dates her love of music to a profound experience as a child when her father took her to a Russian Orthodox church in Paris. From deep within the silence, she writes, "as if from the very womb of the earth, a male voice arose, slowly, tentatively, unfolding, revealing layer after layer of longing, of passion, of supplication, of grateful adoration, and imploration to the Divine Christ." She heard a choir of male voices, moving up and down a scale of harmonic resonances, echoed by angelic female voices, seemingly calling the divine within her soul. From that day, Anand knew that music would always be the power that would carry her spirit to freedom.

In the course of her work, Anand sees many "hopeless" cases. Once in Paris, a couple came to her workshop with their nineteen-year-old son who barely moved, did not speak, and did not respond to anything his parents did. He also had epileptic seizures. For five days, Anand worked with the young man, encouraging him to move, walk, breathe, and make sounds to the beat of her drums. She played joyful music and surrounded him with dancers. A week later, he was transformed. As listening to music and moving his body became a daily ritual, the young man's parents reported sustained improvement, particularly in his ability to anticipate a seizure. He learned to lie on the bed instead of banging his head against a heater. Gradually, his seizures declined in number and severity.

Dr. Robert L. Tusler, professor emeritus, UCLA, is a music therapist and has worked extensively for fifty years with patients with epilepsy. In his book, *Music: Catalyst for Healing*, he presents several successful case histories, including that of M., a thoughtful, gregarious man in his fifties, whose seizures were brought on by a serious automobile accident, as a result of which he also lost the sight in one eye. A brilliant mathematician, M. received the active support of his wife and children, as well as the international firm where he worked. Still, he would often be incapacitated for days.

As most of the attacks occurred at night, Tusler recommended that M. listen to prepared tapes while resting in bed. (Falling asleep was okay.) Tusler also prescribed listening to the same music while commuting to work by train and before any business meeting or conference. The tapes consisted of selections by Bach, Vivaldi, Telemann, Handel, and other Baroque composers who used a stable rhythm, a tempo approximating the normal heartbeat, and little in the way of flashy emotional content. M.'s interest in music was subsequently stimulated, and by the end of the first year, his number of grand mal seizures had been reduced by two-thirds. The attacks were less violent, the recovery quicker, and M. had fewer inhibiting fears.

In the following year, his musical regimen was enlarged to include Chopin, Schumann, Scriabin, and Debussy, as well as Haydn and Bach. M.'s medication was reduced, and he began to play tennis once a week. His sex life also improved. During therapy sessions,

Tusler noticed that M.'s sightless eye was beginning to drift, an indication that nervous energy was still capable of flowing into the area. He referred M. to Rein Bartlema, a practitioner of cranial therapy and Neurolinguistic Programming. By the beginning of the third year, normal coloring and a sensation of feeling returned to M.'s damaged cheek. "After some months, with the aid of a mirror, M. could center the drifting, sightless eye," Tusler related. "Then during one of the sessions, without any prompting on our part, M. verbally relived the accident. It was an outpouring of deeply imbedded fear, an invaluable catharsis, a significant turning point."

For his final program of music, M. listened to compositions with stronger emotional content by Brahms, Bach, Mozart, Corelli, and Ravel. The purpose was to get M. to come to terms with the unconscious dynamics that could be inhibiting his healing. "Abstract music stimulates the cells of the brain, quickens the flow of nervous energy, and stirs up the subconscious while leaving the individual's dream world, his imagination, and his conscious intellect free to express his reactions some other way," Tusler explained. During these sessions, M. arrived at deeper insight into his condition, and twenty years of seizures came to an end.

≀ Grief

Bill became seriously ill shortly after the death of his close friend Roland on Easter Sunday, 1991. The two had been friends for over thirty years, and although Roland had been diagnosed with Lou Gehrig's disease some time earlier, his passing had been a shock. Within days, Bill developed a paralysis on both sides of his face. His eyes regularly filled with tears and the left couldn't blink; he couldn't even whistle. He had seen an M.D., a specialist, and an orthodontist. The physicians suspected Bell's palsy, but Bill's symptoms didn't fit the classic model. In talking to Chris Brewer, a Kalispell, Montana, music therapist, Bill admitted that he had avoided really "focusing" on his friend's death. Brewer suggested a music and guided imagery session to help Bill come to terms with his grief.

In the session, Bill conjured up images of a meeting with Roland, in which farewells were exchanged, and Bill came to see his friend as at peace. As Brewer played Pachelbel's Canon, she watched Bill's body quiver and the tears flow easily down his face. Bill didn't speak, but what he was going through was palpable. Soon after this session, feeling returned to his face, and he has not had any subsequent paralysis. His doctors, who had contemplated surgery, were amazed.

♪ Headaches

Toning can relieve and control headaches. One of my students, Marilyn Utz of Santa Monica, California, came home one day with a ghastly sinus headache. She didn't want aspirin, Tylenol, or other medication, so she sat in a recliner and toned.

I tell students in my classes and workshops that each person must find the tones that are unique to them. There are no specific sounds for specific conditions, nor do the same sounds work for everyone in the same way. You just have to plunge in, which Marilyn did, making random long vowel sounds. "What came out was *Ouuu*," she relates, adding that the tone vibrated her entire head, to the point where, "I could feel my sinuses begin to drain." After a long while, her tongue naturally slid along the roof of her mouth, and she found herself making beautiful overtones. Then she lapsed into quiet meditation and her headache was gone.

Migraines are among the most painful headaches, and music can help sufferers to reduce their intensity, frequency, and duration. Psychologist Janet Lapp of California State University found that sufferers who had special training in the use of music, imagery, and relaxation, in two half-hour sessions per week for five weeks, reported on average 83 percent fewer headaches over the next year, and the episodes were milder and of shorter duration. Lapp also found that music could prevent the onset of a severe headache in those who had taken the training.

In a Polish study of 408 patients with severe headaches and neurological disorders, scientists reported that those who listened to concert music for six months required less medication and fewer painkilling drugs than controls.

Mary Scovel, a music therapist and co-editor of *Music Therapy Perspectives,* a clinical journal published by the National Association for Music Therapy, combines modern medicine with a more holistic approach. Scovel is the founder of Health Harmonics, a new technology that seeks to identify the "keynote" or dominant tone of an individual and supply the needed frequencies with the help of a sound table and headphones. "The key stimulus is sound," she explains. "Not just heard through the ears, but felt as vibrations through the whole body. As tones are reproduced and generated into the body, it causes symptoms to diminish long enough for the body to begin to heal itself."

Recently, Ruth, age forty-five, came to Scovel's office in Tahlequah, Oklahoma. She had a history of severe migraine headaches, and her symptoms included nausea and dizziness. Since her teenage years, doctors had attributed the migraines to stress. With time, they increased in frequency, and one day her husband came home to find her lying on the floor, vomiting. She was rushed to the hospital, where after a CAT scan (normal) and exhaustive testing, doctors attributed her migraines to allergies. However, the treatment for food allergies caused edema, so Ruth was taking fistfuls of medication: Dyazide, a diuretic; Aldactone, a hormone used as a diuretic for water retention; and Xanax, for stress.

Ruth was hopeful that sound and music could help her relax, and Scovel soon "prescribed" two specific frequencies. Ruth listened to these particular frequencies on a cassette tape, as well as to Mozart's *Symphony No. 39 in E flat,* (KV. 543) and piano concerto *No. 12 in A Major* (K. 414). She soon reported that her body "wanted the sound" because it took the headache away and completely relaxed her. After listening to "her" sounds and music for two weeks, her food allergies and edema were alleviated, the migraines subsided, and she was able to stop taking prescription drugs. Ruth still listens to her individualized sound frequency to reduce stress and stay balanced.

Heart disease, modern society's major cause of death, has lent itself to numerous music intervention studies. After installing a music listening system in its six-bed intensive care unit in 1976, Saint Joseph Hospital in New York reported a drop in heart attacks and a death rate 8 to 12 percent below the national average. In 1987, two researchers studied the cardiac rhythm responses of patients with advanced coronary heart disease to taped classical music. In the journal *Heart Lung* they reported a significant decrease in heart rate with no clinical arrhythmias and a change toward a happier emotional state.

As a critical care nurse, Cathie E. Guzzetta, R.N., Ph.D., the director of Holistic Nursing Consultants in Dallas, consultant at Parkland Memorial Hospital, and author of thirteen books, has worked with coronary patients for twenty-five years. On admission to the coronary care unit, she explains, most patients are short of breath, ashen, sweating, with low blood pressure, and a fast heart rate. Often they have an irregular heart rhythm. Sometimes they are close to death. In her pre-music therapy days, she could offer little in the way of mind/spirit care to stabilize their conditions, beyond the usual reassurances that things would be all right and the exhortation to "take a deep breath and try to relax." Guzzetta would watch helplessly as the usual medical interventions failed to put her patients at ease. Terrified of dying, their breathing grew shallow, their fists and jaws clenched tight, and they lost control of their emotions—sometimes with dire physiological consequences.

Guzzetta decided to try a "complementary" approach, and so began relaxation and music therapy sessions with her patients. Her medical colleagues, however, wanted more than personal testimonials and anecdotes. To satisfy them, she designed a research study at three hospitals in Washington, D.C. The study used three groups of patients. The first received relaxation sessions twice a day using Dr. Herbert Benson's "relaxation response" method, in which the practitioner concentrates on the breath, and on the exhale, repeats a simple mantra such as "one" or "relax." The second group received both relaxation and music therapy twice a day, with a choice of soothing popular, classical, or nontraditional music. The third group received no relaxation or music therapy.

One of her patients, Mr. B., a sixty-year-old chief of military police, was admitted to Walter Reed Army Medical Center following a heart attack. He was enrolled in the relaxation-music therapy group but decided to drop out of the study. Guzzetta persuaded him that responses to relaxation and music therapy took practice, just like learning to swim or ride a bike. Mr. B. stuck it out for three more sessions and couldn't believe the changes. "I thought relaxing was having a beer after work and going on a two-week vacation once a year," he told Guzzetta. "I have been walking around my whole life with a tight neck and shoulders and didn't even know it. I think I have learned how to let go of that. I never felt like this before."

Mr. G., another patient, also told Guzzetta he was "scared to death" of the cardiac catheterization procedure to determine whether one has an obstruction of the coronary arteries. Guzzetta counseled him on using the relaxation and music therapy he had learned and arranged for him to take his tapes, recorder, and headphones to the catheterization lab to help him cope with the stress. Afterward, he told her he had still been scared, but that the music and exercises had helped him get through the ordeal. "I felt like I had some control over the situation," he said. "I had something that *I* could do to help with the procedure and control my fear."

Altogether, the study included eighty heart patients. Relaxation and music therapy were effective in lowering mean heart rate from 100 to 82 beats per minute and systolic blood pressure from 150 to 130 mm/Hg. It also reduced cardiac complications and psychological anxiety, and raised peripheral temperatures from 72°F. to 94°F., an indication that patients were more relaxed. "But even before the data were analyzed," Guzzetta boasted, "I knew we had been effective in providing body/mind/spirit care to these patients."

Deepak Chopra, M.D., the mind/body researcher and best-selling author on holistic health, utilizes sound as medicine. In his book *Perfect Health* he describes the case of Agnes Reiner, an elderly woman suffering from angina pectoris, the recurrent dull chest pain that is a common precursor to heart attack. Between January and May when the angina began, Agnes suffered sixty spells of chest pain. Her cardiologist found serious blockage in her coronary arteries and prescribed nitroglycerin pills to relieve the discomfort. In June, Agnes came to see Chopra, who gave her a "primordial sound" to make every day, especially following the onset of angina.

Several months later, Agnes reported that her chest pain had stopped the day she began to practice the sound. It never returned. She stopped carrying nitroglycerin pills and, at age eighty, enrolled in college as a full-time student. "The degree of healing achieved by primordial sound varies from person to person," Chopra observes. "After three years of prescribing it, I have witnessed hundreds of cases where patients with heart disease, cancer, multiple sclerosis, and even AIDS have reported alleviation of pain, anxiety, and various other troubling symptoms." Although he cautioned this does not constitute scientific proof, Chopra concludes that sound healing is grounded in ancient wisdom and "can supplement the benefits of standard medical treatment."

♪ Hypertension (High Blood Pressure)

Hypertension or high blood pressure affects nearly 40 million Americans and is a major risk factor for heart attack, stroke, and peripheral artery disease. In a study with twenty coronary patients at a hospital associated with the University of South Carolina, a researcher reported in 1990 that listening to certain taped music programs lowered blood pressure. The tapes included pieces by Bach, Vivaldi, Bizet, Debussy, Cat Stevens, Nat King Cole, John Denver, Chet Atkins, Willie Nelson, and Judy Collins—all chosen to avoid dynamics that could trigger fearful or compulsive imagery.

In an article on the study in *Applied Research,* Phyllis Updike, R.N., D.N.S., a professor at the University of Colorado, observed that the sedative music reduced systolic blood pressure (from a mean of 124.3 to 118.6), diastolic blood pressure (78.8 to 75.7), heart rate (91.2 to 89.6), mean arterial pressure (94.3 to 75.7), and other improved heart values. Patients' anxiety was also decreased, their pain diminished, and the positive shift in physical and emotional responses outlasted the therapy itself. Several patients said afterward, "It was the only thirty minutes of peace I've known in days."

} Insomnia

Elizabeth was a trained psychotherapist who came to one of my workshops to learn how to use music more effectively with her clients. In a classroom demonstration, I asked her to make a sound and then "glide" it—make it go from high notes to low notes, from the top of her head to the bottom of her feet. As the sound moved, an odd gap of silence appeared in the middle range of her voice—a peculiar block that signaled tension being held. I asked her to lie down, hold a drum on her stomach, and make the sound again as she pounded it.

What happened was dramatic. As she drummed into her body, Elizabeth's voice opened up and a deep, rich sound emerged. She began to cry but continued to drum for five minutes, letting the rhythm enter her body. Afterward, I advised Elizabeth to continue toning, relaxing her jaw, and visualizing the middle of her body being filled with sound. Two weeks later, she confessed that for over five years she had been taking Halcion, one of the most addictive sleeping medications, for chronic insomnia. She believed that, as a result of her toning, the addiction was losing its hold. Within a month, Elizabeth returned to a normal sleep cycle without any medication and has slept soundly ever since.

Sleeping problems lend themselves to music therapy. In a study of twenty-five elderly patients at the University of Louisville's School of Medicine, men and women listened to Baroque and New Age music that was slightly slower than a normal heartbeat. According to a 1996 report in the *Journal of Holistic Nursing*, all patients except one reported an improvement in sleep, and several were able to discontinue their medication for insomnia.

} Learning Disabilities

About 25 percent of the U.S. population is, to some degree, learning disabled. (The figure is as high as 90 percent in the prison population.) Music and listening therapy is helping to correct this condition in schools, clinics, prisons, and other institutions worldwide. The Tomatis method has been particularly successful.

Eric's life was a succession of failures. He barely graduated from high school and drifted from job to job. He spent his days in the street skateboarding and meeting friends, most of whom were as immature as he was. When his mother dragged him to the office of the Tomatis Listening and Learning Center in Lafayette, California, he was twenty-five, unemployed, and dependent on his parents, with whom he had a nasty relationship. His thoughts seemed confused, he had a hard time expressing himself, and he admitted to trainer Pierre Sollier that he smoked pot.

Coming to the Center structured Eric's days, and he was happy about the attention he was receiving. The breakthrough came during the second intensive exercise, when he discovered that what he'd been listening to was a filtered version of his mother's voice. He suddenly felt a tremendous rush of energy, and Sollier and other trainers jumped in with counseling sessions to channel this new energy.

One day Eric announced, to the amazement of his parents, that he was going to college. His grandmother had offered a long time earlier to pay the tuition, and he was now going to use this opportunity. Sollier helped him with the application process, and he went on to enroll at a college for the learning disabled in Vermont. A year later, his mother sent a note to the Tomatis Center reporting that the first year had gone well and that Eric was returning for his second.

Jim Asaff and his wife had always known that their thirteen-year-old son, Harl, was bright. The Dallas youngster expressed himself eloquently in words and was at ease with people, but found it excruciatingly difficult to read, write, or tell time. Specialists labeled his condition *dysgraphic,* and for the eight years since he had been diagnosed, Harl had experienced increasing frustration in school, where a premium is placed on written performance.

Directed to the Tomatis Center in Toronto, the Asaffs were surprised to see changes in their son within three days of beginning the listening program. Harl first developed a sense of direction, which freed him, his parents observed, from the constant fear of getting lost. He asked them about childhood incidents that he previously could not recall. He began to tell time. He played more freely with other children, was more affectionate, and had fewer flashes of anger and frustration. After seven days, his parents asked him to read aloud, a previously terrifying experience. To their amazement, Harl's pronunciation and word punctuation had improved. They noticed that he would laugh at difficult passages rather than cry. Watching a production of Shakespeare, he laughed at all the right jokes, in all five acts of complicated Elizabethan verse!

During the summer, Harl's attention span lengthened and coordination improved. When school began, he completed his assignments and, for the first time, started writing. By the end of the school year, his fluency with written work began to match that of his verbal speech. Harl went on to do volunteer work with learning disabled children a few hours a week and was accepted into a college-sponsored Talented and Gifted (TAG) program. In gratitude, the Asaffs opened and now manage the Tomatis Listening Center in Dallas.

₹ Menopause

Many women experience tremendous discomfort during and after menopause. My student Joy is a good example. For ten years she suffered from hot flashes. Doctors told her that her body had lost its ability to produce and assimilate estrogen, and put her on estrogen-replacement therapy. The therapy helped control the more extreme symptoms, but Joy didn't like the idea of lifelong hormone therapy and began searching for natural alternatives.

Studying with me, she did daily toning exercises to correct the slight auditory decline that accompanies aging and to alleviate her symptoms. She practiced making vowel sounds in various postures for ten to fifteen minutes each day, focusing particularly on the pelvic area. Within three weeks, she felt like a new person. Her hot flashes entirely disappeared. She was amazed when her doctor told her she no longer needed to take medication. Joy continues to be free of symptoms today.

⟩ Neuromuscular and Skeletal Disorders

Neuromuscular and skeletal disorders affect twenty million Americans and are among the most painful and crippling afflictions. Sufferers are prevented from working, studying, traveling, and other daily pursuits. In a recent experiment, music and rhythmic stimulation were used to treat twenty-five people with gait disabilities or abnormal walking speeds. The subjects included sixteen adults, aged fifty-two to eighty-seven, from several nursing homes, a hospital, and a senior citizens' housing project, suffering from stroke, spastic disorders, or painful arthritic or scoliotic conditions. Five marches were selected to provide a strong beat and clear tempo that could easily be matched by walking, among them "Stars and Stripes Forever," "Grand March" from Verdi's *Aida*, "Seventy-six Trombones" from *The Music Man*, and "Semper Fidelis." Subjects were given cassette recorders and headphones and instructed to step either on the first beat, the first and third beat, on all four beats, or once every eight beats according to their ability. The greatest gain was made by a sixty-six-year-old male stroke patient whose walking rate improved from a thirty-second lag between each step to less than one second. Ten achieved a normal rhythm, and nine reduced their lag to only two to three seconds. A small number of children were also included in the study. A seven-year-old child with spina bifida went from a delay of seventeen to eight seconds between steps.

⟩ Overweight

Teenage girls are especially conscious of their weight, and weight-related conditions, including anorexia, bulimia, and obesity are alarmingly widespread. Anna, an overweight and emotionally withdrawn teenager, found herself listening to rock music to ease her depression. The more depressed she felt, the louder she turned up the volume. Eventually, she visited sound healer Joy Gardner-Gordon, who taught her how to tone as a means of expressing her pain. As she verbalized her feelings through sound, her depression lifted, her confidence and self-esteem improved, and she felt like a new person. "[Rock stars] do everything that a teenager's parents tell them not to do," Gardner-Gordon explains. "Once Anna gave herself permission to scream and yell, she no longer needed the rock stars to do it for her." Anna's compulsive overeating stopped, and she lost forty pounds in the next two months. Although she still listens to particular rock artists on occasion, she has no interest in doing so at ruinous volumes or for extended lengths of time.

Nearly one-half of the people in modern society are overweight. In developing countries, overweight and obesity (gross overweight) are also an increasing problem. One of the first studies of the effects of music therapy on weight loss was recently conducted in China. Chen, a thirty-four-year-old physician, stood five-feet-one-and-a-half inches and weighed 168 pounds. She had become progressively fatter over the last four years. Pale, listless, and short of breath, Chen had many symptoms of obesity, including an irregular pulse, swollen hands and feet, a coated tongue, loose stools, and depression.

On May 1, 1993, Chen began a holistic treatment combining music therapy, exercise, and diet. She listened to Section 1 of *Obesity*, a Chinese weight-loss music CD, three times before meals and performed some moderate physical exercises on an empty stomach. Chen also drank some traditional Chinese herbs. One month later, her weight had dropped 7.7 pounds. Beginning on June 5, pressure points were stimulated twice a day on Chen with an electrical apparatus that affected acupuncture points with music. By August 30, her body weight dropped to a more healthful 128 pounds, and researchers attributed her remarkable improvement primarily to the musical component of her treatment.

♩ Paranoia and War Propaganda

Willis Conover is not a household name, at least in the United States. But in Russia and the former Soviet Republics, Conover—even more than Mikhail Gorbachev—is regarded as the man who ended the Cold War. The host of the Voice of America *Jazz Hour* from 1955, Conover treated an estimated thirty million listeners behind the Iron Curtain to a nightly two-hour program of jazz and other rhythmic music officially labeled "decadent" and banned by the authorities. On his death in 1996, the *New York Times* eulogized him as the man "who fought the Cold War with cool music, capturing the hearts and liberating the spirits of millions of listeners trapped behind the Iron Curtain." The editorial went on to say that Conover "proved more effective than a fleet of B-29s. No wonder. Six nights a week he would take the A Train straight into the Communist heartland." In few instances in history has music proven so potent at keeping the spirits of oppressed people alive. Like the walls of Jericho that fell to the trumpets' blast, the Berlin Wall and the edifice of world Communism withered to the accompaniment of Duke Ellington, John Coltrane, and Billy Taylor.

♩ Parkinson's Disease

Ronald Price, Ph.D., a music professor at Northern Illinois University, was struck, in his mid-twenties, with Parkinson's disease, a degenerative neurological disorder. His doctors, who feared for his recovery, also found that he suffered from cerebral palsy. Although he played the French horn, Price was intrigued by the harp, an ancient healing instrument, and discovered that plucking the strings for several hours caused his symptoms to go away. Determined to take his "medicine" more seriously, he became a professional harpist and developed the stamina to play several hours daily. The harp has kept him relatively free of symptoms, but when he does not play music for several days, the symptoms return. His speech becomes garbled, one side of his face slackens, and he loses control of his left arm and leg.

It is clear to medical researchers that harp playing greatly improves the motor skills of those suffering from Parkinson's Disease. The pattern of neuron firings, as we have seen in earlier chapters, is inherently musical. In plain English, the harp music helps the Parkinson patient to retune.

With this in mind, Price has formed Healing Harps, an ensemble that includes other performers with disabilities. The group works actively with medical clinicians to help gain insight into the therapeutic process.

❧ Pregnancy and Labor

The use of music during pregnancy, delivery, and infancy constitutes one of the fastest growing fields of music therapy and intervention. The Tomatis listening method has been shown to be especially successful for expectant mothers. In a study at the Vesoul Hospital in France, researchers reported that pregnant women who participated in four weeks of Tomatis training during the eighth month of pregnancy spent less time in the hospital and had fewer complications. Fifty women were divided into three groups, one with conventional prepartum preparation, one with no preparation at all, and one immersed in Tomatis listening techniques. The first group had an average labor time of three hours and thirty minutes, the second four hours, and the Tomatis group a mere two hours and thirty minutes. Cesarean sections were required in only 4 percent of the Tomatis group, versus 13 percent of the prepared group and 15 percent of the unprepared group. Sixty percent of the Tomatis patients needed no medication, in contrast to 46 percent of the conventionally prepared and 50 percent of the unprepared mothers. Women using the Tomatis method also expressed less worry about giving birth.

As a result of studies like this, hospitals and maternity clinics have begun to make music therapy available. In Austin, Texas, consultants Hope Young and Karen May work with women and their obstetricians to prevent unexpected complications. Prior to delivery, prospective parents select music they enjoy and that is appropriate to the stage of labor. The therapists use a variety of tapes—classical, rock & roll, country-western, and blues, played on piano, guitar, and winds, Young explained in the *Journal of the American Medical Association.*

During labor, the volume of the music is regulated by a handheld remote, which gives the mother a sense of control over her environment. In the early stages of labor, the music is slow, relaxing, and peaceful, with little change in volume or tempo. In the later stages, the tempo increases, and the steady beat helps pace the mother's stronger physical exertions. Following the birth of the child, the woman and her partner listen to a meaningful song or musical selection they have chosen beforehand, as a way of marking the joyful occasion.

Certified childbirth educator Beverly Pierce has taught toning to her classes for three years, and the response from women and couples has been positive. Many of the women who toned during pregnancy describe the experience as calming—a way to stay centered during a time of deep personal change. Belinda, for example, used mostly an *"Mmm"* for five to fifteen minutes in the lowest tones she could reach. The vibrations reverberated through her trunk, from her neck to her lower abdomen. She had an unusually stressful family life, but credits her toning with pulling her (and her baby) through the pregnancy healthy and calm.

Karen, a professional with a distracting, highly stressful job, was in a constant state of doubt about the childbirth choices she had made. She toned for ten minutes eight times a week. The sessions calmed her down and kept her focused on internal sensations. "One could say that, for Karen," says Pierce, "toning was practice in listening to herself."

Priscilla used tone to deal effectively with common pregnancy discomforts. For intensely painful leg cramps, she tried toning *"Oh,"* sending the sound down toward her leg and feeling it vibrate there. "It helped me get through," she says. Another woman, Sarah, toned *"Ah"* and *"Oh"* during Braxton-Hicks (late pregnancy) contractions, and the sounds helped her align her body and stay focused.

Some women don't tone during pregnancy because it makes them feel silly. But once they've been introduced to the technique, you can bet they pull it out when the pain of giving birth becomes intense. Katherine, for whom toning had felt "awkward," found herself using a low *"Uh"* during torturous contractions. Closing her eyes and going deep inside herself, she let the low sound radiate soothingly through her body. Once, while pushing, her tone became high and frantic—which only made things worse. Pierce saw what was happening and guided Katherine in lowering and slowing down the tone, helping her to feel relaxed and open again.

New mothers have found toning to be helpful after birth, sometimes in calming the baby. Linda, who toned every evening during pregnancy, began toning again when her boy was a few months old, and was delighted to hear him join in with her. When he was six months of age, there were nights when he toned himself to sleep!

ᔐ Prejudice and Discrimination

In his autobiography *An Easy Burden*, the Reverend Andrew Young, a close associate of Dr. Martin Luther King Jr., describes the powerful role that music played in the civil rights movement: "We could hear this unity in the singing voices and speaking voices of the people; it seemed we could even hear it in the earth itself, like a soft rumbling, a rhythmic beating of drums from all over the South. It was a knowing, with undeniable and unshakable conviction, that our time had come. The South would never be the same again."

Depicting the struggle as "The Singing Movement," Young goes on to say that, through music, a great secret was discovered: "Black people, otherwise cowed, discouraged, and faced with innumerable and insuperable obstacles, could transcend all those difficulties and forge a new determination, a new faith and strength, when fortified with song."

As an example, Young tells the story of one freedom meeting at a church in rural Georgia that was interrupted by the arrival of the sheriff and his deputies. The people were terrified as the sheriff warned them not to talk about registering to vote, and vowed that there would be no Freedom Riders in his county. Then, slowly, the congregation began to hum "We'll Never Turn Back." As the humming intensified, accompanied by singing and moaning, the sounds in the church entirely drowned out the officers. "The sheriff didn't know what to do," Young notes. "He seemed to be afraid to tell the people to shut up. Finally, he and his men just turned their backs and stomped out. Those beautiful people sang that sheriff right out of their church!'"

⨾ Premature Birth

Besides the mother, siblings and other family members can assist musically in the birthing process. When Kay was pregnant with her second child, her three-year-old son, Michael, would sing a song every night to the unborn baby. Although the pregnancy was normal, complications developed during delivery, and the tiny infant, a girl, was rushed to the Neonatal Intensive Care unit at Saint Mary's Hospital in Knoxville, Tennessee. Despite the doctors' efforts, the baby's condition worsened, and the pediatric specialist told the family her death was imminent.

In the hospital, young Michael constantly asked to see his little sister, and, in the second week, his parents dressed him in an oversize scrub suit and took him to the ICU. The medical staff was angry because a three-year-old had been admitted to the unit, but his mother refused to remove him, saying, "He is not leaving until he sings to his sister." Michael made his way to the bassinet that held his little sister and began to sing:

> You are my sunshine, my only sunshine,
> You make me happy when skies are gray.
> You'll never know, dear, how much I love you,
> Please don't take my sunshine away.

Woman's Day magazine later called it the "miracle of a brother's song." Kay, a devout Methodist, called it a miracle of God's love. The doctor just called it a miracle. The next day, when they might have been planning a funeral, they took Michael's little sister home. She had responded immediately to the familiar voice of her brother.

Birth weight is a major predictor of survival and development, and Dr. Lee Salk, one of the first researchers to study the effect of sound in the womb and after birth, reported that babies who hear heartbeats gain more weight and develop more quickly than those who are separated from their mothers. Jacqueline Sue Chapman, a New York University doctoral student, found that music could help premature babies gain weight and become stronger. In a study of 153 "premies" in three hospitals, the group of babies exposed to Brahms's "Lullaby" six times a day were ready to go home a week earlier on average than those who heard no lullaby. As *American Health* reported, the music soothed the babies, reducing their crying and extraneous movements, enabling them to conserve the energy necessary for survival.

♪ Psychosocial Development

Handicapped children often lag behind other children, become withdrawn, and have poor social skills. In a study of music's effect on socialization, twelve handicapped children, aged three to five, were invited to participate in a music program with fifteen four-year-olds from a preschool. The students met together once a week for eight months. Social interaction among the students increased from 69 percent at the beginning of the study to 93 percent at the end. Students who chose partners from the other group increased from 7 percent to 46 percent. The researcher concluded that when children with disabilities listen to music and play with other children they loosen up and become friendlier.

♪ Rehabilitation

At Bryn Mawr Rehab, a rehabilitation center in Malvern, Pennsylvania, music therapist Connie Eichenberg uses music and imaging techniques to help patients focus on mastering their pain. During a recent group session, she and volunteer Peter Patane let patients select musical instruments from a shopping cart that included drums, cow bells, and other homemade instruments.

Ed Ghamyem, who had spinal meningitis and suffered from a pounding inside his head, selected a wooden drum and drumsticks, while Richard Fleming, a former beekeeper recovering from a stroke, chose a large, white, latex house paint bucket that he beat with a large, sponge-tipped drumstick. While Eichenberg and Patane accompanied them with soothing instruments simulating the sound of ocean waves, the two men played their drums. By visualizing their pain and developing the ability to mask it with sound, they gained control over their physical disabilities and developed a sense of deep inner peace.

⟩ Schizophrenia

Nearly forty years ago, Paul Moses, M.D., an ear, nose, and throat specialist who studied vocal sounds and neurosis at Stanford University School of Medicine, discovered a recurring pattern in his schizophrenic patients. He found that their voices were more rhythmic than melodious. Higher tones dominated, and there was little nasal resonance. The voice could not glide; it jumped from scale to scale, and words were accented strangely.

As new styles were introduced into patients' speaking and humming voices, Moses found that some of their neurotic and psychotic patterns disappeared. Singing was of little help, but humming, speaking, and creative vocal dialogue with patients did modify their behavior.

Following up on Moses' insights, the U.S. Alcohol, Drug Abuse, and Mental Health Administration reported the results of a study in which schizophrenics proved less likely to hear hallucinatory voices if they hummed softly. Doctors at the UCLA Research Center at Camarillo State Hospital found that humming masked other sounds, including normally inaudible muscular activity that might be perceived as voices. They found that humming the *Mmmm* sound very quietly resulted in a 59 percent reduction in auditory hallucinations in hospitalized patients with this disease.

In a large case-control study of forty-one adults with schizophrenia, researchers at the Royal Edinburgh Hospital and the University of Edinburgh in Scotland reported that patients who attended a series of individual music therapy sessions experienced clinical improvement. Experimental subjects received one individual music therapy session a week for ten weeks, while controls received the therapy only in the first and tenth week.

The patients were encouraged to improvise on a variety of instruments, including bongo drums, bass drums, side drums, cymbals, marimbas, and xylophones. In the course of these sessions, as they began to improvise, they improved their abilities to listen and cooperate with each other. Interestingly, the most severely ill patients showed the most improvement, as the music making supported the development of an intimate, nonverbal interaction and enhanced the quality of patients' communications skills.

⟩ Stroke

Music has been especially helpful in stroke rehabilitation. In a study reported in the *Journal of the American Medical Association*, Colorado researchers found that stroke patients who were given rhythmic auditory stimulation a half hour a day for three weeks had improved cadence, stride, and foot placement compared with a control group. The rhythmic stimulation, or cueing, was delivered by metronome pulses embedded in music of the patients' choice, which was recorded on audiotapes and listened to over headphones. The researchers further found that the effect of the music therapy was lasting. They found that the patients retained the walking pattern they acquired during the training and could accurately reproduce their new stride thereafter. Dr. Michael Thaut, a prominent music therapist and the chief researcher, attributed the improvement to an entrainment effect that enhances the normal mechanism in the brain damaged by the stroke.

The journal further reported that in a case-controlled study in

Scotland of long-term institutionalized stroke patients, subjects chosen randomly and given music therapy had less depression and anxiety and more emotional stability and motivation to communicate than patients receiving standard care.

⟨ Substance Abuse

Sound and music can play an important role in treating alcoholism, drug addiction, and smoking, as well as the codependency issues surrounding substance abuse. Ginny Helfrich, a nationally certified chemical dependency counselor in the Seattle area, has helped many clients with the daily maintenance of a recovery lifestyle. Helfrich has found that teaching people to "sound" the emotions they feel—and thereby listen to their unresolved pain— makes it easier for them to connect with issues surrounding their addiction. "Often these unresolved issues have plagued them for many years," she says, "and they have tried to medicate their inner pain with drugs, alcohol, overeating, or various denial or transference behaviors or attitudes. Having expressed these locked-up negative emotions, they can move on to develop more positive and healthy ways of living."

One of her clients was Ted, a severely depressed, thirty-four-year-old recovering alcoholic and drug addict with two years sobriety as an active AA member. His chemically addicted wife of fourteen years was leaving him, having decided that she liked him better during his "carefree," irresponsible years. Ted was deeply worried about how the separation would affect their three children. Beyond that, it brought up traumatic, unresolved feelings from his childhood. Since sixth grade, he had learned to control his emotional pain by smoking marijuana and drinking alcohol. During his active years of substance abuse, he had often raged and been physically destructive.

As his therapeutic relationship with Helfrich grew, Ted learned to identify and connect with his suppressed feelings and to release his negative energy by exhaling on a long vowel sound. One toning session became the turning point in his recovery process: He recalled, toned through, and released a violent childhood experience of physical and sexual abuse. Ted found that he could tone daily during his AA meditation time, when he got frustrated on the job, or when his impending divorce threatened to send him back into the depression from which he had so triumphantly emerged.

Another recovering alcoholic, Trudi, a sixty-five-year-old "war bride" of a retiring army general, had found that a daily glass or two or wine helped her cope with the anxiety attacks she had suffered for years with the demands of being a commander's wife. Now, however, the attacks were growing worse, and the "wine remedy" didn't work anymore. As Trudi gained some abstinence time, she found that "breathing on a tone" when she felt anxiety helped her remain connected to her positive thoughts and empowering energy. The toning helped her to stay sober as well.

Listening to music can also play a role in helping people to stop smoking, especially in conjunction with guided imagery and meditation. Loretta, a mother of four, had returned to school to finish her degree at a small community college in Kalispell, Montana, and was taking a classical music appreciation class with Chris Brewer, a musician and music therapist. Asked to isolate an aspect of her life that she would like to change, Loretta chose to focus on her smoking, and on what it would be like to give it up.

As part of the class, students listened to three musical selections and had the option of sitting, lying quietly, or drawing images within circles. Following the experience, they recorded their insights in their journal. Loretta later told Brewer that she had seen herself "filled with blackness," as if she were being suffocated by tobacco smoke. A vision of her children filled her with the urge to be free of this "darkness." When she envisioned herself no longer smoking, she felt a wonderful sensation of freedom, cleanliness, and lightness. Her desire to smoke, she told Brewer, had vanished. Any time she was confronted with her habit, the picture and feeling of that darkness returned, and she lost any thought of or craving for cigarettes.

} Tinnitus

One of the most common hearing disorders is tinnitus, or ringing in the ears. An estimated 10 percent of the population will, at some time in their lives, suffer from this painful—and maddening—affliction. Well-known sufferers include William Shatner and Leonard Nimoy of *Star Trek*, actor Steve Martin, and former First Lady Rosalynn Carter.

A wide variety of things can trigger this condition, including high blood pressure, arteriosclerosis, respiratory infection, muscular sclerosis, nutritional deficiencies, TMJ, migraines, anemia, and Paget's disease. Sounds in the ears can also be caused by an explosion or exposure to loud noise, or even by medication. *The Physician's Desk Reference* lists more than seventy drugs that can generate or worsen tinnitus, including aspirin, Quinine, diuretics, and aminoglycoside antibiotics. Coffee, tea, and cigarettes, as well as MSG, birth control pills, artificial food colors, and marijuana have all been thought to worsen ringing in the ears.

Tinnitus takes many forms, and there is no standard treatment. Chronic cases can last years, and the intensity of the sounds has completely disabled many sufferers, even driving some to suicide. Seldom cured, it can be made more manageable. Current treatments include hearing aids, biofeedback, drug therapy, nutritional supplements, electrical suppression, and acupuncture.

One of the most promising new treatments is "masking." From ancient times, it has been known that external sounds can inhibit tinnitus. "Why is it," asked Hippocrates, the father of medicine, "that buzzing in the ears ceases if one makes a sound?" The contemporary application of this principle dates to a providential meeting between Jack Vernon, a scientist researching tinnitus for the National Institutes of Health, and Dr. Charles Unice, the head of the American Tinnitus Association and himself a tinnitus sufferer. During one of their meetings in Portland, the two men walked through a park to have lunch. As they passed a cascading fountain, Unice realized that he could not hear the ringing in his ears. The gentle sounds of splashing water completely overrode it!

Out of this encounter came the idea for a small hearing-aidlike device that could emit its own sound and drown out unwanted ringing. Vernon contacted major hearing aid companies, and the upshot was a small, portable invention called a masker. Early models generated a spectrum of sound that included the specific frequency of the tinnitus. Subsequent research in Japan has found that some patients get better results with frequencies similar but not identical to the pitch of their ringing. Both kinds of model are now available, and 70 percent of tinnitus patients report at least partial relief.

≀ Toilet Training

Like a lot of children, Sherri was not properly toilet trained. Desperate, her parents and teachers approached Deforia Lane, a music therapist at the Rainbow Babies and Children's Hospital in Cleveland. Noting that Sherri would focus and settle down when she heard music, Lane rigged up a small portable toilet that played a tune. When Sherri urinated, "Mary Had a Little Lamb" would be played. Realizing that she had caused this, the little girl reacted gleeflully, and stopped wringing her hands as she had done previously. "Eventually," notes Lane, in her book *Music as Medicine,* "she learned not only to go in the potty but also to pee slowly, so that she could make the music last longer."

≀ Tooth Problems

In many dental offices, music is moving from the waiting room to the operating room. A quarter century ago, Dr. Wallace J. Gardner, a Boston dentist, reported that music and sound were "fully effective" in suppressing pain for 65 percent of 1,000 patients who had previously required nitrous oxide or a local anesthetic. For another 25 percent, audio-analgesia was sufficiently effective that nothing else was needed. The patients held a small control box and listened to music and sound, including a waterfall-like noise, on headphones. Eight other doctors in the Boston area who joined Gardner's experiment reported that sound was the only analgesic required in 5,000 operations. In an article in *Science,* Gardner further reported that he had extracted over 200 teeth "without encountering any difficulty or report of objectionable pain."

Putting the Mozart Effect into action, Robert A. Wortzel, D.M.D., a dentist from Summit, New Jersey, was doing a root canal on a patient named Dave, who played guitar at local clubs. After the first session, Dave admitted to feeling considerable fear and expressed a desire to hold his guitar and play it during treatment. Wortzel agreed that this might counter the loud and irritating sounds of the root canal, and he ordered a travel electric guitar that was two feet long, along with a headphone amplifier. At the next visit, all went harmoniously. "Dave was off in another world," Wortzel reports. "His body and jaw were totally relaxed, and I was able to easily perform my dental work." Wortzel went on to produce a children's tape, *A Trip to the Dentist Can Be Fun!,* that pokes fun at many of the fear-enhancing sounds associated with a visit to the dentist.

Toning, or even simple groaning exercises, can mask and offset the chaotic sounds of the random pink noise (for example, the roar of thunder and loud winds) generated during drilling. Sometimes self-generated sounds can even make dental treatment unnecessary. Alex Jack, a teacher at the Kushi Institute in Becket, Massachusetts, developed a painful abcess above his top left front tooth. The dietary remedies that he had employed successfully in the past didn't work. One morning, he started humming to *Ancient Noels,* a cassette of traditional Christmas carols that he was listening to in his car. After fifteen minutes, the level of pain dropped dramatically, affording him the first relief in several days. "Humming 'Silent Night' worked wonders," he says. "Through a combination of sound diet and nutritious sounds, the abcess proceeded to clear up."

❬ Trauma

Maria was born prematurely, with a harelip, into a German Catholic family in 1939. Her mother died in the hospital shortly afterward, and she was raised by her mother's sister, who consented to marry the father in order to care for the child. Because of her disability, Maria almost choked in the hospital's incubator when she couldn't drink from the nipple of the bottle stuck into her mouth.

As a small child, Maria's speech was so severely affected that only her parents could understand her. Germany in the early 1940s was caught up in genocidal madness, which marked for death not only Jews, but all others not considered "good stock" for the fatherland. This included the disabled and handicapped, whom the Nazis shipped off to "hospitals," where they inevitably disappeared.

One day, when little Maria was playing in the garden, she heard her neighbor say, "How could they let that thing live?" Maria says she knew then that she must never cry, complain, or make sounds that were "not right"; otherwise, she could be killed. It was as though a trap door had snapped shut, locking her in a transparent cage where she could be seen but never heard.

Years later, Maria had an operation on her lip and learned to speak intelligibly, if not with full expression. Molly Scott, M.Ed., a psychotherapist, singer, composer, and creator of Resonance Therapy, a mind/body practice focused on the voice, met Maria in Hamburg when she came in for counseling. Scott invited her to get in touch with her body, which she believed contained the wisdom she needed to heal herself. Maria stood up, trembling. First, she made small *"Uh"* sounds. Then came *"Ah."* With that opening, the tones crescendoed, alternating with choking sobs as the anguish and fear of that muffled childhood flowed from her body on her voice. From time to time, she would stop sounding and stand as though frozen, and Scott would ask if she wished to continue. Maria said yes. She knew she had to push herself beyond her own physical instrument.

After several sessions in the safety of the studio, Maria gained confidence in her ability to open her voice without eliciting punishment or reprisal. It was of critical importance that this process occur in the presence of another person. Maria now had tools that she could use on her own, sounding her feelings in the privacy of her home, her car, or her office—tools that allowed her to reclaim the sonic birthright of the child who thought she must be silent in order to live.

Elena suffered from enforced silence, too. Like Anne Frank in

Holland, her life changed in the space of a day, when her family was forced out of its comfortable Belgium home and into hiding from the Nazis. During daylight hours, the family had to huddle in a dark basement, the windows covered so that no one would suspect anyone of living there. Elena was two years old—an age when most children are beginning to learn and enjoy speaking. Now she needed to be absolutely quiet: her life and the lives of her family depended on it. At night, on rare occasions, they would venture cautiously out to the street, but during the day the family remained silent in the darkness.

Many years later, Elena, a therapist herself, came to see Molly Scott because she felt blocked vocally and had a feeling that sound held the key to her healing. Scott demonstrated a basic, voice-opening technique—a long sweep of the voice from very low to very high and back again. Elena hit the floor in terror, trembling and in tears. The sound had awakened memories of the sirens in the city before the bombs hit. "Because of her confinement and enforced silence, she had experienced no peals of laughter, no childhood screams of rage or frustration, no giggles of delight," Scott observes. "It was no wonder that sound held such secrets for her."

In the course of her musical sessions, Elena relived and released suppressed memories and feelings surrounding the two years that she and her family lived in that cellar. The work of opening her voice was arduous, but ultimately revelatory. "Regaining a lost part of her resonance," Scott concludes, "Elena began to regain not only a missing part of her development, but access to renewed resources of vitality, creativity, and joy."

Sister Mary Elizabeth had a bad knee, damaged in an accident twenty years earlier that had necessitated the removal of loose carti-lage. Subsequently, stiffness and arthritic pain set in. She was espe-cially aware of it in church, where she would have to kneel stiffly with her right leg extended behind her. Sister Mary Elizabeth was also a music therapist in a large city hospital. She believed in the healing powers of music and had seen its effects on children, adoles-cents, and the terminally ill. To enhance her skills, she enrolled in a two-year certification program using music and imagery. She hoped it would prove helpful at the hospital, especially the burn ward.

During her training, she was surprised at what she learned about herself—at the images and feelings that bubbled up relating to her childhood. Adopted as an infant, she had spent years trying to find her birth mother, whom she finally found when she was twenty-one, in a nursing home, in the last stages of encephalitis. Her birth mother, fifty-five years old, was unable to talk and stared numbly at the daughter she had given up long ago. Relatives told her the story. Her mother had gotten pregnant four years after the death of her husband. Since, at the time, out of wedlock pregnancy was a disgrace, she went off to have the baby in secret. Mary was put up for adoption immediately after birth.

Working with imagery and music, Mary encountered emotionally charged images of fear and abandonment. During one session, she suddenly stiffened in a spasm, reporting later that she felt as if an electrical current had shot through her body. Carol A. Bush, Mary's trainer, became concerned she was having a seizure. But after the session, Mary appeared calm, almost beatific. "We had no time to discuss the details of this journey, since she had to hurry to attend an evening mass at a nearby convent," Bush observed. "Later as we discussed that session she recalled with awe that she had been peacefully kneeling through half of the mass when she realized she was on her damaged knee. For the first time in twenty years, it was pain free!"

Later, Mary's doctor expressed amazement at how flexible and pain-free her knee had become. From the medical view, it was not clear how the knee problem related to the release of long-held emotions. However, in Oriental medicine, knees (and elbows) are governed by the liver, which is considered the seat of anger. It's possible that by releasing her childhood anger over her abandonment, Mary let go of stiffness that had accumulated over many years in this region of her body. Concluded Bush, "Sister Mary Elizabeth feels her life has changed as a result of her work with imagery and music. She has become lighter in body and spirit, and the healing of her knee told her that indeed God and music had always been there for her."

⸲ Writer's Block

Elaine, a middle-aged, single mother, came to the Sound Listening and Learning Center in Phoenix for help with her nine-year-old son Ross. He was not reading yet, had experienced many problems in school, and could not communicate with her. After attending the first thirty minutes of the free parent listening program, Elaine asked to be switched to her own individual full-length program, sensing intuitively that the Tomatis Method would help her as well as her son. She told director Billie M. Thompson that for years she felt weary, unmotivated, and unhappy with her job as a scientific word processor. She was discouraged by her and her son's problems and had a recurring pattern of getting excited about something, starting, stopping, then getting depressed.

Elaine vividly described a recurring dream of watching a grasshopper jumping from place to place in a field, but getting nowhere. One of her goals was to be a writer, but she feared the same cycle of defeat. She felt she couldn't write well enough to take a university level poetry class.

Elaine began writing fluidly during the Tomatis listening training, and afterward submitted a portfolio of poems to the university and was accepted for the course. She did so well that she was asked to enroll for a master's degree in writing at the University of New Mexico. Quitting her dead-end job to become a full-time student and pursue her dream of becoming a writer, Elaine is now working on two major projects, including a book. Imbued with self-confidence, she sent the Tomatis staff a poem about the new relationship that she has with her son. Many people like Elaine need only a catalyst to overcome anxiety and self-doubt and give themselves permission to be creative.

In ancient Greece, Apollo was recognized as both the God of Medicine and the God of Music. The celestial harmony and the earthly harmony were considered one. Since then, healing and art, body and mind, the analytical and the intuitive, have gradually separated. As Novalis, the Enlightenment philosopher quoted at the beginning of this section observed, every illness is a musical problem. As these many case reports, scientific studies, and anecdotes show, every type of music has healing potential. Ideally, there is a musical solution for every person, if not for every illness.

Sound Resources

Music and Medicine

Institute for Music and Neurologic Function
Beth Abraham Family of Health Services
612 Allerton Avenue
Bronx, NY 10469
(718) 519-5840
www.musichaspower.org
> *Offers a wide range of therapies, research, and education under the guidance of Concetta M. Tomaino, D.A., MT-BC, Vice President of Music Therapy at Beth Abraham and Director of the Institute for Music and Neurologic Function.*

International Society for Music in Medicine
Ralph Sprintge, Director
Sportkrankanhaus Hellerson
Paulmannshoher Strasse 17
D-5880 Ludenscheild, Germany
> *Leading international organization involved in research, conferences, and publishing.*

MuSICA (Music and Science Information Computer Archive)
c/o Dr. Norman M. Weinberger
Center for the Neurobiology of Learning and Memory
University of California, Irvine
Irvine, CA 92717

E-mail: mbic@mila.ps.uci.edu
> Formerly MBIC (Music and Brain Information Center), this re-
> source has many thousands of entries and is updated regularly.

Music and Healing

The Mozart Effect® Resource Center
3526 Washington Avenue
Saint Louis, MO 63103-1019
(800) 721-2177 (U.S./CANADA)
(314) 531-4756
Email for orders: music@mozarteffect.com
Email for information: info@mozarteffect.com
www.mozarteffect.com
> For information on seminars, workshops, and classes by Don G.
> Campbell, as well as books and tapes by mail order.

Music for the Mozart Effect®, Vols. I–V
Spring Hill Music
P.O. Box 800
Boulder, CO 80306
(800) 721-2177
(303) 938-1188
Email: info@springhillmedia.com
www.springhillmedia.com

The Mozart Effect®—Music for Children, Vols. I–IV
Music for Newborns, Babies, and Moms and Moms-to-Be
The Children's Group
1400 Bayly Street, #7
Pickering, ON L1W 3R2
CANADA
(800) 668-0242 (U.S.)
(800) 757-8372 (CANADA)
(905) 831-1995
Email: moreinfo@childrensgroup.com
www.childrensgroup.com

The Open Ear Center
Pat Moffitt Cook, Director
P.O. Box 10276
Bainbridge Island, WA 98110
(206) 842-5560
Email: openear@nwlink.com
www.openearcenter.com
> *Offers courses, seminars, and resources for music and healing.*

Chalice of Repose Project
Therese Schroeder-Sheker, Coordinator
School of Music-Thanatology
312 E. Pine Street
Missoula, MT 59802
(406) 542-0001, ext. 2810
Email: chalice1@saintpatrick.org
www.saintpatrick.org/chalice
> *Offers music-thanatology services to the dying and administers a training program at Saint Patrick's Hospital in Missoula.*

The Bonny Foundation
P.O. Box 39355
Baltimore, MD 21212
(866) 345-5465
Email: info@bonnyfoundation.org
www.bonnyfoundation.org
> *Offers trainings in the Bonny Method of Guided Imagery and Music (G.I.M.).*

Tomatis International Headquarters
Christian Tomatis, Director
21 bis, rue Lord Byron
Paris 75008, France
Telephone: 01 53 53 42 40
Email: c.tomatis@tomatis.groupe.com
> *International headquarters for the Tomatis method and training.*

Sound Listening & Learning Center, Tomatis USA
Billie Thompson, Ph.D., Director
301 E. Bethany Home Road
Suite A-107
Phoenix, AZ 85012
(602) 381-0086
Email: info@soundlistening.com
www.soundlistening.com
> *A principal Tomatis center in the U.S. and frequent host for semi-nars and information source for Tomatis centers throughout the U.S. and Europe.*

The Listening Centre, Tomatis Canada
Paul Maudaule, Director
599 Markham Street
Toronto, ON M6G 2L7
CANADA
(416) 588-4136
Email: listen@idirect.com
www.listeningcentre.com
> *The oldest North American center and principal Canadian resource for the Tomatis Method.*

Music Therapy

American Music Therapy Association
8455 Colesville Road, Suite 1000
Silver Spring, MD 20910
(301) 589-3300
Email: info@musictherapy.org
www.musictherapy.org
> *Over seventy schools nationwide offer degree programs in music therapy. For more information, contact the American Music Therapy Association.*

The Nordoff-Robbins Center for Music Therapy
82 Washington Square East
Fourth Floor
New York, NY 10003
(212) 998-5151
Email: nordoff.robbins@nyu.edu
www.nyu.edu/education/music/nrobbins
> *Offers treatment programs for children, adolescents, and adults with various disabilities. Also offers a fine program in music therapy.*

Temple University
c/o Kenneth Bruscia, Ph.D., RMT, DC
Department of Music Education and Therapy
2001 North 13th Street
Philadelphia, PA 19122
(215) 204-8314
www.temple.edu/music

Arizona State University School of Music
c/o Barbara Crowe, MNT, MT-BC
Department of Music Therapy
Box 870405
Tempe, AZ 85287-0405
(480) 965-7413
Email: Barbara.J.Crowe@asu.edu
www.asu.edu/cfa/music

Naropa University
c/o Laurie Rugenstein, MMT, RMT-BC
2130 Arapahoe Avenue
Boulder, CO 80302
(303) 444-0202
Email: info@naropa.edu
www.naropa.edu
> *The only transpersonal music therapy program available for graduate study and full licensing accreditation.*

Music and Children

Music Educators National Conference (MENC)
1806 Robert Fulton Drive
Reston, VA 20191
(800) 336-3768
(703) 860-4000
www.menc.org
> *The largest association that addresses all aspects of music education, with more than 90,000 members.*

The American Orff-Schulwerk Association
P.O. Box 391089
Cleveland, OH 44139
(440) 543-5366
www.aosa.org
> *Offers training in the Orff method at fifty-three locations in the U.S. and many other countries, featuring wooden xylophones, metal glockenspeils as well as poems, rhymes, games, storytelling, songs, and dances.*

The Suzuki Association of the Americas
1900 Folsom Street, Suite 101
Boulder, CO 80302
(303) 444-0948
www.suzukiassociation.org
> *American headquarters for the Suzuki method and training of string and keyboard instruments.*

Organization of American Kodály Educators
1612 29th Avenue South
Moorhead, MN 56560
(218) 227-6253
Email: oakeoffice@aol.com
www.oake.org
> *Offers training in the Kodály method, invented by a Hungarian composer and collector of folk music who developed an approach modeled after the way children learn language, including hand movements synchronized to pitch and dynamics.*

Kindermusik International
P.O. Box 26575
Greensboro, NC 27415
(800) 628-5687
www.kindermusik.com
> Provides an early childhood music and movement curriculum, with
> programs for parents and teachers.

Musikgarten
409 Blandwood Avenue
Greensboro, NC 27401
(800) 216-6864
www.musikgarten.org
> Provides early childhood music educators with training and cur-
> riculum, classroom materials, and instruments.

Center for Music and Young Children
Ken Guilmarten, Director
66 Witherspoon Street
Princeton, NJ 08542
(800) 728-2692
www.musictogether.com
> Offers teacher training for early childhood and music professionals
> and requires parents to be involved in the learning process.

The Children's Group
1400 Bayly Street #7
Pickering, ON L1W 3R2
CANADA
(800) 668-0242 (U.S.)
(800) 757-8372 (in Canada)
(905) 831-1995
Email: moreinfo@childrensgroup.com
www.childrensgroup.com
> Excellent resources for classical music and putting the Mozart
> Effect to work for children.

Kindling Touch Publications
Dee Coulter, Director
4850 Niwot
Longmont, CO 80503
(303) 530-5058
Email: dcoulter@ecentral.com
> *Tapes and publications on the brain and music development for children. Fax requests to (303) 530-2357.*

Transitions Music
Fred J. Schwartz, M.D.
1930 Monroe Drive
Atlanta, GA 30324
(404) 355-4242
Email: wombsnd@mindspring.com
www.transitionsmusic.com

Audio-Therapy Innovations, Inc.
P.O. Box 550
Colorado Springs, CO 80901
(719) 473-0100
Email: sandman@audiotherapy.com
www.babygotosleep.com
> *The supplier of Terry Woodford's* Baby-Go-to-Sleep *recordings, described on page 25 of* The Mozart Effect®.

Music and Society

Music for People
P.O. Box 295
Boynton Beach, FL 33425-0295
(877) 446-8742
(561) 330-9561
Email: mfp@musicforpeople.org
www.musicforpeople.org
> *Promotes music making and improvisational performance through workshops for all levels, from beginners to professionals. Founded by cellist David Darling and Bonnie Insull.*

Hospital Audiences, Inc.
548 Broadway, 3rd Floor
New York, NY 10012
(212) 575-7676
Email: hai@hospand.org
www.hospitalaudiences.org
> *Offers hope and inspiration to hospitalized patients through music and the arts.*

Books on Music Healing

MMB Music, Inc.
Contemporary Arts Building
3526 Washington Avenue
St. Louis, MO 63103
(314) 531-9635
www.mmbmusic.com
> *Publishes specialized books not widely available.*

Periodicals

Early Childhood Connections: Journal of Music- and Movement-Based Learning
Foundation for Music-Based Learning
P.O. Box 4274
Greensboro, NC 27404-4274
(336) 272-5303
Email: econnect@aol.com
> *Excellent resource for teachers and musicians, with current research and diverse approaches to childhood development and education.*

Hearing Health Magazine
P.O. Drawer V
Ingleside, TX 78362
(361) 776-7240
Email: ears2u@hearinghealthmag.com
www.hearinghealthmag.com

Bi-monthly newsletter covering a range of topics important for living with hearing impairment and deafness. Many interesting articles on music and healing.

International Arts-Medicine Association Newsletter
714 Old Lancaster Road
Bryn Mawr, PA 19010
(610) 525-3784
Email: iama.org@aol.com
www.iamaonline.org

Informative newsletter for health professionals and membership organizations.

International Journal of Arts Medicine
MMB Music, Inc.
Contemporary Arts Building
3526 Washington Avenue
St. Louis, MO 63103
(314) 531-9635
www.mmbmusic.com

Journal of Music Therapy
8455 Colesville Road, Suite 930
Silver Spring, MD 20910

Quarterly research journal on music and healing.

Music Therapy Perspectives
American Music Therapy Association
8455 Colesville Road, Suite 1000
Silver Spring, MD 20910
(301) 589-3300
Email: info@musictherapy.org
www.musictherapy.org

Quarterly research journal on music and health.

Music Educators Journal—Teaching Music
Music Educators National Conference (MENC)
1806 Robert Fulton Drive
Reston, VA 20191
(800) 336-3768
(703) 860-4000
www.menc.org

Open Ear Journal
The Open Ear Center
Pat Moffitt Cook, Director
P.O. Box 10276
Bainbridge Island, WA 98110
(206) 842-5560
Email: openear@nwlink.com
www.openearcenter.com
    Annual journal dedicated to sound and music in health education.

Tinnitus Today
American Tinnitus Association
P.O. Box 5
Portland, OR 97207
(800) 634-8979
(503) 248-9985
Email: tinnitus@ata.org
www.ata.org
    Newsletter devoted to tinnitus and related conditions.

Recommended Reading

Imagery

Achterberg, J., and Lawlis, G. F., *Imagery and Disease*. Champaign, Il. Institute for Personality and Ability Testing, 1984.

——, Dossey, B., and Kolkmeier, L. *Rituals of Healing*. New York: Bantam Books, 1994.

——. *Imagery in Healing*. Boston: New Science Library, 1985.

Bonny, H. L., and Savary, L. M. *Music & Your Mind*. (Barrytown, N.Y.: Station Hill Press, 1990).

Bush, Carol. *Healing Imagery & Music*. Portland, Ore.: Rudra Press, 1995.

Epstein, Gerald, M.D. *Healing Visualizations*. New York: Bantam Books, 1989.

Merritt, Stephanie. *Mind, Music and Imagery*. Santa Rosa, Calif.: Aslan Publishing, 1996.

Rossi, Ernest Lawrence. *The Psychobiology of Mind-Body Healing: New Concepts of Therapeutic Hypnosis*. New York: W. W. Norton & Co., 1986.

Rossman, Martin L. *Healing Yourself*. New York: Pocket Books, 1987.

Voice

Appelbaum, David. *Voice*. Albany, N.Y.: State University of New York Press, 1990.

Campbell, Don G. *The Roar of Silence*. Wheaton, Il.: Theosophical Publishing House, 1989.

Chun-Tao Cheng, Stephen. *The Tao of Voice: A New East-West Approach to Transforming the Singing and Speaking Voice.* Rochester, Vt.: Destiny Books, 1991.

Gardner-Gordon, Joy. *The Healing Voice.* Freedom, Calif.: The Crossing Press, 1993.

Hale, Susan E. *Song & Silence.* Albuquerque, N.M.: La Alameda Press, 1995.

Hayden, Robert C. *Singing for All People: Roland Hayes, A Biography.* Boston: Select Publications, 1989.

Jindrak, Karel F. and Heda. *Sing, Clean Your Brain and Stay Sound and Sane: Postulate of Mechanical Effect of Vocalization on the Brain.* Forest Hills, N.Y.: Jindrak, 1986.

Keyes, Laurel Elizabeth. *Toning: The Creative Power of the Voice.* Marina del Rey, Calif.: DeVorss & Co., 1973.

Le Mée, Katharine. *Chant.* New York: Bell Tower, 1994.

Linklater, Kristin. *Freeing the Natural Voice.* New York: Drama Book Publishers, 1976.

McCallion, Michael. *The Voice Book.* New York: Routledge, 1988.

Moses, Paul J. *The Voice of Neurosis.* New York: Grune & Stratton, 1954.

Newham, Paul. *The Singing Cure.* Boston, MA: Shambhala, 1993.

Newman, Frederick R. *MouthSounds.* New York, NY: Workman Publishing, 1980.

Steindl-Rast, David. *The Music of Silence.* San Francisco: HarperSanFrancisco, 1995.

Werbeck-Svärdström, Valborg. *Uncovering the Voice,* 2nd ed. London, Eng.: Rudolf Steiner Press, 1985.

Education

Campbell, Don G. *100 Ways to Improve Teaching Using Your Voice & Music.* Tucson, Ariz.: Zephyr Press, 1992.

————, and Brewer, C. *Rhythms of Learning.* Tucson, Ariz.: Zephyr Press, 1991.

————. *Introduction to the Musical Brain,* 2nd ed. St. Louis, Mo.: MMB Music, 1983.

————. *Master Teacher, Nadia Boulanger.* Washington, D.C.: Pastoral Press, 1984.

————. *The Mozart Effect for Children.* New York: William Morrow, 2000.

Choksy, L., Abramson, R. M., Gillespie, A. E., and Woods, D. *Teaching Music in the Twentieth Century.* Englewood Cliffs, N.J.: Prentice-Hall, 1986.

Clynes, Manfred, Ph.D. *Sentics: The Touch of the Emotions,* 2nd ed. Dorset, Eng.: Prism Press, 1989.

Elliott, David J. *Music Matters.* New York: Oxford University Press, 1985.

Green, Barry. *The Inner Game of Music.* Garden City, N.Y.: Anchor Press, 1986.

Machover, Wilma and Marienne Uszler. *Sound Choices: Guiding Your Child's Musical Experiences.* New York: Oxford University Press, 1996.

Ostrander, S., and Schroeder, L. *Superlearning 2000.* New York: Delacorte Press, 1994.

Listening

Ackerman, Diane. *A Natural History of the Senses.* New York: Random House, 1990.

Bérard, Guy, M.D. *Hearing Equals Behavior.* New Canaan, Conn.: Keats Publishing, 1993.

Berendt, Joachim-Ernst. *The Third Ear.* London, Eng.: Element Books, 1988.

Burley-Allen, Madelyn. *Listening: The Forgotten Skill.* New York: John Wiley & Sons, 1982.

Madaule, Paul. *When Listening Comes Alive.* Norval, Ont.: Moulin Publishing, 1993.

Mathieu, W. A. *The Listening Book.* Boston: Shambhala, 1991.

Retallack, Dorothy. *The Sound of Music and Plants.* Santa Monica, Calif.: DeVorss & Co., 1973.

Stehli, Annabel. *The Sound of a Miracle.* New York: Doubleday, 1991.

Tomatis, Alfred A., M.D. *Ecouter l'Univers.* Paris: Editions Robert Laffont, 1996.

————. *L'Oreille et la Voix.* Paris: Editions Robert Laffont, 1987.

————. *La Nuit Utérine.* Paris: Editions Stock, 1981.

————. *Nous Sommes Tous Nés Polyglottes.* Paris: Editions Fixot, 1991.

————. *The Conscious Ear.* Barrytown, N.Y.: Station Hill Press, 1991.

————. *The Ear and Language.* Norval, Ont.: Moulin Publishing, 1996.

Verny, Thomas, M.D. *The Secret Life of the Unborn Child.* New York: Dell Publishing Co., 1981.

Wolvin, A. D., and Coakley, C. G., eds. *Perspectives on Listening.* Norwood, N.J.: Ablex Publishing Corporation, 1993.

Music Therapy, Health, and Psychology

Bruscia, Kenneth E. *Defining Music Therapy.* Phoenixville, Pa.: Barcelona Publishers, 1984.

————. ed. *Case Studies in Music Therapy.* Phoenixville, Pa.: Barcelona Publishers, 1991.

Campbell, Don G. *Music and Miracles.* Wheaton, Ill.: Theosophical Publishing House, 1992.

————. *Music: Physician for Times to Come.* Wheaton, Ill.: Theosophical Publishing House, 1991.

Cook, Pat Moffitt. *The Open Ear Journals: Guide to Music and Healing.* Portland, Or.: Rudra Press, 1997.

————. *Traditional Music Healers: A Sacred Legacy.* Roslyn, New York: Ellipsis Arts, 1997.

Davis, W., Gfeller, K., and Taut, M. *An Introduction to Music Therapy. Dubuque, Iowa: Wm. C. Brown Publishers, 1992.*

Deutsch, Diana, ed. *The Psychology of Music.* New York: Academic Press, 1982.

Dewhurst-Maddock, Olivea. *The Book of Sound Therapy.* New York: Simon & Schuster, 1993.

Gardner, Kay. *Sounding the Inner Landscape: Music as Medicine.* Stonington, Maine: Caduceus Publications, 1990.

Garfield, Laeh Maggie. *Sound Medicine: Healing with Music, Voice and Song.* Berkeley, Calif.: Celestial Arts, 1987.

Gilroy, A. and Lee, C., eds. *Art and Music: Therapy and Research.* New York: Routledge, 1995.

Goldman, Jonathan. *Healing Sounds.* Rockport, Mass.: Element, 1992.

Goleman, Daniel. *Emotional Intelligence.* New York: Bantam Books, 1995.

Halpern, Steven. *Sound Health: The Music and Sounds That Make Us Whole.* San Francisco: Harper & Row, 1985.

Hamel, Peter Michael. *Through Music to the Self: How to Appreciate and Experience Music Anew.* Boulder, Colo.: Shambhala, 1979.

Heimrath, Johannes. *The Healing Power of the Gong,* trans. by Susan Bawell Weber. St. Louis, Mo.: MMB Music, 1994.

Hodges, Donald A., ed. *Handbook of Music Psychology.* Lawrence, Kans.: National Association for Music Therapy, 1980.

Hoffman, Janalea. *Rhythmic Medicine.* Leawood, Kans.: Jamillan Press, 1995.

Jourdain, Robert. *Music, the Brain and Ecstacy.* New York: William Morrow, 1997.

Lane, Deforia. *Music as Medicine.* Grand Rapids, Mich.: Zondervan Publishing House, 1994.

Lee, Colin. *Music at the Edge.* New York: Routledge, 1996.

Maranto, Cheryl Dileo, ed. *Music Therapy: International Perspectives.* Pipersville, Pa.: Jeffrey Books, 1993.

Nordoff, P. and Robbins, C. *Therapy in Music for Handicapped Children,* 3rd ed. London, Eng.: Victor Gollancz, 1992.

Priestley, Mary. *Music Therapy in Action,* 2nd ed. St. Louis, Mo.: MMB Music, 1985.

Rouget, Gilbert. *Music and Trance.* Chicago: University of Chicago Press, 1985.

Spintge, R., M.D., and Droh, R., M.D., eds. *MusicMedicine.* St. Louis, Mo.: MMB Music, 1992.

Standley, Jayne. *Music Techniques in Therapy, Counseling and Special Education.* St. Louis, Mo.: MMB Music, 1991.

Tomatis, Alfred A., M.D. *Education and Dyslexia,* trans. by Louise Guiney. Fribourg, Switzerland: AIAPP, 1978.

Watson, A., and Drury, N. *Healing Music.* Bridport, Dorset, Eng.: Prism Press, 1987.

Wheeler, Barbara L. *Music Therapy Research: Quantitative and Qualitative Perspectives.* Phoenixville, Pa.: Barcelona Publishers, 1995.

Music and Creativity

Bayles, Martha. *Hole in Our Soul.* Chicago: University of Chicago Press, 1994.

Cameron, Julia. *The Vein of Gold.* New York: Putnam Books, 1996.

————. *The Artist's Way: A Spiritual Path to Higher Creativity.* New York: Tarcher/Putnam Books, 1992.

Carlinsky, D., and Goodgold, E. *The Armchair Conductor.* New York: Dell Publishing, 1991.

Floyd Jr., Samuel A. *The Power of Black Music.* New York: Oxford University Press, 1995.

Gardner, Howard. *Frames of Mind.* New York: Basic Books Publishers, 1983.

Hart, Mickey. *Drumming at the Edge of Magic.* San Francisco: HarperSanFrancisco, 1990.

James, Jamie. *The Music of the Spheres.* New York: Grove Press, 1993.

Jenny, Hans. *Cymatics.* Vol. 2. *Wave Phenomena, Vibrational Effects, Harmonic Oscillations with Their Structure, Kinetics, and Dynamics.* Basel, Switz.: Basilius Presse AG, 1974.

Judy, Stephanie. *Making Music for the Joy of It.* Los Angeles: Jeremy P. Tarcher, 1990.

Kittelson, Mary Lynn. *Sounding the Soul.* Einsiedeln, Switz.: Daimon, 1996.

Kristel, Dru. *Breath Was the First Drummer.* Santa Fe, N.M.: QX Publications A.D.A.M. Inc., 1995.

Lanza, Joseph. *Elevator Music.* New York: St. Martin's Press, 1994.

Neuls-Bates, Carol, ed. *Women in Music.* Boston: Northeastern University Press, 1996.

Oliveros, Pauline. *Software for People.* Baltimore: Smith Publications, 1984.

Ristad, Eloise. *A Soprano on Her Head.* Moab, Utah: Real People Press, 1982.

Storr, Anthony. *Music and the Mind.* New York: Ballantine Books, 1992.

Titon, Jeff Todd, ed. *Worlds of Music,* 2nd ed. New York: Schirmer Books, 1992.

Toop, David. *Ocean of Sound.* New York: Serpent's Tail, 1995.

Philosophy and Theory

Berendt, Joachim-Ernst. *Nada Brahma: The World Is Sound,* Inner Traditions International, Ltd. Rochester, Vt.: Destiny Books, 1987.

Hunt, Valerie V. *Infinite Mind.* Malibu, Calif.: Malibu Publishing Co., 1995.

Khan, Hazrat Inayat. *The Music of Life.* Santa Fe, N.M.: Omega Press, 1983.

Rothstein, Edward. *Emblems of Mind.* New York: Random House, 1995.

Mozart

Gutman, Robert W. *Mozart: A Cultural Biography.* New York: Harcourt Brace and Company, 1999.

Harris, Robert. *What to Listen for in Mozart.* New York: Simon & Schuster, 1991.

Marshall, Robert L. *Mozart Speaks.* New York: Schirmer Books, 1991.

Parouty, Michel. *Mozart: From Child Prodigy to Tragic Hero.* New York: Harry N. Abrams, 1993.

Solomon, Maynard. *Mozart: A Life.* New York: HarperCollins, 1995.

Tomatis, Alfred A., M.D. *Pourquoi Mozart?* Paris: Editions Fixot, 1991.

Notes

Introduction
A Healing Breeze of Sound

11   from the Greek roots *per son:* Paul Newham, *The Singing Cure: An Introduction to Voice Movement Therapy* (Boston: Shambhala, 1993), p. 37. See also Paul J. Moses, *The Voice of Neurosis* (New York: Grune and Stratton, 1954), p.7.

11   one out of three Americans: D. M. Eisenberg, et al., "Unconventional Medicine in the United States—Prevalence, Costs, and Patterns of Use," *New England Journal of Medicine,* 328 (1993): 246–52.

Chapter 1
Sound Beginnings

14   In monasteries in Brittany: Alfred Tomatis, *Pourquois Mozart?*, my translation.

14   In Washington State: Sheila Ostrander and Lynn Schroeder with Nancy Ostrander, *Superlearning 2000* (New York: Delacorte Press, 1994), p. 76.

14   "Beethoven Bread": "Bread and Noodles Exposed to Classical Music Are 'Tastier'"; Asahi News Service, n.d.

14   At Saint Agnes Hospital: Ostrader, *Superlearning 2000,* p. 82.

14   The city of Edmonton, Canada: "Music—Let's Split," *Newsweek,* 1990.

14 In Tokyo, noodle makers: "Bread and Noodles Exposed to Classical Music Are 'Tastier' ": Asahi News.

14 Mozart makes the best sake: Ibid.

15 Mozart's "Sonata for Two Pianos in D Major" (K. 448): In the 19th century, each of Mozart's compositions was assigned a chronological number by the Austrian musicologist Ludwig von Köchel. Since then, the catalog of Mozart's works has been revised several times, but each composition still bears a Köchel listing.

15 music and spatial reasoning: Frances H. Rauscher, Gordon L. Shaw, and Katherine N. Ky, "Music and Spatial Task Performance," *Nature*, 365 (1993): 611. See also Frances Rauscher, "Can Music Make Us More Intelligent?" *Billboard*, 15 October 1994.

15 Mozart's music "may 'warm up' the brain": "Brief Intellectual Gains Sparked by Classical Music," *Brain/Mind Bulletin* (October/November 1994): 1–2.

15 In a follow-up study: Rauscher, Shaw, and Ky, "Listening to Mozart Enhances Spatial-Temporal Reasoning: Towards a Neurophysiological Basis," *Neuroscience Letters* 185 (1995): 44–47.

16 In their most recent study: Rauscher, Shaw, Linda J. Levine, Eric L. Wright, Wendy R. Dennis, Robert L. Newcomb, "Music Training Causes Long-Term Enhancement of Preschool Children's Spatial-Temporal Reasoning," *Neurological Research* 19 (1997): 208.

17 Following the Irvine studies: Material in this chapter was supplemented with a telephone interview with Gordon Shaw, summer 1996. Despite the significant work done by the Irvine research group, they were not aware of the multitude of listening procedures that might have enhanced their results. For example, they did not administer listening tests before testing, as many researchers in the field recommend. Nor did they examine how posture, food intake, or the time of day modified their listening. The Mozart Effect is far more dramatic when one controls for these factors, and when one evaluates which ear is dominant in listening to the music. Also the positive results might have been even greater if the researchers had played Mozart's violin concertos, which offer a much wider range of frequency stimulation, rather than the piano sonatas.

17 Over the last half century, the French physician: Alfred A. Tomatis, M.D., *The Conscious Ear: My Life of Transformation Through Listening* (Bar-

rytown, N.Y.: Station Hill Press, 1991). Translated from *l'Oreille et la vie* (Editions Robert Laffont, S. A., 1977, 1990) by Stephen Lushington, final editing by Billie M. Thompson. Material and quotations in this and subsequent chapters are largely drawn from his autobiography unless otherwise noted.

22 "Mozart is a very good mother . . .": Ron Minson, M.D., "A Sonic Birth," ed. Don Campbell, *Music and Miracles* (Wheaton, Ill.: Quest Books, 1992), p. 95.

22 "Listening to Mozart is like a kiss from my mom . . ." Judith Belk, "The Tomatis Method," ibid, p. 244.

22 "Now I know where learning to take turns comes from.": Belk, "The Tomatis Method," ibid., p. 245.

22 Premature infants: Tomatis, *The Conscious Ear*, pp. 211–212.

22 "Each child must truly know": Tomatis, *Pourquoi Mozart?*, p. 92.

23 In 1962, Dr. Lee Salk demonstrated: "Mother's Beat as an Imprinting Stimulus," in R. O. Benezon, ed., *Music Therapy Manual* (Springfield, Ill.: Charles C. Thomas, 1981).

23 In *The Secret Life of the Unborn Child:* Dr. Thomas Verney, *The Secret Life of the Unborn Child* (New York: Dell, 1981).

23 psychologists at the Pacific Medical Center: "Music Is Refined to Quiet Babies, Relieve Stress, Enhance Sport," *Brain/Mind Bulletin* (21 January and 11 February 1985): 1–2.

24 In a study of fifty-two premature babies: Janet Caine, "The Effects of Music on the Selected Stress Behaviors, Weight, Caloric and Formula Intake, and Length of Hospital Stay of Premature and Low Birth Weight Neonates in a Newborn Intensive Care Unit," *Journal of Music Therapy,* 28 (1991): 180–192.

25 At Helen Keller Hospital in Alabama: Lance W. Brunner, "Testimonies Old and New," in *Music and Miracles,* ed. Campbell, pp. 82–84; Caine, "The Effects of Music," 180–192.

25 "I could hardly breathe . . .": Lance W. Brunner, "Theme and Variation: Testimonies Old and New," in *Music and Miracles,* ed. Campbell, pp. 74–88.

26 new research describing electrical activity: B. Bower, "Babies' Brains Charge Up," *Science* 146 (1993): 71.

26 asked pregnant women to read Dr. Seuss's *The Cat in the Hat:* Gina

Kolata, "Rhyme's Reason: Linking Thinking to Train the Brain?" *New York Times,* 19 February 1995.

26 "Each day in the womb represents about 10 million years' of evolution": Michio Kushi with Alex Jack, *The Book of Macrobiotics* (New York and Tokyo: Japan Publications, 1986), p. 74, and lectures at the Kushi Institute.

27 Although Mozart shares affinities: Dr. Alfred Tomatis, *Pourquoi Mozart?*

28 A gifted performer from the age of four: One of the most insightful recent biographies is Maynard Solomon's *Mozart: A Life* (New York: HarperCollins, 1995), which presents a highly psychoanalytic view of Mozart's relationship with his father. The letters between father and son, invaluable for an understanding of the familial ties and environment in which Mozart lived, are available in many editions, including Hans Mersmann, ed., *Letters of Wolfgang Amadeus Mozart* (New York: Dover, 1972). ed. Robert L. Marshall, *Mozart Speaks: Views on Music, Musicians, and the World* (New York: Schirmer Books, 1991) includes not only letters but also contemporary accounts and valuable commentary. Robert Harris's *What to Listen for in Mozart* (New York: Penguin Books, 1991) analyzes several major works and provides a listening guide to fifty others. William Stafford's *The Mozart Myths* (Stanford, Calif.: Stanford University Press, 1991) offers a critical reassessment of the myths and legends that have grown up around the composer, including his mysterious death (which scholars generally regard as medically related and not caused by the murderous designs of a court rival, Salieri, as dramatized in Peter Shaffer's controversial play *Amadeus*). The unexpurgated Mozart, which includes risqué songs and canons, is included in *Scatological Songs and Canons of Wolfgang Amadeus Mozart,* accompaniments by Thomas Z. Shepard and English texts by Anne Grossman (New York: Walton Music Corp., 1969).

28 "Everything has been composed . . ." Marshall, *Mozart Speaks,* p. 30.

28 "Soon notions of Mozart's irresponsibility . . ." Solomon, *Mozart,* p. 14.

28 Drs. Rauscher and Shaw explained: Rauscher, Shaw, and Ky, "Listening to Mozart," 44–47. See also, Shaw, "Music Training Enhances Spatial-Temporal Reasoning in Pre-School Children: Educational Im-

plications" (Proceedings of the Fourth Greek Conference of Pre-School Education, Athens, 15–17 March 1996).

Chapter 2
Sound Listening

32 In Africa, the Maabans: "Noise in Our Environment," *Hearing Health,* (October/November 1994): 13.

33 Hans Jenny, a Swiss engineer: Hans Jenny, *Cymatics* (Basel: Basilius Presse, 1974), pp. 7–13.

36 Dr. Samuel Rosen: quoted in R. Murray Schafer, *The Tuning of the World* (New York: Alfred A. Knopf, 1977), p. 185.

36 A study at a public elementary school: Diane Ackerman, *A Natural History of the Senses* (New York: Vintage, 1990), p. 187.

37 On the other side of the country, a California study: "Noise in Our Environment," *Hearing Health* (October/November 1994): 13.

37 The opera star Maria Callas: With an early version of the Electronic Ear, Dr. Tomatis was able to modify Maria Callas's voice subtly at a time of great stress in her life and she went on to recover her magnificent register onstage.

37 Although headphones are convenient: Michelle Vittiow, "Influence of Physical Exercise During Noise Exposure on Susceptibility to Temporary Threshold Shift," master's thesis, University of Louisville, 1991; see also *Women's Day,* 13 August 1991.

38 In Paris, the French Parliament: "In France: More Piano, Less Forte," *New York Times,* 3 May 1996: A4.

38 Amid all the clamor of modern life: "Searching for Enticing Sound," *SICA Bulletin, No. 18* (Hong Kong: Spark International Culture Agency, 1996).

38 Preliminary research at the Medical College of Wisconsin: Jon Van, "Drowning Out the Din," *Boulder Camera,* 17 September 1996, Business section, 9.

38 natural foods pioneer Michio Kushi tells: lectures by Michio Kushi at the Kushi Institute, Becket, Mass.

39   Finnish researchers: Ackerman, *A Natural History,* p. 187.

39   Based on a study of more than 1,400 persons with inner ear symp-
      toms: J. T. Spencer, "Hyperlipoproteinemia, Hyperinsulinism, and
      Meniere's Disease," *Southern Medical Journal,* 74 (1981): 1194–97.

39   Although he recommends a more traditional diet: Although there
      have been few scientific studies in this field, Gale Jack, a dietary
      counselor and author of *Promeanade Home,* a macrobiotic approach to
      women's health, explains the traditional Far Eastern approach to diet
      and hearing: "Eating dairy food is particularly bad for the ears. Too
      much fat, cholesterol, and mucus can interfere with smooth hearing.
      Cold foods such as ice cream and cold drinks are particularly bad for
      the ears and can contribute to colds, flu, and ear infection. In the
      Far East, seaweed, unrefined sea salt, and good quality well or spring
      water, as well as beans and bean products such as tofu and tempeh,
      are considered especially beneficial for hearing."

40   Evelyn Glennie: Lana Williams and Paula Bonillas, "Interviews: Eve-
      lyn Glennie," *Hearing Health* (April/May 1993): 8–9.

41   At Saint Joseph Institute for the Deaf: Paula Bonillas, "Roll Over,
      Beethoven!" *Hearing Health* (November/December 1995): 6.

42   Tomatis used the great Italian tenor: Tomatis, *The Conscious Ear: My
      Life of Transformation Through Listening* (Barrytown, N.Y.: Station Hill
      Press, 1991), pp. 45–66.

44   listening absorbs an average of 55 percent: 1975 study by Elyse K.
      Werner cited in Chris Brewer and Don G. Campbell, *Rhythms of Learn-
      ing* (Tucson: Zephyr Press, 1991), p. 19.

45   Once Oliver Sacks, the celebrated neurologist: Oliver Sacks, *A Leg to
      Stand On* (New York: HarperPerennial, 1992), pp. 91–122.

49   Nearly deaf, the French actor Philip Bardi: "Envoyé Special," Paris
      TV–2, 1992.

54   "The ear is not a differentiated piece of skin": Material in this chapter
      is from my interviews with Dr. Tomatis and from his autobiography,
      The Conscious Ear, especially pp. 140–169.

58   Scientists have recently reported: "Infants Tune Up to Music's Core
      Qualities," *Science News,* 7 September 1996: 151.

58   researchers at the State University of New York: Ibid.

Chapter 3
Sound Healing

63   In *Anatomy of an Illness:* Norman Cousins, *Anatomy of an Illness as Per-
      ceived by the Patient* (New York: Norton, 1979), pp. 72–74.

66   Performer-composer Kay Gardner: Kay Gardner, *Sounding the Inner
      Landscape: Music as Medicine* (Stonington, Maine: Caduceus Publica-
      tions, 1990), p. 93.

67   "My objections to Wagner's music": Nietzsche, quoted in Jacques
      Barzum, editor, *Pleasures of Music* (Chicago: University of Chicago
      Press, 1977), p. 312.

67   a Louisiana State University study: cited in Bill Gottlieb, ed., "Sound
      Therapy," *New Choices in Natural Healing* (Emmaus, Pa.: Rodale Press,
      1995), p. 127.

67   In another study, on the effects of rock music: Claire V. Wilson and
      Leona S. Aiken, "The Effect of Intensity Levels upon Physiological
      and Subjective Affective Response to Rock Music," *Journal of Music
      Therapy* 14 (1977): 60–77.

68   In a third recent study, female undergraduates: Makoto Iwanaga, "Re-
      lationship Between Heart Rate and Preference for Tempo of Music,"
      Perceptual and Motor Skills 81 (1995): 435–440.

68   Like Mozart's music: Michio Kushi and Alex Jack, *Diet for a Strong
      Heart* (New York: St. Martin's Press, 1985), pp. 207-208.

68   Music can also change blood pressure: Gottlieb, "Sound Therapy,"
      New Choices, p. 126.

68   medical researchers reported that my album: Olav Skille, "Vibroa-
      coustic Research 1980–1991," in *MusicMedicine,* ed. Ralph Spintge and
      R. Droh (Saint Louis: MMB Music, 1991), p. 249.

68   Other experiments using a variety: Tony Wigram, "The Psychologi-
      cal and Physiological Effects of Low Frequency Sound and Music,"
      Music Therapy Perspectives 13 (1995): 16–35.

69   In a study at Colorado State University in 1991: Gottlieb, "Sound
      Therapy," *New Choices,* p. 127; Michael Thaut, Sandra Schleiffers, and
      William Davis, "Analysis of EMG Activity in Biceps and Triceps
      Muscle in an Upper Extremity Gross Motor Task under the Influence
      of Auditory Rhythm," *Journal of Music Therapy,* 28 (1991): 64–88.

69 in a study of seventy university students: Kate Gfeller, "Musical Components and Styles Preferred by Young Adults for Aerobic Fitness Activities," *Journal of Music Therapy* 25 (1988): 28–43.

69 educator Olav Skille began using music: Olav Skille, "Vibroacoustic Research."

71 At the Addiction Research Center: "Music/Endorphin Link," *Brain/Mind Bulletin* (21 January and 11 February 1985): 1–3.

71 expectant mothers who listened: Droh and Spintge, *Anxiety, Pain, and Music in Anesthesia* (Basel: Roche Editions, 1983).

71 natural highs . . . may at times elevate the levels of T-cells: S. C. Gilman, et al., "Beta-Endorphin Enhances Lymphocyte Proliferate Response," *Proceedings of the National Academy of Sciences* 79 (July 1982), 4226–4230.

72 Anesthesiologists report: Spintge, "Music as a Physiotherapeutic and Emotional Means in Medicine," *Musik, Tanz Und Kunst Therapie* (2 March 1988): 79.

72 "I cannot listen to music too often," Lenin confessed: Richard Pipes, ed., *The Unknown Lenin: From the Secret Archive* (New Haven: Yale University Press, 1996).

72 vocal exercises that can increase the lymph circulation: Buddha Gerace, "So, You'd Like to Sing," *Macrobiotics Today* 35 (May/June 1995): 21–22.

72 listening to music . . . could increase levels of interleukin-1: Dale Bartlett, Donald Kaufman, and Roger Smeltekop, "The Effects of Music Listening and Perceived Sensory Experiences on the Immune System as Measured by Interleukin-1 and Cortisol," *Journal of Music Therapy* 30 (1993): 194–209.

75 The University of Washington: these studies are described in *Business Music: A Performance Tool for the Office/Workplace* (Seattle: Muzak, 1991).

76 rock music causes people to eat faster: Johns Hopkins study cited in Don G. Campbell, ed., *Music—Physician for Times to Come* (Wheaton, Ill.: Quest Books, 1991), p. 246.

77 a recent musically paced transcontinental bicycle race: "Music, Healing," *Brain/Mind Bulletin* 8 (13 December 1982): 2.

82   Dorothy Retallack . . . also began to experiment: Dorothy Retallack, *The Sound of Music and Plants* (Marina Del Ray, Calif.: DeVorss & Co., 1973).

83   Mickey Hart, longtime drummer for the Grateful Dead: Mickey Hart, *Drumming at the Edge of Magic* (San Francisco, Harper, 1990).

Chapter 4
Sound Voice

91   Laurel Elizabeth Keyes wrote: Laurel Elizabeth Keyes, *Toning: The Creative Power of the Voice* (Santa Monica, Calif.: DeVorss, 1973).

95   Humming an *m* sound: Jean Westerman Gregg, "What Humming Can Do for You," *Journal of Singing* 52 (1996): 37–38.

95   In a letter explaining his method: quoted in the liner notes to the album *Mozart for Your Mind* (Philips Recordings, 1995).

97   He considered the voice: Paul J. Moses, *The Voice of Neurosis* (New York: Grune & Stratton, 1954), pp. 1–6.

98   "Vocal dynamics truthfully reflect psychodynamics": Paul Newham, *The Singing Cure* (Boston: Shambhala, 1994), p. 76.

99   At the first utterance of a friend or family member: In traditional Oriental medicine and philosophy, it is believed that the condition of the internal organs can be diagnosed by listening to the voice. A rapid, fluttery voice, for example, is associated with a heart murmur or weakness, while a deep, groaning voice suggests kidney problems. This method of voice diagnosis is taught at the Kushi Institute in Becket, Massachusetts.

100   The whole purpose of psychoanalysis. . . .: interview in London, April 1996.

100   For women, Newham argues: Newham, *The Singing Cure*, p. 198–200.

102   Another approach to voice therapy was pioneered: Newham, *The Singing Cure*, pp. 86–96.

103   After arriving on the scene and finding: interview with Alfred Tomatis, M.D., by Tim Wilson, "Chat: The Healing Power of Voice and Ear," in *Music—Physician for Times to Come,* ed. Don Campbell (Wheaton, Ill.: Quest Books, 1991), pp. 11–28.

107 "It is as if there is no actual singer . . .": Katharine Le Mée, *Chant: The Origins, Form, Practice, and Healing Power of Gregorian Chant* (New York: Bell Tower, 1994), p. 122.

110 "There is a particular exercise . . .": "Mysteries of the Spiritual Voice: An Interview by Don G. Campbell with the Abbot of the Gyuto Tantric College, Khen Rinpoche," in Campbell, ed., *Music and Miracles* (Wheaton, Il.: Quest Books, 1992), pp. 176–184.

113 "Rap in its beginnings . . .": *New York Times,* undated article of America Online, 1996.

116 Depardieu, the French actor: Paul Chutkow, *Depardieu: A Biography* (New York: Alfred A. Knopf, 1994), pp. 135–151.

117 "Before Tomatis, I could not complete any of my sentences": In the late 1980s, Depardieu returned to the Tomatis Center to work on his English pronunciation for the movie, *Green Card,* which was filmed in America. He reported that, because of the Tomatis Method, he could better understand the English of Andie MacDowell, the actress starring opposite him. Not only could he connect the sounds and meaning, he also felt able to sense the feeling behind the words.

119 in high school Elvis Presley: Peter Guralnick, *Last Train to Memphis: The Rise of Elvis Presley* (New York: Little Brown, 1994), p. 36.

119 In a study of "untuned" singers: Marvin Greenberg, "Musical Achievement and the Self-Concept," *Journal of Research in Music Education* 18 (1970): 57–64.

Chapter 5
Sound Medicine

121 American medicine first experimented: William B. Davis, "Music Therapy in 19th Century America," *Journal of Music Therapy* 24 (1987): 76–87; Dale B Taylor, "Music in General Hospital Treatment from 1900 to 1950," *Journal of Music Therapy* 18 (1981): 62–73; E. Thayer Gaston, ed., *Music in Therapy* (New York: Macmillan, 1968).

126 Seventy American colleges: Kenneth E. Bruscia, Ph.D., co-director of music therapy at Temple University in Philadelphia and author of an entire book on the definition of music therapy, admits to the

difficulty of delineating the profession because it is a dynamic combination of many disciplines. "Music therapy is an interpersonal process in which the therapist uses music and all of its facets—physical, emotional, mental, social, aesthetic, and spiritual—to help clients to improve or maintain health," he concludes. "In some instances, the client's needs are addressed directly through music; in others they are addressed through the relationships that develop between the client and therapist." Kenneth E. Bruscia, Ph.D., *Defining Music Therapy* (Phoenixville, Pa.: Barcelona Publishers, 1984).

127   the Institute for Music and Neurologic Function: "Music Has Power," Institute for Music and Neurologic Function (Bronx, N.Y.: Beth Abraham Hospital, 1995). Sacks quoted on Parkinson's in "Music, Health, and Well-Being," *Journal of the American Medical Association* 26 (1991): 32.

127   In 1991, Sacks testified: Hearing Before the Senate Special Committee on Aging, "Forever Young: Music and Aging," U.S. Senate, 1 August 1991, *Music Therapy Perspectives* 10 (1992); 59–60.

128   Linda Rodgers, a clinical social worker: Linda Rodgers, "Music for Surgery," *Advances: The Journal of Mind-Body Health* 11 (1995): 9–57.

132   At Charing Cross Hospital in London: *New Scientist* 1339: 20.

132   the impact of music on fifty male surgeons: K. Allen and J. Blascovich, "Effects of Music on Cardiovascular Reactivity Among Surgeons," *Journal of the American Medical Association* 272 (1994): 882–84.

132   At Saint Luke's Hospital: Judy Simpson, RMT-BC, "Applying Music Therapy," *Healing Healthcare Network Newsletter* 3 (1992): 3.

132   At Saint Mary's Hospital in Green Bay: Nancy Whitfield, R.N., "Music Therapy—Melody of Caring," *Healing Healthcare Network Newsletter* 3 (1992): 3.

133   Dr. Paul Robertson: Paul Robertson, "Music and the Mind," *Caduceus* 31 (spring 1995): 17–20.

133   At the University of Massachusetts Medical Center: "Music Facilitates Healing, Bodymind Coordination," *Brain/Mind Bulletin 8* (13 December 1982) 1–2.

133   surgeons are famous for toting boom boxes: Dick Kankas, "Music as Medicine," *Louisville Courier-Journal,* 7 January 1996.

133   The Multisensory Sound Lab: Kimberly V. Fisher and Barbara J. Par-

ker, "A Multisensory System for the Development of Sound Awareness and Speech Production," *Journal of the Academy of Rehabilitative
Audiology* 27 (1994): 13–24.

134 The world's oldest musical instrument: John Noble Wilford, "Playing
of Flute May Have Graced Neanderthal Fire," *New York Times,* 29
October 1996, C1.

134 practically every ear in the world recognizes: Howard Gardner, "Do
Babies Sing a Universal Song?" *Psychology Today,* December 1981. For
the musically minded, it is the descending minor third and then up
a fourth, better known as the sol-mi-la sequence.

136 From Siberian shamanism: E. Métraux, "The Myths and Tales of the
Mataco Indians," *Ethnological Studies* 9 (1939): 107–108.

139 One of the most charismatic figures: "Musical Qi Gong," *SICA Bulletin
No. 8* (Hong Kong: Spark International Culture Agency, 1996); "Obesity," booklet with album, Wind Records, Los Angeles, 1994.

141 At hospitals, universities, and healing centers: M. D. Riti and S. Ak-
hila, "Getting Well to Music," *The Week,* 18 August 1996.

141 When he was twelve years old: "Musical Medicine," *Skylife,* September 1995, pp. 26–28.

143 Traditional African music: Samuel A. Floyd, Jr., *The Power of Black
Music* (New York: Oxford University Press, 1995).

146 the Boys Choir of Harlem: Dr. Walter Turnbull, *Lift Every Voice* (New
York: Hyperion, 1995).

146 Dr. Joy Berger uses gospel music with patients: Dick Kankas, "Music
as Medicine," *Louisville Courier-Journal,* 7 January 1996.

148 At the Senate Hearings on the Elderly, Mickey Hart: Senate Special
Committee, "Forever Young."

149 hundreds of testimonials extolling: Andrew Weil, M.D., *Spontaneous
Healing* (New York: Alfred A. Knopf, 1995), p. 53.

150 what constitutes therapy, medicine, and healing: Larry Dossey, M.D.,
"Whatever Happened to Healers?" *Alternative Therapies* 1 (1995): 6.

151 the Office of Alternative Medicine: *Alternative Medicine: Expanding
Medical Horizons, A Report to the National Institutes of Health on Alternative
Medical Systems and Practices in the United States* (Washington, D.C.: U.S.
Government Printing Office, 1994); see especially the section on
music therapy, pp. 27–29.

151 In a report to the National Institutes of Health: Ibid.

Chapter 6

Sound Images

154   Jerry was a twenty-six-year-old African-American man: Ginger Clarkson, "Adapting a Guided Imagery and Music Series for a Nonverbal Man with Autism," *Association for Music and Imagery Journal,* (1995): 123–137.

158   there are times when a DNA sequence is altered: Deepak Chopra, M.D., *Perfect Health* (New York: Harmony Books, 1991), pp. 133–37.

158   "Her body had become frozen": Joy Gardner-Gordon, *The Healing Voice* (Freedom, Calif.: Crossing Press, 1993), pp. 100–102.

159   "Opera buffs go to hear favorite singers": Laeh Maggie Garfield, *Sound Medicine: Healing with Music, Voice, and Song* (Berkeley: Celestial Arts, 1987), p. 57.

159   a fascinating guided-imagery project by Dr. Victor Beasley: Dr. Victor Beasley, *Your Electro-Vibratory Body* (Boulder Creek, Calif.: University of the Trees Press, 1978).

161   "As our world gets faster and more crowded": Joseph Lanza, *Elevator Music* (New York: St. Martin's Press, 1994), p. 224.

161   In a ten-week experiment, the Florida: Liesi-Vivoni Ramos, "The Effects of On-Hold Telephone Music on the Number of Premature Disconnections to a Statewide Protective Services Abuse Hot Line," *Journal of Music Therapy* 30 (1993): 119–29.

162   In a book on the psychology of medicine: Norman Cousins, *The Healing Heart: Antidotes to Panic and Helplessness* (New York: W. W. Norton, 1983), pp. 199–221.

164   The placebo effect: The most comprehensive survey on the placebo effect is Howard M. Spiro, *Doctors, Patients, and Placebos* (New Haven: Yale University Press, 1986).

164   *Hooper's Medical Dictionary* in 1811 defined placebo: *The Compact Edition of the Oxford English Dictionary* (New York: Oxford University Press), p. 2192.

164   Sir Walter Scott used it in a romance: ibid.

165   In research on the effects of guided imagery: Jeanne Achterberg and G. Frank Lawlis, *Imagery and Disease* (Champaign, Ill.: Institute for

Personality and Ability Testing, 1984); Mark Rider, J. Achterberg, and G. F. Lawlis, et al, "Effect of Biological Imagery on Antibody Production and Health" (unpublished manuscript, 1988); Chin Chung Tsao, Thomas F. Gordon, Cheryl D. Maranto, Caryn German, and Donna Murasko, "The Effects of Music and Biological Imagery on Immune Response (S-GI)," in *Applications of Music in Medicine,* Cheryl Maranto, ed. (Washington, D.C.: National Association for Music Therapy, 1991), pp. 85–121; Cheryl Maranto and Joseph Scartelli, "Music in the Treatment of Immune-Related Disorders," in *Music-Medicine,* ed. Ralph Spintge and R. Droh (St. Louis: MagnaMusic Baton, 1992), pp. 142–54.

166 one of the most prominent researchers . . . has been Jean Houston.: Jean Houston and Robert Masters, *Listening to the Body* (New York: Dell Publishing, 1978); Don G. Campbell, "Sound and the Miraculous: An Interview with Jean Houston," in *Music and Miracles,* ed. Don Campbell (Wheaton, Ill.: Quest Books, 1992), pp. 9–17.

169 Jung came to regard music: Patricia Warming, "The Use of Music in Jungian Analysis," in *Music and Miracles,* ed. Campbell (Wheaton, Ill.: Quest Books, 1992), pp. 231–234.

169 "We know that the creative power of the unconscious": Warming, ibid, 234–241.

170 The leading therapeutic use of music: Helen L. Bonny, *Facilitating GIM Sessions* (Port Townsend, Wash.: ICM Press, 1978); Bonny and Louis M. Savary, *Music and Your Mind: Listening with a New Consciousness* (Port Townsend, Wash.: ICM Press, 1983).

173 from those with multiple personality disorder: GIM uses primarily European classical music, but as its influence spreads, music from other traditions is being integrated into its basic therapeutic framework. Pat Moffitt Cook, director of the Open Ear Center near Seattle, Washington, successfully uses Indian music in her GIM sessions and training. The Mid-Atlantic Institute in Virginia Beach, Virginia, directed by Sarah Jane Stokes and Carol Bush, trains dozens of people each year in both Mexico and the United States in how to use music-evoked imagery and art. Ginger Clarkson, who guided Jerry through his sessions, now directs an integrated program in music therapy, toning, and GIM in central Mexico.

Chapter 7
Sound Intellect

177   The College Entrance Examination Board reported: "Music Is Key,"
      Music Educators Journal (January 1996): 6.

177   In a study of approximately 7,500 students: Peter H. Wood, "The
      Comparative Academic Abilities of Students in Education and in
      Other Areas of a Multi-focus University," unpublished paper, ERIC
      Document Number ED327480.

178   the combination of music and art: Myra J. Staum and Melissa Bro-
      tons, "The Influence of Auditory Subliminals on Behavior: A Series
      of Investigations," *Journal of Music Therapy* 29 (1992): 149–160.

178   lessened children's inappropriate behavior: Robert Cutietta, Donald
      L. Hamann, and Linda Miller Walker, *Spin-offs: The Extra-Musical Ad-
      vantages of a Musical Education* (Elkhart, Ind.: United Musical Instru-
      ments U.S.A., Inc., for the Future of Music Project, 1995), pp. 29–32.

178   primarily songs by the Beatles: Claire V. Wilson and Leona S. Aiken,
      "The Effect of Intensity Levels upon Physiological and Subjective
      Affective Response to Rock Music," *Journal of Music Therapy* 14
      (1977): 60–77.

178   the notion that we have multiple intelligences: Howard Gardner,
      Frames of Mind (New York: Basic Books, 1983).

179   In 1997, during the debate: Howard Gardner quoted in Susan Black,
      "The Musical Mind," *The American School Board Journal,* January 1997,
      pp. 20–22.

179   music instruction aids reading: Robert Cutietta, Donald L. Hamann,
      and Linda Miller Walker, *Spin-Off: The Extra-Musical Advantage of a
      Musical Education* (Elkhart, Ind.: United Musical Instruments, 1995).

181   A 1993 study found that African-American high school students: D.
      L. Hamann and L. M. Walker, "Music Teachers as Role Models for
      African-American Students," *Journal of Research in Music Education* 41
      (1993): 303–314.

181   Other studies have found: B. S. Hood III, "The Effect of Daily In-
      struction in Public School Music and Related Experiences upon Non-
      musical Personal and School Attitudes of Average Achieving Third-
      Grade Students" (doctoral dissertation, Mississippi State University,

1973); N. H. Barry, J. A. Taylor, and K. Walls, "The Role of the Fine and Performing Arts in High School Dropout Prevention" (Tallahassee, Fla.: Center for Music Research, Florida State University, 1990).

182 The most in-depth use of music: Georgi Lozanov, *Suggestology and Outlines of Suggestopedy* (New York: E. P. Dutton, 1978); Sheila Ostrander and Lynn Schroeder with Nancy Ostrander, *Superlearning 2000* (New York, Delacorte Press, 1994); the Lozanov Report to Unesco excerpted in Appendix 2, Chris Brewer and Don G. Campbell, *Rhythms of Learning* (Tucson: Zephyr Press, 1991), pp. 291–305.

185 modern music education has come a long way: Edgar W. Knight, *Education in the United States* (Boston: Ginn, 1941), p. 319.

185 Thanks to Mann and Lowell Mason: National Education Association, Department of Superintendence, *The Nation of Work on the Public School Curriculum*, 4 yearbook (Washington, D.C.: 1926), p. 300.

186 "Just as humus": Carl Orff, *His Life and Work (Schulwerk*, vol. 3), trans. Margaret Murray (New York: Schott Music Corporation, 1978).

192 the corpus callosum of musicians: "Brain: Music of the Hemispheres," *Discover*, March 1994, p. 15.

192 The *planum temporale*: James Shreeve, "Music of the Hemispheres," *Discover*, October 1996, pp. 90–100.

193 Studies like this . . . are "part of a growing body of evidence": Richard A. Knox, "Sweet Taste in Music May be Human Trait, Harvard Study Finds," *Boston Globe*, 5 September 1996.

195 "Playing jazz means learning how to reconcile differences": Tony Scherman, "The Music of Democracy," *Currents* (March-April 1996): 29–35.

195 Brazilian music, which fuses: Lee Cobin, "Cheremoya Escola de Samba," *Think Drums*, January 1996, pp. 1–4.

199 Music in the workplace has been shown: "Business Music: A Performance Tool for the Office/Workplace" (Seattle: Muzak Corporation, 1991) and Joseph Lanza, *Elevator Music: A Surreal History of Muzak, Easy-Listening, and Other Moodsong* (New York: St. Martin's Press, 1994).

199 Designer music can also be a valuable tool: "Business Music: A Merchandising Tool for the Retail Industry" (Seattle: Muzak Corporation, 1991).

200 A liquor store reported: report on National Public Radio, summer
     1996.

206 proposed a Millennial Symphony: Bernard Holland, "A Modest Pro-
     posal for the Millennium," *New York Times*, 7 July 1996.

207 it may be more useful to see the sciences: In a survey of 538 regis-
     tered voters, the majority agreed that schools spend too little money
     on music programs; the number of music classes and activities
     should be expanded; music education should be included in the cur-
     riculum rather than being offered after school; and that music was
     as important as science and other academic subjects. R. Radocy, "A
     Survey of General Attitudes Toward Music and Music Education,"
     unpublished paper, 1991.

Chapter 8

Sound Spirit

211 Therese tells the story of her first patient: Therese Schroeder-Sheker,
     "Music for the Dying: A Personal Account of the New Field of Music-
     Thanatology—History, Theories, and Clinical Narratives," *Journal of
     Holistic Nursing* 12 (1994): 83–99.

213 "It was a moment of truth.": Therese Schroeder-Sheker, "Musical-
     Sacramental-Midwifery: The Use of Music in Death and Dying," in
     Music and Miracles, ed. Don G. Campbell (Wheaton, Ill.: Quest Books,
     1992), pp. 25–26.

215 The concluding refrain: David Steindl-Rast, *The Music of Silence* (San
     Francisco: HarperCollins, 1995).

215 American psychic Edgar Cayce: Shirley Rabb Winston, *Music As the
     Bridge* (Virginia Beach, Va.: Edgar Cayce Foundation, 1972).

216 As his symptoms worsened: Kitti K. Outlaw, M.D., and J. Patrick
     O'Leary, M.D., "Wolfgang Amadeus Mozart 1756–1791: A Mysteri-
     ous Death," *American Surgery* 61 (1994): 1025–1027.

217 "A creative force": Goethe, 3 February 1980, quoted in Gernot
     Gruber, *Mozart and Posterity* (New York: Quartet Books, 1991), p. vii.

Coda
The Eternal Song

218 a tribe in Africa in which music is the thread of life: Jack Kornfield, *A Path with Heart: A Guide Through the Perils and Promises of Spiritual Life* (New York: Bantam, 1996), p. 120.

Postlude
Miracle Stories of Treatment and Cure

224 victims of domestic violence: Michael David Cassity and Kimberly A. Kaczor Theobold, "Domestic Violence: Assessments and Treatments by Music Therapists," *Journal of Music Therapy* 27 (1990): 179–94.

227 Music, combined with imagery, has been particularly helpful: Kenneth E. Bruscia, Ph.D.; "Embracing Life with AIDS: Psychotherapy through Guided Imagery and Music (GIM)," *Case Studies in Music Therapy* (Phoenixville, Pa.: Barcelona Publications, 1989), pp. 581–602.

229 In a study of ten elderly men and women with dementia: Carol A. Prickett and Randall S. Moore, "The Use of Music to Aid Memory of Alzheimer's Patients," *Journal of Music Therapy* 28 (1991): 101–110.

230 One of the most widespread therapeutic uses of music: J. F. Thompson and P. C. A. Kam, "Music in the Operating Room," *British Journal of Surgery* 82 (1995): 1586–1587.

231 the effects of music on nearly 97,000 patients: International Arts-Medicine Association Newsletter, March 1995; see also, "Sound Therapy," in *New Choices in Natural Healing*, ed. Bill Gottlieb (Emmaus, Pa.: Rodale Press, 1995), p. 127.

231 At the University of Massachusetts Medical Center: Pamela Bloom, "Soul Music," *New Age Journal*, March/April 1987, p. 60.

231 One of my associates, Jeanne Achterberg: "An Interview with Jeanne Achterberg," in *Music and Miracles*, ed. Don Campbell (Wheaton, Ill.: Quest Books, 1992), pp. 123–127.

232 For years, Jack: Stephanie Merritt, "The Healing Link: Guided Imagery and Music and the Body/Mind Connection," *Journal of the Associa-*

tion of Music for Music and Imagery 2 (1993); see also Stephanie Merritt, *Mind, Music, and Imagery* (Santa Rosa, Calif.: Aslan Publishing, 1996).

232   An immunological disease that strikes older people: Elizabeth Jacobi, Ph.D. and Gerald Eisenberg, M.D., "The Efficacy of Guided Imagery and Music in the Treatment of Rheumatoid Arthritis," Department of Pastoral Care and Division of Rheumatology, Department of Medicine, Lutheran General Hospital, Chicago.

233   In a study of nineteen children: Rosalie Rebollo Pratt, Hans-Henning Abel, and Jon Skidmore, "The Effects of Neurofeedback Training with Background Music on EGG Patterns of ADD and ADHD Children," *International Journal of Arts Medicine* 4 (1995): 24–31.

234   Annabel Stehli's life was a nightmare: Annabel Stehli, *Sound of a Miracle* (New York: Doubleday, 1991).

235   Brain-damaged, blind, and autistic at birth: Paul Robertson, "Music and the Mind," *Caduceus 31* (Spring 1995): pp. 14–17.

236   medical researchers in Wales: Dawn Wimpory, Paul Chadwick, and Susan Nash, "Brief Report: Musical Interaction Therapy for Children with Autism: An Evaluative Case Study with Two-Year Follow-up," *Journal of Autism and Developmental Disorders* 25 (1995): 541–49.

237   nonverbal communication: Charles Marwick, "Leaving Concert Hall for Clinic, Therapists Now Test Music's Charms," *Journal of the American Medical Association* 265 (1995): 267–68.

238   A pioneer in harp therapy: Sarajane Williams, "Harp Therapy: A Psychoacoustic Approach to Treating Pain and Stress," *Open Ear,* Winter/Spring 1994, pp. 25–30.

239   George's asthma had gotten progressively worse: Joy Gardner-Gordon, *The Healing Voice*: (Freedom, Calif.: Crossing Press, 1993), pp. 95–96.

240   Excruciating pain usually accompanies severe burns: Christenberry, Elizabeth Bolton, "The Use of Music Therapy with Burn Patients," *Journal of Music Therapy* 16 (1979): 138–39.

241   music has been used in cancer treatment primarily as a palliative: J. D. Cook, "Music as an Intervention in the Oncology Setting," *Cancer Nursing* 1986: 23–28; J. M. Frank, "The Effects of Music Therapy and Guided Visual Imagery on Chemotherapy Induced Nausea and Vomiting," *Oncology Nursing Forum* 12 (1985): 47–52.

241 Since the era of Galen: Fabien Maman, interview, autumn 1995.

243 Music therapist Deforia Lane: Deforia Lane with Rob Wilkins, *Music As Medicine* (Grand Rapids, Mich.: Zondervan, 1994), pp. 194–195.

244 In a study of twenty developmentally disabled children: Suzanne Evans Morris, Ph.D., "Music and Hemi-Sync in the Treatment of Children with Developmental Disabilities," *Open Ear* 2 (1996): 14–17.

244 a study conducted at United Cerebral Palsy: Joseph P. Scatelli, "The Effects of Sedative Music on Electromyographic Biofeedback Assisted Relaxation Training on Spastic Cerebral Palsied Adults," *Journal of Music Therapy* 19 (1982): 210–218.

245 a study of twenty-two patients undergoing cervical examinations: Cynthia Allison Davis, "The Effects of Music and Basic Relaxation Instruction on Pain and Anxiety of Women Undergoing In-Office Gynecological Procedures," *Journal of Music Therapy* 29 (1992): 202–216.

246 Floyd suffered from chronic fatigue syndrome: Floyd Skloot, "Thorns into Feathers: Coping with Chronic Illness," *The Sun,* June 1994, pp. 30–33.

248 Brigitte had been obsessed with death: Guy Bérard, M.D. *Hearing Equals Behavior* (New Canaan, Conn.: Keats Publishing, 1993), pp. 140–141.

250 Michael lagged far behind: David Manners, *Music to the Ears* (East Sussex, Eng.: Tomatis Centre, n.d.); see also Paul Madaule, *When Listening Comes Alive: A Guide to Effective Listening* (Norval: Moulin Publishing, 1993).

254 Dr. Robert L. Tusler: Robert L. Tusler, "Music and Epilepsy," *Open Ear* (Winter/Spring 1994): 3–8. In the original article, the patient was referred to as Mr. X. However, in this book I refer to him as Mr. M.

256 Migraines are among the most painful headaches: Paul Chance, "Music Hath Charms to Soothe a Throbbing Head," *Psychology Today,* February 1987, p. 14.

256 In a Polish study: Dina Ingber, Robert Brody, and Cliff Pearson, "Music Therapy: Tune-Up for Mind and Body," *Science Digest* (January 1982): 78.

258 After installing a music listening system: Jayne Standley, "Music

Research in Medical/Dental Treatment: Meta-analysis and Clinical Applications," *Journal of Music Therapy* 23 (1986): 61.

258   As a critical care nurse: Cathie E. Guzzetta, R.N., Ph.D., "Effects of Relaxation and Music Therapy on Patients in a Coronary Care Unit with Presumptive Acute Myocardial Infarction," *Heart Lung* 18 (1989): 609–616.

259   the case of Agnes Reiner: Deepak Chopra, M.D., *Perfect Health* (New York: Harmony Books, 1991), pp. 133–136.

260   sedative music reduced systolic blood pressure: Phyllis Updike, R.N. D.N.S., "Music Therapy Results for ICU Patients," *Applied Research* 9 (1990): 39–45.

261   Sleeping problems lend themselves to music therapy: Dick Kankas, "Music as Medicine," *Louisville Courier Journal,* 7 January 1996.

262   The Dallas youngster expressed himself eloquently: Jim and Harl Asaff, "Listening Therapy for Our Son," *Open Ear* (Fall 1991), pp. 9–10.

264   twenty-five people with gait disabilities or abnormal walking speeds: Myra J. Staum, "Music and Rhythmic Stimuli in the Rehabilitation of Gait Disorders," *Journal of Music Therapy* 20 (1983): 69–87.

265   Anna, an overweight and emotionally withdrawn teenager: Joy Gardner-Gordon, *The Healing Voice* (Freedom, Calif.: Crossing Press, 1993), pp. 102–103.

265   Chen began a holistic treatment: "Musical Qi Gong," *SICA Bulletin No. 8* (Hong Kong: Spark International Culture Agency, 1996); "Obesity," booklet with album, Wind Records, Los Angeles, 1994.

266   the man who ended the Cold War: Robert Thomas, "Willis Conover Is Dead at 75; Aimed Jazz at the Soviet Bloc," *New York Times,* 20 May 1996.

266   Ronald Price, Ph.D., a music professor: Lance W. Brunner, "Testimonies Old and New," *Music and Miracles,* ed. Don Campbell (Wheaton, Ill.: Quest Books), pp. 79–81.

267   In a study at the Vesoul Hospital in France: reported in "Tomatis Centre U.K. Ltd." (Lewis, U.K.: n.d.).

267   In Austin, Texas: Marwick, "Leaving Concert Hall for Clinic, Therapists Now Test Music's Charms," *Journal of the American Medical Association,* 265 (4) 1995: pp. 267–68.

269   the powerful role that music played in the civil rights movement:

Andrew Young, *An Easy Burden* (New York: HarperCollins, 1996), pp. 156–157, 183.

271 Handicapped children often lag behind: Marcia Humpal, "The Effects of an Integrated Early Childhood Music Program on Social Interaction Among Children with Handicaps and Their Typical Peers," *Journal of Music Therapy* 28 (1991): 161–77.

271 At Bryn Mawr Rehab: Leah Ariniello, "Music's Power May Be More than Emotional," *Philadelphia Inquirer,* 6 Nov. 1995.

272 a recurring pattern in his schizophrenic patients: Moses cited in *Music and Miracles,* ed. Campbell, p. 118.

272 The U.S. Alcohol, Drug Abuse, and Mental Health Administration: M. F. Green and M. Kinsbourne, "Subvocal Activity and Auditory Hallucinations: Clues for Behavioral Treatments?" *Schizophrenia Bulletin* 16 (1990): 617–25.

273 In a large case-control study of forty-one adults: Mercedes Pavlicevic, Colwyn Trevarthen, and Janice Duncan, "Improvisational Music Therapy and the Rehabilitation of Persons Suffering from Chronic Schizophrenia," *Journal of Music Therapy* 31 (1994): 86–104; "Tune Therapy," *USA Today,* 30 May 1991.

273 improved cadence, stride, and foot placement: Marwick, "Leaving Concert Hall for Clinic."

276 The contemporary application of this principle: Michael D. Seidman, M.D., "Doctor to Doctor: A Medical Evaluation of the Tinnitus Patient," *Tinnitus Today,* September 1995; Barbara Tabachnick, "The Miracle of Masking," *Tinnitus Today,* December 1995, pp. 9–13.

277 Sherri was not properly toilet trained: Deforia Lane, *Music As Medicine* (Grand Rapids, Mich.: Zondervan, 1994), p. 101. It should be noted that although Sherri was seven years old and retarded, her difficulties with toilet training are not uncommon.

277 music and sound were "fully effective" in suppressing pain: Dr. Wallace J. Gardner, "Suppression of Pain by Sound," *Science* 132 (1960): 32–33.

Index

Don Campbell has produced four sets of recordings of Mozart's music for those who want to take advantage of the Mozart effect. Each set is available both on compact disc and cassette.

Music for the Mozart Effect®

Volume I—Strengthen the Mind:
Music for Intelligence and Learning

Volume II—Heal the Body:
Music for Rest and Relaxation

Volume III—Unlock the Creative Spirit:
Music for Creativity and Imagination

Available from Spring Hill Music (800)427-7680

The Mozart Effect®—Music for Children

Volume I—Tune Up Your Mind

Volume II—Relax, Daydream, and Draw

Volume III—Mozart in Motion

The Mozart Effect®—Music for Newborns

The Mozart Effect®—Music for Babies

Available from the Children's Group (800)668-0242

BOOKS BY DON CAMPBELL

THE MOZART EFFECT®
Tapping the Power of Music to Heal the Body, Strengthen the Mind, and Unlock the Creative Spirit

ISBN 0-06-093720-3 (paperback)

Drawing on medicine, Eastern wisdom, and the latest research on learning and creativity, Campbell reveals how exposure to sound, music, and other forms of vibration can have a lifelong effect on health, learning, and behavior.

"Practical, mystical, and visionary, he makes the world of music accessible, friendly, and profoundly healing."
—Julia Cameron, author of *The Artist's Way*

THE MOZART EFFECT®
FOR CHILDREN
Awakening Your Child's Mind, Health, and Creativity With Music

ISBN 0-380-80744-0 (paperback)

In this book, Campbell follows a child's life from pre-birth through age 10, demonstrating ways in which music can be used to activate new neural pathways in the brain of the fetus and infants, promote language acquisition, prepare the brain for reading, and much more.

"A bountiful compendium of research, teaching, and learning strategies, and innumerable other resources." —Dee Dickinson, CEO, New Horizons for Learning